The Gallery at Cleveland House

MATERIAL CULTURE OF ART AND DESIGN

Material Culture of Art and Design is devoted to scholarship that brings art history into dialogue with interdisciplinary material culture studies. The material components of an object – its medium and physicality – are key to understanding its cultural significance. Material culture has stretched the boundaries of art history and emphasized new points of contact with other disciplines, including anthropology, archaeology, consumer and mass culture studies, the literary movement called 'Thing Theory,' and materialist philosophy. **Material Culture of Art and Design** seeks to publish studies that explore the relationship between art and material culture in all of its complexity. The series is a venue for scholars to explore specific object histories (or object biographies, as the term has developed), studies of medium and the procedures for making works of art, and investigations of art's relationship to the broader material world that comprises society. It seeks to be the premiere venue for publishing scholarship about works of art as exemplifications of material culture.

The series encompasses material culture in its broadest dimensions, including the decorative arts (furniture, ceramics, metalwork, textiles), everyday objects of all kinds (toys, machines, musical instruments), and studies of the familiar high arts of painting and sculpture. The series welcomes proposals for monographs, thematic studies, and edited collections.

Volumes in the Series

British Women and Cultural Practices of Empire, 1775–1930, Edited by Rosie Dias and Kate Smith

Jewellery in the Age of Modernism, 1918–1940: Adornment and Beyond, Simon Bliss

Childhood by Design: Toys and the Material Culture of Childhood, 1700–Present, Edited by Megan Brandow-Faller

Material Literacy in Eighteenth-Century Britain: A Nation of Makers, Edited by Serena Dyer and Chloe Wigston Smith

Sculpture and the Decorative in Britain and Europe, Seventeenth Century to Contemporary, Edited by Imogen Hart and Claire Jones

Georges Rouault and Material Imagining, Jennifer Johnson

The Versailles Effect: Objects, Lives and Afterlives of the Domain, Edited by Mark Ledbury and Robert Wellington

Domestic Space in Britain, 1750–1840: Materiality, Sociability and Emotion, Freya Gowrley

Domestic Space in France and Belgium: Art, Literature and Design, 1850–1920, Edited by Claire Moran

Enlightened Animals in Eighteenth-Century Art: Sensation, Matter, and Knowledge, Sarah R. Cohen

Materials, Practices, and Politics of Shine in Modern Art and Popular Culture, Edited by Antje Krause-Wahl, Petra Löffler, and Änne Söll

Lead in Modern and Contemporary Art, Edited by Sharon Hecker and Silvia Bottinelli

Transformative Jars, Edited by Anna Grasskamp and Anne Gerritsen

Material Cultures of the Global Eighteenth Century, Edited by Wendy Bellion and Kristel Smentek

Intimate Interiors: Sex, Politics, and Material Culture in the Eighteenth-Century Bedroom and Boudoir, Edited by Tara Zanardi and Christopher M. S. Johns

The Material Landscapes of Scotland's Jewellery Craft, 1780–1914, Sarah Laurenson

Ceramics in the Victorian Era: Meanings and Metaphors in Painting and Literature, Rachel Gotlieb

The Art of Mary Linwood: Embroidery and Cultural Agency in Late Georgian Britain, Heidi A. Strobel

The Gallery at Cleveland House

Displaying Art and Society in Late Georgian London

Anne Nellis Richter

BLOOMSBURY VISUAL ARTS
LONDON • NEW YORK • OXFORD • NEW DELHI • SYDNEY

BLOOMSBURY VISUAL ARTS
Bloomsbury Publishing Plc, 50 Bedford Square, London, WC1B 3DP, UK
Bloomsbury Publishing Inc, 1359 Broadway, New York, NY 10018, USA
Bloomsbury Publishing Ireland, 29 Earlsfort Terrace, Dublin 2, D02 AY28, Ireland

BLOOMSBURY, BLOOMSBURY VISUAL ARTS and the Diana logo are trademarks of Bloomsbury Publishing Plc

First published in Great Britain 2024
Paperback edition published 2026

Cover design: Elena Durey
Cover image: 'The Cabinet', P.W. Tomkins, from William Young Ottley, *Engravings of the Most Noble the Marquis of Stafford's collection of pictures in London* (London: Longman, Hurst, Rees, Orme, and Brown, 1818), engraving. Yale Center for British Art, Paul Mellon Collection.

A catalogue record for this book is available from the British Library.

A catalog record for this book is available from the Library of Congress.

ISBN: HB: 978-1-3503-7275-7
PB: 978-1-3503-7278-8
ePDF: 978-1-3503-7274-0
eBook: 978-1-3503-7276-4

Series: Material Culture of Art and Design

Typeset by RefineCatch Limited, Bungay, Suffolk

For product safety related questions contact productsafety@bloomsbury.com.

CONTENTS

ILLUSTRATIONS

ACKNOWLEDGEMENTS

This book was written over the course of many years in distinct spaces and places and during very different eras of my own life. These acknowledgements offer an opportunity to reflect on these different moments and all the people who helped me and encouraged me to keep going along the way.

The first of these was graduate school at Brown University in Providence, Rhode Island, and I have many people from that now seemingly distant period to whom I must express proper and long-delayed appreciation. Dian Kriz was a wonderful and generous advisor who always pushed me to look at the big picture, and I think this book demonstrates the wisdom of her guidance in that regard. The late Kermit Champa's wry smile and provocative questions made their mark on my dissertation and his keen interest in the language of art writing and criticism had a lasting influence. Andrew McClellan showed an enthusiasm for my topic and approach that was incredibly encouraging. My heartfelt thanks to all of them. From my community at Brown, I must also thank Daniel Harkett in particular – he was not only a great friend but an excellent reader and editor who spent hours with me discussing and working through the ideas that formed the original framework for this book. I am also grateful to Alanna Hildt for friendship, moral support and intellectual companionship.

In London, I must start by acknowledging my respect and debt to the late Giles Waterfield, who carried out the first serious work on the gallery at Cleveland House. Over the years he encouraged me at every turn and I wish he were able to see the finished product. David, Ben & Mia Solkin were extraordinarily patient and kind to a graduate student who was in personal and professional disarray. Without them I could not have spent the sustained period of time in London during which I first planted the seeds of core research that grew into my dissertation and eventually flowered into this book. The staff at the Paul Mellon Centre for Studies in British Art, including Brian Allen, Steven Parissien, Frank Salmon, and librarian Emma Floyd, who allowed me to stash my moribund and un-transportable laptop computer in her office while I saved up for a new one. Also, in London over many years I benefited from conversations and friendship from Douglas Fordham, Vittoria di Palma and Helen Dorey. I would particularly like to thank Helen and Markus Geisser for their warm and enthusiastic hospitality. And finally in London I give special thanks to Charles Sebag-Montefiore FSA, who showed me his unsurpassed collection of guidebooks and *catalogues raisonnés*, especially his hand-coloured edition of William Young Ottley's *catalogue raisonné*. He has been both extremely generous with his time and genuinely interested in my work over the years, for which I am very grateful.

In Washington DC I encountered many more people who encouraged me on both a personal and professional level to continue my work. I thank Therese O'Malley, Nicholas Penny, Kim Butler, Lynn Clement-Bremer, Sarah Gordon, Tammany Kramer, Bénédicte Miyamoto, Kate Roach, Amy Freund, and Meredith Gamer. I've also benefited from participating in a number of academic conferences and meetings in London and in the US, and met people there whose work has been incredibly important and stimulating, including Michael Yonan, Kate Retford, Susanna Avery-Quash, Julia Armstrong-Totten, Peter Humfrey, Denise Baxter, Meredith Martin, Anca Lasc, Änne Söll, Lela Graybill, Andrea Gáldy, Susan Bracken, Adriana Turpin, Margaret Iacono Wertz, Esmée Quodbach, Helen McCormack, Jenny Gray, Joe Friedman and Susannah Brooke Homer, who generously shared her unpublished dissertation with me. I would also like to give special thanks to the late historian Eric Richards, who generously shared his knowledge about the Sutherland archives.

For research support over the years, I thank Brown University, Historians of British Art, the Huntington Library, Museum & Gardens, Amy Meyers, the Attingham Trust and the Paul Mellon Centre for Studies in British Art. I'd also like to thank Smith College for the exceptional library services that helped get this project over the finish line. I also thank the staffs at the National Library of Scotland, especially Kerry Eldon, the Staffordshire Record Office and its senior archivist Tim Groom, Claudia Hopkins, Tico Seifert, Robert Copley, Sue Stern, Alex Kidson, Clare Pye at the Tabley House Trust, Lena Newman at the Avery Architectural and Fine Arts Library at Columbia University, and Laura Callery at the Yale Center for British Art.

Finally, I must single out a few people who have been exceptionally steadfast in their support and encouragement over the years from graduate school to the present. First among them must be Morna O'Neill. We first met researching our dissertations in London in the early days of the 21st century, and since have become fast friends and co-conspirators, not to mention co-bloggers and co-authors. Morna has read more drafts than any person should reasonably agree to and her encouragement and patience over the years have kept me on track with this project. I would also put Stacey Sloboda, Melinda McCurdy and Craig Ashley Hanson in this category. They are all exceptionally supportive, kind, and encouraging people, and all have offered friendship, conversation, and insightful feedback on my work, often just when I needed it most.

And last and most importantly, my parents Merrilee and Steve Nellis for their support and encouragement, my husband Kurt and my children Will & Charlotte who, as little ones, cheered me on to finish writing about the 'loo' of London. This is for them.

Introduction: 'The Finest in England'

'The Finest in England': Cleveland House and its Gallery of Art

In 1805, a visitor to London wondering where to go and what to see might have consulted *The Picture of London*, a popular travel guide. The subtitle of this book, *Being a Correct Guide to All the Curiosities, Amusements, Exhibitions, Public Establishments and Remarkable Objects in and Near London*, signalled its ambition to list all sites of significance the city offered, including royal palaces, shopping districts, pubs and prisons. Included amongst these attractions were 23 private houses, of which a few – though certainly not all – were open for 'proper persons to apply to view them'.[1] Our imagined visitor might learn from his or her guidebook that private residences were particularly important places to seek out '*chef d'œuvres* of art'. London's masterpieces included Raphael's Cartoons for the Sistine Chapel tapestries, which were on display to polite audiences upon application at the Queen's Palace in St James's Park. Our visitor might also consider the Marquis of Lansdowne's house in Berkeley Square where pictures were hung amidst 'busts, antiques, and library', Thomas Hope's 'very valuable collection' in Mansfield Street, Portland Place, or Charles Townley's house in Park Street, where he had installed his esteemed collection of sculpture.[2]

It was the collection at Cleveland House, however, that *The Picture of London* deemed 'perhaps, the finest in England'.[3] In the late 1790s, a much-admired collection of Italian and French Old Master paintings, including a large and valuable cache of paintings from the famed Orléans Collection, came into the possession of Francis Egerton, Third Duke of Bridgewater ('Bridgewater'). Bridgewater soon set about making arrangements to display them. In the late 1790s, Bridgewater had Cleveland House's existing façade refurbished in a sober, neoclassical idiom, as depicted in views of the building's exterior (see Figure 0.1). As early as 1802, *The Picture of London* reported that 'his Grace has lately fitted up a gallery for the reception of pictures, and they may be seen by permission, at his house in Cleveland-row, St. James's's'.[4]

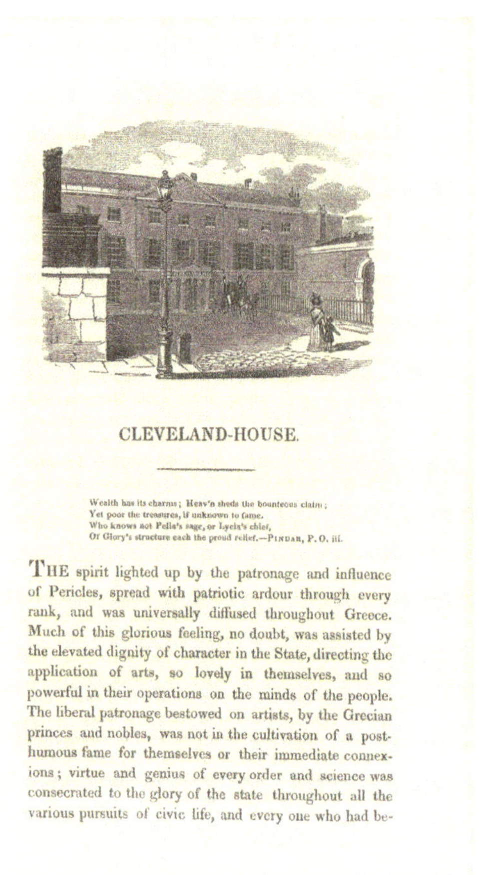

CLEVELAND-HOUSE.

Wealth has its charms; Heav'n sheds the bounteous claim;
Yet poor the treasures, if unknown to fame.
Who knows not Pella's sage, or Lycia's chief,
Or Glory's structure each the proud relief.—PINDAR, P. O. iii.

THE spirit lighted up by the patronage and influence of Pericles, spread with patriotic ardour through every rank, and was universally diffused throughout Greece. Much of this glorious feeling, no doubt, was assisted by the elevated dignity of character in the State, directing the application of arts, so lovely in themselves, and so powerful in their operations on the minds of the people. The liberal patronage bestowed on artists, by the Grecian princes and nobles, was not in the cultivation of a posthumous fame for themselves or their immediate connexions; virtue and genius of every order and science was consecrated to the glory of the state throughout all the various pursuits of civic life, and every one who had be-

FIGURE 0.1 *'Cleveland-House' from Charles Molloy Westmacott,* British Galleries of Painting and Sculpture *(London: Sherwood, Jones & Co, 1824). Getty Research Institute, Los Angeles (83-B7743).*

After Bridgewater died, his nephew and heir, George Leveson-Gower, the Marquess of Stafford ('Stafford') renovated and expanded the gallery at Cleveland House with the intention of opening it to the public on a more predictable basis than had been typical practice amongst his peers.[5] When Cleveland House opened to the public in 1806, our visitor – should he or she have been fortunate enough to obtain a ticket – would have seen more than 250 artworks by artists like Raphael, Titian, Claude and Carracci arranged according to a hierarchy of national schools and displayed in a luxurious interior that only one of Britain's richest families could have produced.

Stafford was not following his personal inclinations alone but was responding to general pressures that had built over the previous century to open collections to the public, a concept which appeared straightforward but was, in practice, fraught with complexity. From the beginning, the tensions inherent in the act of making a private dwelling open to 'the public' – an elastic category that could be as restrictive as it appeared inclusive – led to inevitable friction between men who owned important collections and constituencies who claimed a need for access. Even so, the gallery at Cleveland House offered a valuable model for making art available to the public, spurring other collectors who were thinking of opening their houses to act. As the practice was more widely adopted, collectors began to regard it as an essential component of their civic duty. By 1820 the number of houses in London that were open to the public had increased dramatically. The example of Cleveland House had been widely influential and thereafter private art galleries set the standard for conventions of display and access to public and private museums and art galleries for more than a century.

Cleveland House and the Nineteenth-century Culture of Art in London

This book seeks to restore the gallery at Cleveland House as a key cultural site in early nineteenth-century London. It was a space for displaying and experiencing art, for intellectual engagement and spirited sociability and for establishing and exhibiting cultural and political influence. Private houses and galleries played a critical role in the building of Britain's national culture during a period of political transformation, yet the tendency in the historical literature has been to focus on the development of public spaces for the display of contemporary art, like the Royal Academy and the Society of Artists and public-facing art galleries, including the British Institution and the National Gallery, that proliferated during the same period.[6] Cleveland House is the best documented example of the workings of a private gallery – that is to say, a 'public' art gallery situated in a private dwelling – in this period. The gallery was written about regularly in the newspapers of the day and was documented in no fewer than six books and catalogues, several of which were lavishly illustrated. Giles Waterfield, whose pioneering work on private galleries and the London townhouse laid the foundation for this book, called Cleveland House the 'first nobleman's house to be. . .opened in London', the impact of which he called 'enormous'.[7]

Cleveland House was a large freestanding townhouse built around 1630, named for one of its earliest residents, Barbara Villiers, Duchess of Cleveland, a prominent mistress of King Charles II. Occupying a site on Cleveland Row adjacent to St James's Palace with views to Green Park, it was acquired by the Egerton family at the beginning of the eighteenth century and passed by descent to the Third Duke of Bridgewater in 1748. As aristocratic London continued to develop westward during the late seventeenth and eighteenth centuries, the surrounding area filled with a number of equally impressive

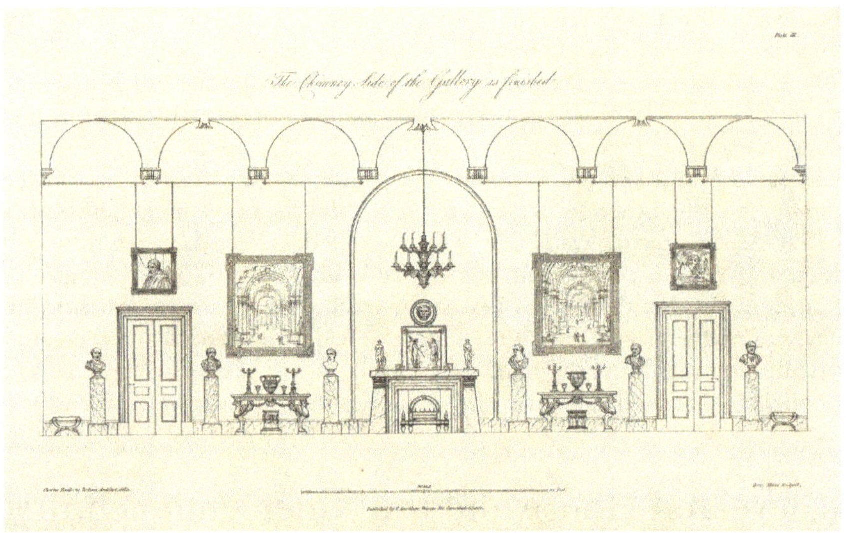

FIGURE 0.2 *Charles Heathcote Tatham, 'Chimney Side of the Gallery as finished' from* The Gallery at Castle Howard in Yorkshire *(London: T Gardiner, 1811). Avery Classics, Avery Architectural & Fine Arts Library, Columbia University.*

residences, including Burlington House, Devonshire House, Spencer House, Carlton House and Buckingham House (later Palace).[8] In 1803, Bridgewater left the house and the collection of continental masterpieces he had amassed to his nephew Stafford, who immediately undertook the renovation and expansion of the house's existing gallery. Stafford hired architect Charles Heathcote Tatham, who had experience designing galleries, such as that built at Castle Howard for Frederick Howard, Fifth Earl of Carlisle, to design and oversee its construction (see Figure 0.2). The construction of the gallery suite transformed Cleveland House into one of early nineteenth-century London's most glittering addresses. For a period of 20 years after the gallery opened in 1806, its status as London's most important private art gallery was widely acknowledged.

Stafford died in 1833 and Cleveland House was demolished less than a decade later. Unusually, Cleveland House passed to Stafford's second son, Francis Leveson-Gower. Francis changed his surname to Egerton and took control of the house and the portion of the collection bequeathed by Bridgewater, according to the terms of his 1803 will. Cleveland House was pulled down around 1840 and Egerton hired architect Charles Barry to design a new building for the site.[9] To maintain what was now a family tradition of three generations, the lavish new residence, called Bridgewater House, was outfitted with a spacious art gallery with an external entrance for the general public (see Figure 0.3). (This gallery is long defunct, but the door and bell bearing the words 'Picture Gallery' are still visible to the alert

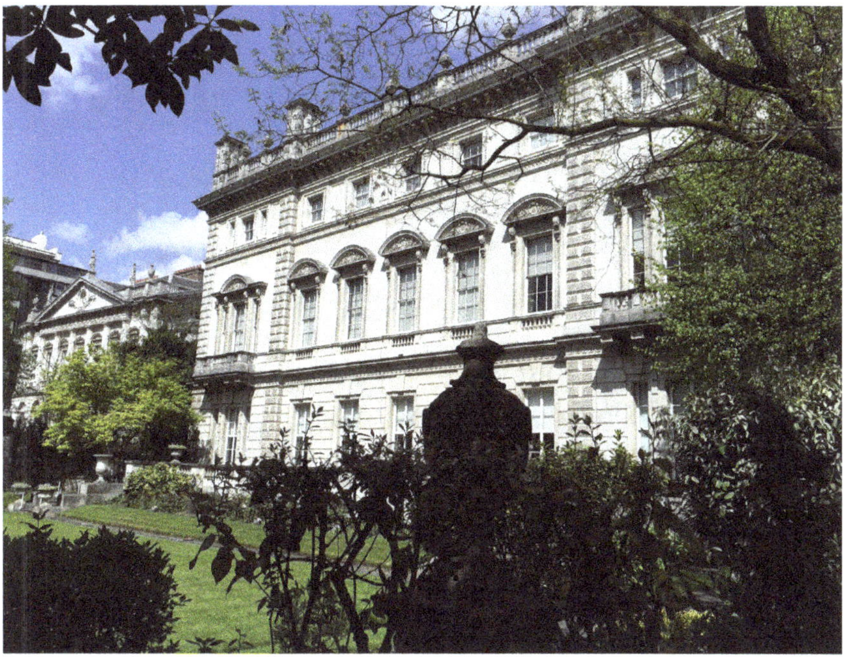

FIGURE 0.3 *Bridgewater House, photographed by flickr user Shakespearesmonkey 28 April 2015. Creative Commons Attribution 2.0 Generic license.*

passer-by in Little St James's Street) (see Figure 0.4). Meanwhile, Egerton's elder brother George, Second Duke of Sutherland, had been instrumental in building Stafford House (now renamed Lancaster House) on an adjacent site (see Figure 0.5).[10] Side by side, the brothers' houses functioned as a hub of political and cultural authority centred on the activities of one extraordinarily rich aristocratic family; indeed, they occupied the heart of St James's, a neighbourhood which represented an 'extraordinary nexus of wealth and social prestige'.[11]

In part due to Cleveland House's demolition, its significance within London's social, cultural and political landscape has been overshadowed by houses from the same period that have survived.[12] For example, Lancaster House, mentioned above, is now a frequent filming location (especially as a stand-in for Buckingham Palace) and is operated by the Foreign, Commonwealth and Development Office as a setting for diplomacy and entertaining. Lancaster House has remained visible in the historical record and the public imagination in a way Cleveland House has not. Even houses that have survived however, usually bear little trace of their original architecture or decoration. As Joe Friedman puts it, 'in almost every case, [townhouses have] been stripped of their contents and generally demolished or altered beyond recognition, so that even the context for the collections

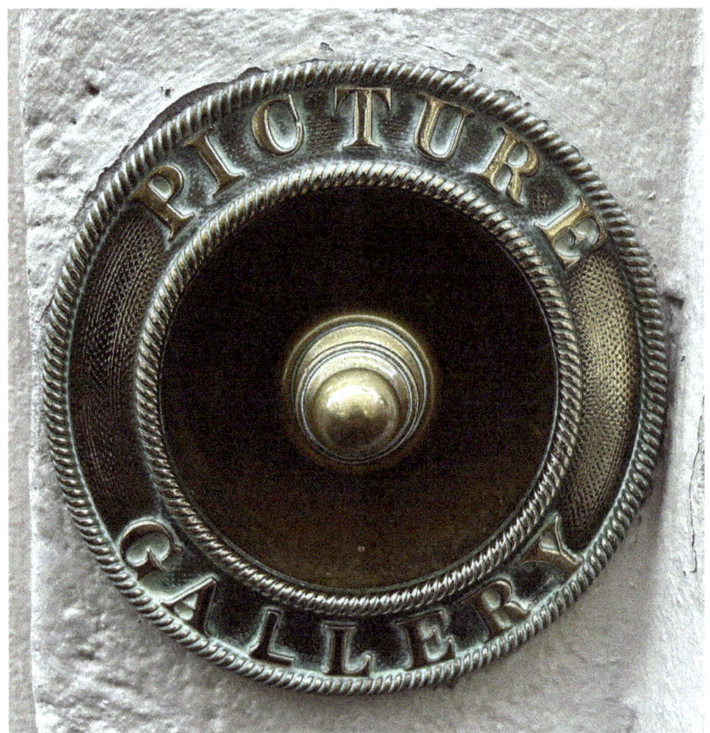

FIGURE 0.4 *Doorbell marking the entrance to the defunct picture gallery at Bridgewater House, Little St. James's Street.*

they once contained is now lost or severely compromised'.[13] Further complicating matters, in general townhouses have been overshadowed in the historical record by country houses, which have survived intact in greater numbers and, as popular tourist destinations, are often in a state of relatively good preservation thanks to the work of bodies like the National Trust.[14] In recent years, research and writing about the London townhouse by art and architectural historians like Friedman, Rachel Stewart, Adriano Aymonino and Manolo Guerci, to name a few, has increased dramatically to redress these gaps and imbalances. The work of these scholars and many others has begun to restore our understanding of the townhouse's centrality to the political and social culture of Britain in the seventeenth, eighteenth, and nineteenth centuries.[15]

Although the gallery at Cleveland House is often mentioned in passing in institutional histories of the period, the role it played in London's art world is generally treated as that of an extra in a drama whose epic sweep ultimately eclipsed its contemporary significance. For these reasons, our understanding of what Cleveland House symbolized – in the minds of the public it was ostensibly meant to serve and for the upper classes whose tastes and habits

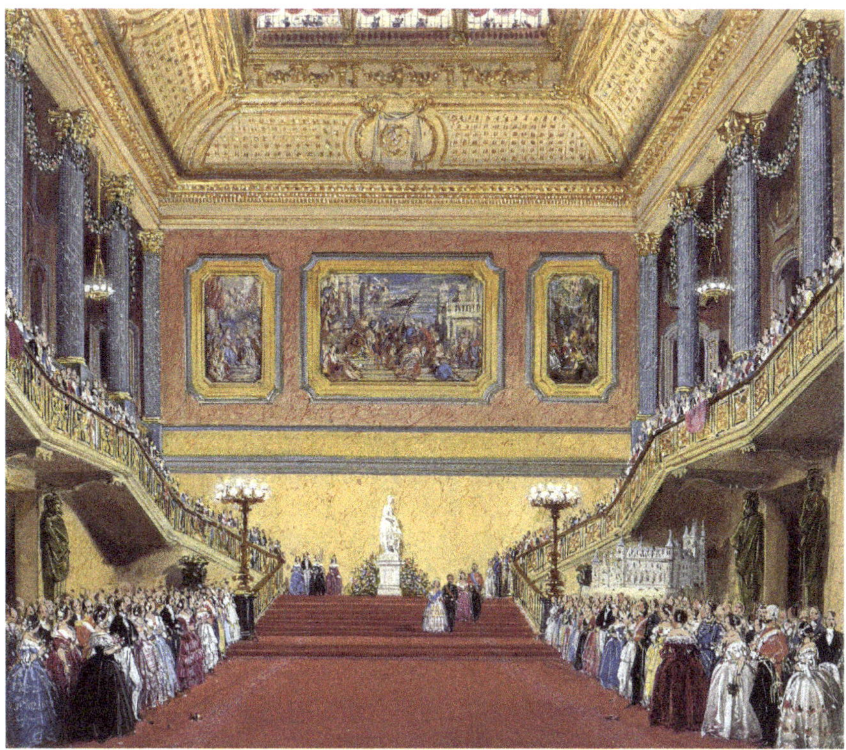

FIGURE 0.5 *Joseph Nash,* Stafford House: The staircase at the Ball, 16 June 1847, *1847. Watercolour and bodycolour | 22.4 × 26.3 cm (whole object) | RCIN 920194. Royal Collection Trust / © His Majesty King Charles III 2023.*

it represented – has remained opaque. The picture collection has been written about extensively, but the house itself has never been subjected to a sustained history, nor has there been any inventory or analysis of its interiors (aside from the pictures), nor critical analysis of the numerous publications that memorialised it. As a result, scholars have underestimated its importance – and that of privately-owned art galleries more generally – in shaping the very conversations about the practices of display, appropriate publics for art and the meaning of the nation's patrimony that permitted the creation of the durable public institutions that arose alongside it.

Accessing the Gallery: Public and Private Space

Cleveland House stood out in the London art scene not only because of its availability to the public, but also because of the unparalleled quality of the collection displayed on its walls; although the house has been overlooked by historians, its collection of paintings has most certainly not. It was widely regarded as having no equal in Britain and was said to rival even those on the continent. After visiting in 1818 American envoy to the Court of St. James Richard Rush wrote: 'There is said to be no such private collection in Europe. It comprehends the productions of the first masters of the different schools. . .These works of genius glowing from every part of the walls, formed a high attraction'.[16] Still ranked among the world's greatest collections of Old Master paintings, it has long attracted keen interest from scholars.[17] Focusing on the collection of paintings, however, has obscured the house and the role it played as a site of urban display and sociability during a dynamic period in the history of British art. One important goal of this book is to try to look past the astonishing collection – which has survived – to look more carefully at the house and gallery – which have not – as spaces that framed the collection's reception and cultural meanings. In a country in which no National Gallery yet existed and no viable plan had emerged for building one, Cleveland House represented the ambition to offer the public an alternative to state-owned or commercial institutions for looking at art.

The tensions between the exigencies of public and private patronage and the display of art to all kinds of audiences has been amongst the most pressing questions animating the story of British art in recent decades, which has generally flowed from the theoretical model of the 'public sphere' established by Jürgen Habermas and deployed by David Solkin in his seminal study, *Painting for Money*.[18] These writers have used this concept to describe a network of sites where the cultural and political identities of the middle classes were able to develop and flourish. Following their lead, art historians have fleshed out a narrative suggesting that the progress of the 'British School' of painting in the eighteenth century, in the absence of organized or predictable state patronage of the arts, was largely facilitated by its display in an array of idiosyncratic public-private venues, such as schools, religious charities and pleasure gardens.[19] The establishment of numerous artist-driven commercial exhibition spaces and small academies, not to mention the Royal Academy and its annual exhibitions which began in 1768, meant that by the turn of the nineteenth century London was rich in venues for looking at contemporary art. The expansion of metropolitan art venues (in London and regionally) worked hand-in-hand with the development of educated, middle-class audiences, eventually making possible the emergence of a range of national, regional and municipal museums and art galleries, funded both by private individuals and the British government.[20]

The 'public sphere' for art outlined above is only part of the story of art in Britain and Habermas' now-classic theorization of the public sphere has undergone thoroughgoing reappraisal.[21] The gallery at Cleveland House offers an opportunity for detailed analysis of an intersectional space in which the signs of private ownership and public-facing mission were fundamentally intertwined. A tangible example of Linda Colley's oft-cited observation that in order to avoid a repeat of the French Revolution in their own country, British elites wished to make it appear that 'aristocratic property was in some magical and strictly intangible way the *people's property also'*, Cleveland House permits in-depth study of the processes through which this 'magical' transformation could take place.[22] Enthusiasts of gentlemen's galleries, who tended to be educated, 'polite' men or artists who would have qualified for entry, never assumed that private houses should or would be open freely to the general public. On the contrary, in writing and image, they leant heavily on notions of privacy and domesticity to affirm Cleveland House as private space and its contents as private property, even as both house and collection enjoyed high visibility in the public arena.

'Privacy' and 'domesticity', concepts that were once considered the province of women's history and therefore outside of mainstream historical concern have, in the last several decades, attracted considerable interest from historians in the fields of politics, art, material culture, literature and sociology.[23] What has emerged from this incredibly rich body of scholarship is a nuanced picture of how these concepts worked as cultural constructs in relation to gender and social class. Historians like Leonore Davidoff, Catherine Hall, Stella Tillyard and Amanda Vickery have convincingly demonstrated that the private house played a fundamental role in the rise of the concept of domesticity, which has been linked to the expansion of the middle classes and their cultural influence during the eighteenth century.[24]

In recent years art historians have energetically addressed themselves to questions of art and material culture and what they can tell us about the role of the private house in constructing and attenuating the roles described above. The private dwelling, as the physical manifestation of the values inherent in the domestic ideal, was a site of particular interest and investment for members of the polite middle classes who could afford to decorate and improve their houses as a public reflection of private virtue.[25] Enthusiasm for domesticity as a cultural concept was expressed in myriad ways, not least through building houses and decorating their interiors with the wide array of material objects the expanding empire made available to Georgian consumers.[26] These objects, which ranged from tea sets made by pioneers of mass production like Josiah Wedgwood to furniture made from imported woods sourced abroad thanks to the economic networks enabled by imperialism, were widely understood to increase the comfort of the interior. Kate Retford has demonstrated the exquisite nuance with which portraiture could be used to define and exhibit gender roles for intimate and public audiences alike.[27] Others, including Vickery and social and economic historian Jon Stobart, have excavated the role men and women played in commissioning the art, furniture and other durable and ephemeral items that filled private interiors, lending tremendous insight into the ways that such activity allowed people to perform class and gender identity, social identities that were at times dressed up in the language of privacy.[28]

How were these objects – once they had been acquired – arranged, understood and used within the space of the private interior? This question is, by its nature, challenging to approach, not least because these are aspects of the historic interior and domestic life that are only obliquely visible to historians, who have nevertheless shed important light on these questions across a wide range of places and time periods.[29] Until Nicholas Tromans' recent book *The Private Lives of Pictures*, however, there had been few attempts to put forth an overarching narrative about the display, meaning and use of pictures in British houses, especially those occupied by people who did not belong to the uppermost echelon of the class system.[30] In the twenty-first century, many people think of paintings as isolated masterpieces to be viewed in museums in a state of quiet contemplation, but how this idea developed over the course of centuries is one question that underpins those addressed by this book.

As domesticity became more deeply embedded into cultural perceptions of British identity, the question of which class could most convincingly claim the moral authority that domesticity represented became one of vital political importance. Dror Wahrman has argued that the gentry and aristocracy were increasingly concerned to promote and protect the privacy of their own families and to espouse domesticity as a signifier of their continued fitness as a ruling class, especially after the French Revolution.[31] Yet, the idea that the home was a site of retreat and intimate family life did not fit comfortably with the traditional demands and expectations of the ruling classes. The enormous townhouses that dotted London, like Cleveland House, functioned primarily as stages for the performance of public duty and played a critical role in the production of elite metropolitan culture that adherents of domesticity were keen to deflect.[32] The scale of these houses and the expectation that they would be used for balls and assemblies throughout the social season, welcoming a constant stream of visitors and guests, meant they were different in nature and kind from the typical London house.

It is important not to overstate the extent to which Cleveland House would have been regarded by anyone, including its owners, as a 'domestic' space. Despite these caveats, personal privacy – glossed as domesticity – was increasingly embraced amongst the upper classes who understood the need to balance it with the duty to participate in public life. Cleveland House was hailed in the press as a 'national' collection and was publicised as open to the public – as limited as this public was in practice – thanks to the sense of duty embraced by its magnanimous owner. Yet, even during the height of its fame, the gallery was designated as 'open' for only one afternoon a week, a few months of the year during the London season. The rest of the time it was closed, available for the use of the family when they were in town and for private, invitation only, social events.

Materialising the Gallery: Issues of Representation

It is enormously challenging to recover what it meant to encounter renowned masterpieces of art in any glamorous London townhouse in the early nineteenth century. This objective is made more daunting in light of Cleveland House's demolition and a dearth of written documentation regarding the gallery's initial design and construction. Fortunately, an unusually abundant selection of images and texts representing and describing Cleveland House enable study and analysis of the issues raised above. Cleveland House was written about in guidebooks and *catalogues raisonnés*, in newspapers and magazines, and in diaries and letters. Likewise there is a profusion of visual material to consider, including a perspectival view, a floor plan, detailed individual room plans and engravings of the pictures in the collection, all created for distribution to the general public and supported by a range of texts. The interdependence of the gallery's private and public faces was subtly expressed in such texts and images, which proliferated after 1806 when the gallery officially opened for public afternoons during the late spring and summer.

Picture lists and catalogues are a particularly important source of evidence for how the gallery was organized, decorated and thought about at any given moment. At least six different guidebooks and catalogues were produced during the gallery's first two decades. These took multiple forms, from simple picture lists designed to be used while walking in the gallery to multi-volume, fully illustrated *catalogues raisonnés*. The first to appear, *A Catalogue of Pictures at Cleveland House*, was a picture list in the form of a pocket-sized book printed for J Hays of Marylebone Street in 1806. Catalogues were distributed at the door and this is certainly the one that early visitors would have received upon entry.[33] Household account books show a payment to Hays for these catalogues on 23 May 1806, a few days after the gallery opened on 21 May.[34] After 1808, however, the primary source on all matters related to the gallery was antiquarian John Britton's *catalogue raisonné*-cum-guidebook.[35] Printed in octavo format, a convenient size for carrying by hand, Britton's book encapsulated all of the practical information a visitor could possibly need. It contained a list of conditions for entry, a floor plan, a perspectival view of the interior and detailed notes on many of the pictures. The floor plan could be used to navigate its spaces and Britton's exegeses on the paintings could be read in front of the artworks they described. The next major project addressing the collection appeared in 1818 in the form of collector William Young Ottley's monumental four-volume, fully illustrated *catalogue raisonné*. In contrast to Britton's hand-held guidebook, Ottley's folio-sized catalogue was an expensive collector's item intended to proclaim Cleveland House's national and international significance.[36] Though they differ in important respects, Britton and Ottley's catalogues were both elaborate and ambitious attempts to record the quality and depth of Cleveland House's collection and the gallery itself as a space for looking at art.[37]

The wealth of the visual and written testimony outlined above enables wide-ranging analysis of how the gallery was understood by both its owners and the public. Looking closely at Ottley's luxurious *catalogue raisonné* as an object in its own right, for example, offers the opportunity to consider how visitors and readers experienced and engaged with the gallery as a space to look at art and as a private interior. As a physical object Ottley's catalogue was impressive, comprising four volumes in atlas folio size. The most deluxe edition was available fully hand-coloured in 1818 at the (astronomical) price of £178 10s, but even the least expensive black-and-white editions were advertised for the substantial sum of £35.[38] The exceptional example of the book illustrated here, one of only two known hand-coloured copies, is opulently bound and signed by Dawson & Lewis, a prominent luxury bookbinder active during the late 1810s and 1820s (see Figure 0.6).[39] Its

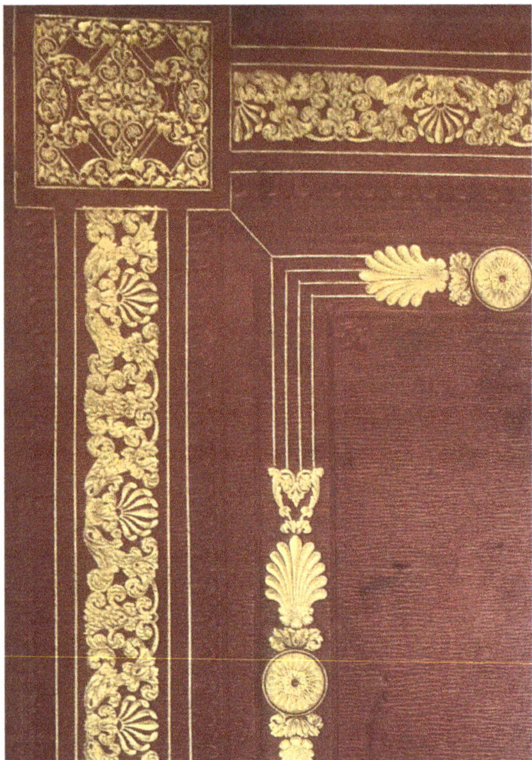

FIGURE 0.6 *Regency binding signed by Dawson for William Young Ottley,* Engravings of the Most Noble the Marquis of Stafford's collection of pictures in London, *London: Longman, Hurst, Rees, Orme, and Brown, 1818. Courtesy of Charles Sebag-Montefiore, London.*

physical size, not to mention its weight, means that the catalogue can only be read resting on a table; simply turning one of the enormous pages requires two hands. It contained a set of thirteen floor plans depicting the interior of each room in the gallery, as well as nearly 300 individual engravings made after every picture on display at the time of publication.

This brief description of the plates and the book that contained them does not explain why the floor plans themselves are so compelling and invite close, sustained looking. The plans evocatively recreate in miniature the aristocratic world to be found inside Cleveland House, depicting the pictures in the context of the furnishings and family heirlooms that surrounded them (see Figure 0.7) The richly furnished interiors visually echo descriptions that appeared in the periodical press, which dwelt at length on the furniture and other decorative objects the gallery contained. Writers offered detailed accounts of the lighting, mirrors, sculpture, wall colours, silver plate, even plants and other ephemeral objects that filled its spaces. These material markers of the lived, social life of the gallery were a source of intense interest for a variety of audiences; author Priscilla Wakefield best summarised the public fascination with the house's interior when she wrote that Cleveland House 'is admired still more for the superb furniture within, than for its magnificence without'.[40]

Bringing together the disparate forms of evidence described above – objects, printmaking, newspaper archives, first-hand accounts – requires casting the methodological net widely to encompass approaches drawn not only from art history but also anthropology, sociology and economics. All contribute to building up a holistic picture of Cleveland House as a physical location filled with the material objects that attended upper-class life, including paintings, chandeliers and silk draperies. It is crucial, however, that we not interpret such images and texts as transparent documents of a space that no longer exists. Certainly, images of the interior communicate many factual details about how the rooms were decorated, where paintings were hung and how they were organised, but by subjecting catalogues and their contents to rigorous visual and historical analysis they can also reveal the ideological framework that underpinned the gallery and allow recontextualization of the collection within the exigencies of taste, style and social practice.[41] As Michael Yonan has written, 'the long-held belief that certain classes of objects are somehow intrinsically more worthy of close analysis' has been a barrier to fully integrating the discipline of art history with material culture studies.[42] This book takes seriously the notion that all of the different types of objects that occupied and documented the gallery have something to tell us about its architecture, decoration, social function and cultural meaning.

The methodological approach outlined above would not be possible without the enormous body of work devoted to the study of consumption and material culture that has developed since the 1980s. The anthropologist Arjun Appadurai has offered the 'social life of things' as a valuable

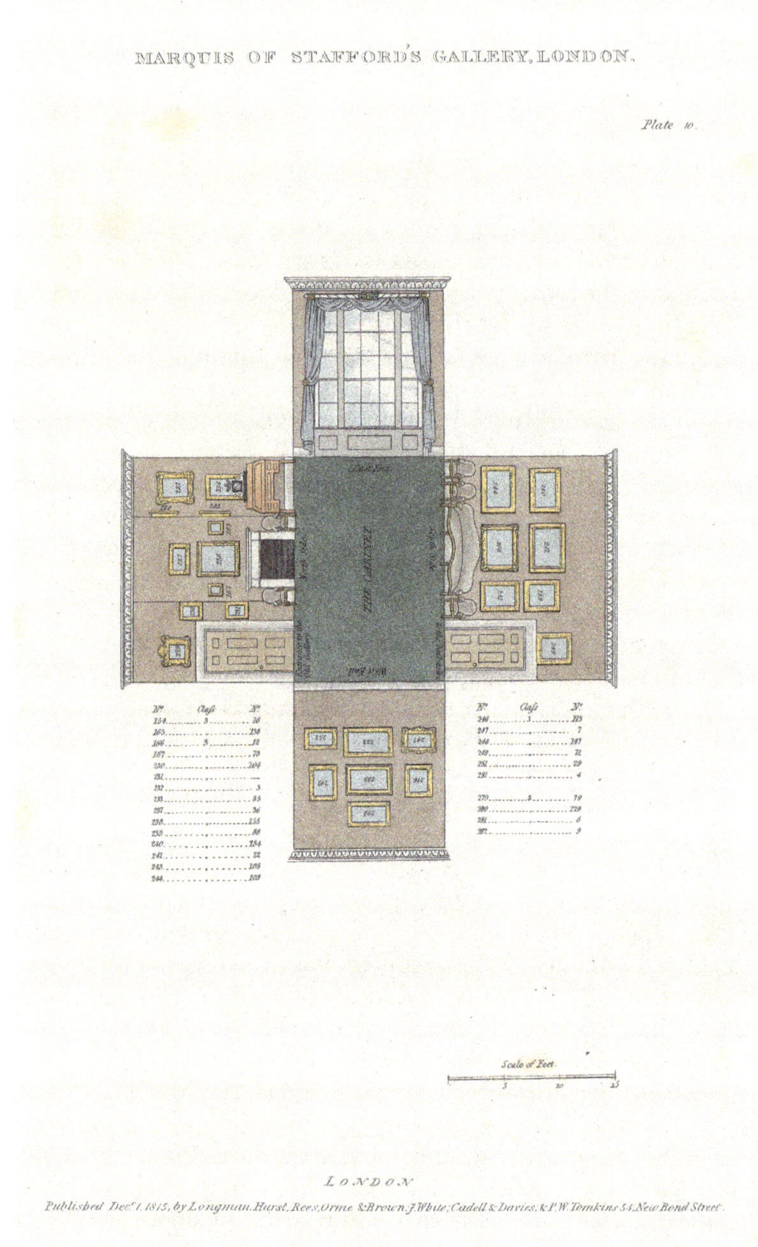

FIGURE 0.7 *[P.W. Tomkins, engr.] 'The Cabinet' from William Young Ottley,* Engravings of the Most Noble the Marquis of Stafford's collection of pictures in London, *London: Longman, Hurst, Rees, Orme, and Brown, 1818, engraving. Yale Center for British Art, Paul Mellon Collection.*

framework for theorizing the way that people and objects interact in complex systems and can shed light on the role luxury objects played within the space of the London townhouse.[43] Neil McKendrick, John Brewer and JH Plumb's *The Birth of a Consumer Society* set the stage for scholars to understand the proliferation of consumer goods in eighteenth and early nineteenth-century British culture.[44] Another critical strand of scholarship revolves around the commission, making and disposition of the multitude of objects that furnished the upper-class house; tables and chairs, bed hangings, clocks and silver and china services, to name but a few examples.[45] In turn, sensitive and historically-informed consideration of how these objects were used reveals how style and functionality were sometimes intertwined with cultural meaning.[46] This book will place considerations of style and design into the contexts of both political ideology and social practice to unlock new perspectives on the cultural practices surrounding the making, display and appreciation of art.

Animating the Gallery: Social Space

The private townhouse gallery was a distinctive type of social space in the early nineteenth century, putting a socially-diverse group of people into motion in the context of the aristocratic interior. Its closest analogue might be the *salon*, which has been explored in British and French cultural life in the eighteenth and early nineteenth centuries especially as an outlet for women's intellectual pursuits.[47] As noted above, townhouses played a critical role in the social and political activities of the elite. Townhouses on the scale of Cleveland House were the province of only the richest and highest-ranking families, their magnificent exteriors functioning as public statements of wealth and political authority. Their interiors, however, were mostly inaccessible to the general public. Access to such spaces was tightly controlled; admission to a house bestowed substantial social cachet on the fortunate recipient.

Yet news of the sumptuous furnishings, lavish assemblies and political dealings that took place within circulated widely in engravings and periodical literature and, in the case of Cleveland House, the possibility of acquiring a ticket to the gallery offered people from a range of social classes the promise of a peek inside. An aquatint by John Bluck after a drawing by Thomas Rowlandson and AC Pugin, for example, depicts a 'Drawing Room' where members of the aristocracy mingle in a sumptuous interior at St James's Palace, the royal coat of arms clearly visible on the rich scarlet canopy in the background. Textiles, portraits in gilded frames, chandeliers and mirrors installed between large, sun-filled windows evoke an interior that only the richest could create (see Figure 0.8). Bluck's aquatint, like images of Cleveland House's interior, circulated in an economy of print aimed at

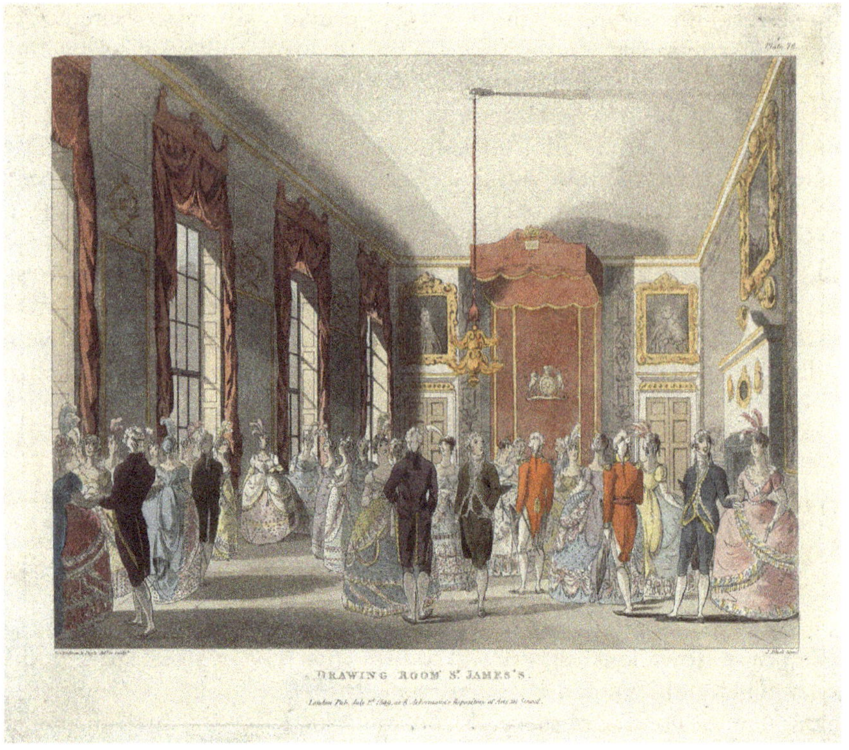

FIGURE 0.8 *John Bluck after Thomas Rowlandson and Augustus Charles Pugin, 'Drawing Room, St. James's,' hand-coloured aquatint, 1809. Yale Center for British Art, Paul Mellon Collection, B1977.14.18152.*

audiences who would never be invited to such an assembly themselves, making visible the social world that such interiors enabled.

The work of anthropologists Mary Douglas and Baron Isherwood suggests a route to explore how objects were used to negotiate social regimes governing access to spaces like St. James's Palace or Cleveland House.[48] Likewise, social geographers Bill Hillier and Julienne Hanson have written, 'however much we may prefer to discuss architecture in terms of visual styles, its most far-reaching practical effects are . . . at the level of space . . . it provides the material preconditions for the patterns of movement, encounter and avoidance which are the material realization – as well as sometimes the generator – of social relations'.[49] Buildings like Cleveland House functioned as stages on which the public lives of London's most important landowning families played out; the specifics of their decoration were but one aspect of the spectacle. Through her work on the *beau monde*, historian Hannah Greig proposes a nuanced framework for understanding how the deployment of money in the pursuit of social and political prestige shaped metropolitan culture in the eighteenth and early nineteenth centuries.[50] Most of what we know about the experience of visiting Cleveland House comes from the visitors who meandered, studied, sketched and gossiped in its spaces. We must rely on these visitors – artists, ticket holders, members of the press, the family's aristocratic friends – to understand how the gallery looked and how it made visitors feel. If we understand such accounts as performances of social capital, visitors experienced the thrill of seeing the interior of a glamorous townhouse and the possibility of chance encounters with some of the most well-known figures of the day.

Past and Present

By drawing on techniques of visual analysis that are amongst the art historian's most compelling methodological tools, this book aims to understand more deeply what images can tell us about how Cleveland House functioned as a space, not only for displaying and looking at art in the early nineteenth century, but also for claiming territory in the cultural debates that characterized the period. The issues at stake included the fundamental nature of public institutions, the primacy of private collectors in forming national taste and the development of a national cultural life in which private houses and the collections they contained embodied the moral authority of the ruling class, somehow speaking to and for 'the nation'. When displayed to the public in a magnificent private house, Old Master paintings could be transformed into national treasures, a status which their very position in London's most prestigious dwellings helped to confer. Put another way, only a private house, which symbolically encapsulated the principles of hereditary privilege and constitutional monarchy that formed the foundation of the British political system, could fulfil the expectations raised by the phrase the '*Louvre* of London', as Cleveland House was dubbed shortly after it opened in 1806.

During subsequent decades, the cultural pressures that had initially prompted the Marquess of Stafford to open his collection to the public began to yield as commercial art galleries and public art museums proliferated around the country. Bridgewater House and its gallery enjoyed a slowly fading reputation for glamour and prestige until the 1930s, featuring prominently in E Beresford Chancellor's illustrated volume *The Private Palaces of London Past and Present* (1908), in which it was described as a 'palace of art'.[51] The gallery at Bridgewater House remained open to the public until sometime around 1940, when the prospect of war prompted its closure and the evacuation of the pictures from the city. (A wise decision, it turned out, as the gallery was severely damaged in a German bombing raid in 1941. Annibale Carracci's *Danaë*, one of the few pictures to remain *in situ* after the evacuation, was destroyed in the blast (see Figure 1.2).[52])

After the war, the Duke of Sutherland sold Bridgewater House. It is presently owned by a family that is not associated with either the Duke or his descendants. Having moved his collection to Scotland where it was no longer accessible to the public, the Duke arranged to place the most important pictures on long-term loan with the National Gallery in London and the Scottish National Gallery. Pictures like Raphael's *Holy Family with a Palm Tree*, Titian's *Diana and Actaeon* and *Diana and Callisto* and JMW Turner's *Dutch Boats in a Gale* became beloved stalwarts of their permanent collections (see Figures 1.19, 2.3 and 2.5). As a result, over the course of the past 75 years, pictures that once hung in Cleveland House have remained steadily in the public eye. Many came to be understood as 'public' property in the popular imagination, if not by any legal standard, even as most people who saw them in public institutions had little idea of the richness of the history sketched above.

By the end of the twentieth century, Cleveland House and its role in London's art world had become a historical footnote. In 2009 and 2012, however, the collection – if not the gallery that once displayed it to an eager public – came back into the news when the Duke of Sutherland decided to sell the two highly-prized pictures by Titian mentioned above, *Diana and Actaeon* and *Diana and Callisto*, throwing their status as long-term loans to the National Gallery into doubt. The pictures were eventually purchased for the nation for the combined price of £95 million after a widely-publicized fundraising campaign, but the sale prompted a debate about the use of public funds to purchase pictures that had already become accepted as 'public' property.[53] Yet, the question as to whether these paintings should most rightly be considered the property of an individual or the cultural heritage of a nation can be traced back to the first days and weeks that the gallery was open in 1806. The tensions between public and private interests that bedevilled the concept of the gallery at the moment of its inception are still being played out, as the question of when a private possession morphs into public patrimony animates the art market of the twenty-first century.

1

'A very complete business': Designing and Building the Gallery

In 1808, antiquarian John Britton published a guidebook and *catalogue raisonné* of the gallery at Cleveland House. It featured JC Smith's view of the New Gallery as its frontispiece (see Figure 1.1). As the only perspectival view made of the gallery's interior, Smith's view is one of the few pieces of evidence available regarding its architecture and decoration. Smith depicts the gallery from an angle permitting a clear view of several of the collection's prized masterpieces. Annibale Carracci's *Danaë* (see Figure 1.2) dominates the wall at the image's upper left while a trio of paintings by Raphael, including *Holy Family with a Palm Tree* (see Figure 1.19), are arranged symmetrically below. The room is spacious and light, thanks to the large rectangular skylight depicted at the top of the image, and is mostly clear of furniture and other decorative objects, allowing visitors to circulate freely, as they might in a twenty-first century museum. Prioritising the room's status as a 'gallery', Smith records elements that were essential to its effective functioning as a space for displaying art, such as the skylight and picture rails, which engraver William Bond renders in straightforwardly legible black and white.

Smith's image is a valuable primary source documenting the gallery's interior, but it is also a cultural artifact in its own right expressing how its patron and his supporters thought about the meaning and purpose of the collection and the gallery built to display it. In this chapter, I will use close reading of Britton's guidebook, including Smith's image, to explore what we know about the gallery's architecture, which was designed by architect Charles Heathcote Tatham and to explore the cultural meaning of the 'art gallery' in the early nineteenth century. Tatham was an ardent student of classical antiquity, having lived in Rome for many years and later publishing books of drawings and designs made after ancient architecture and decorative objects. The decorative mouldings, coffered ceilings, furniture and light fixtures he used for the interior of Cleveland House betokened the

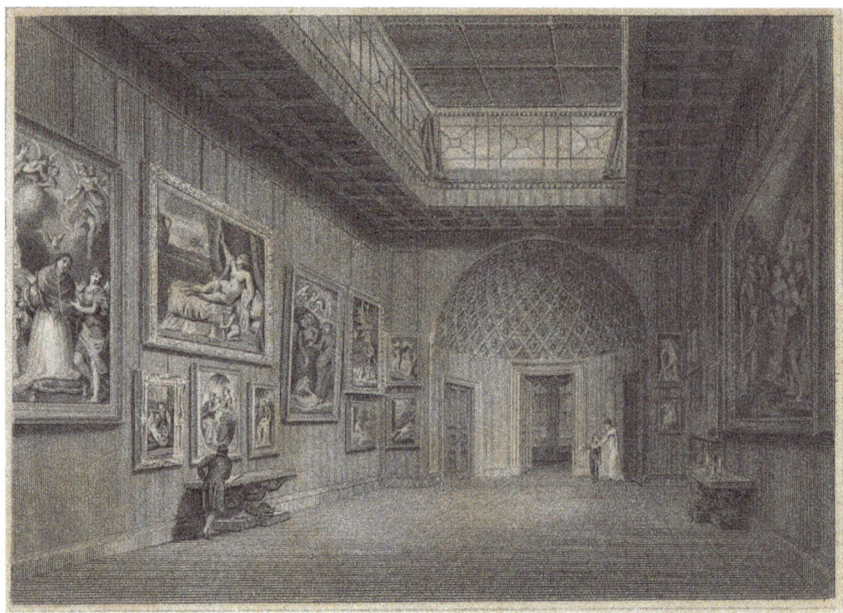

FIGURE 1.1 *William Bond (engr.) after JC Smith,* The New Gallery at Cleveland House *in John Britton,* Catalogue Raisonné of the Pictures Belonging to the Most Honourable the Marquis of Stafford, in the Gallery of Cleveland House *(London: Longman, Hurst, Rees, and Orme, 1808), National Gallery of Art, Washington, DC.*

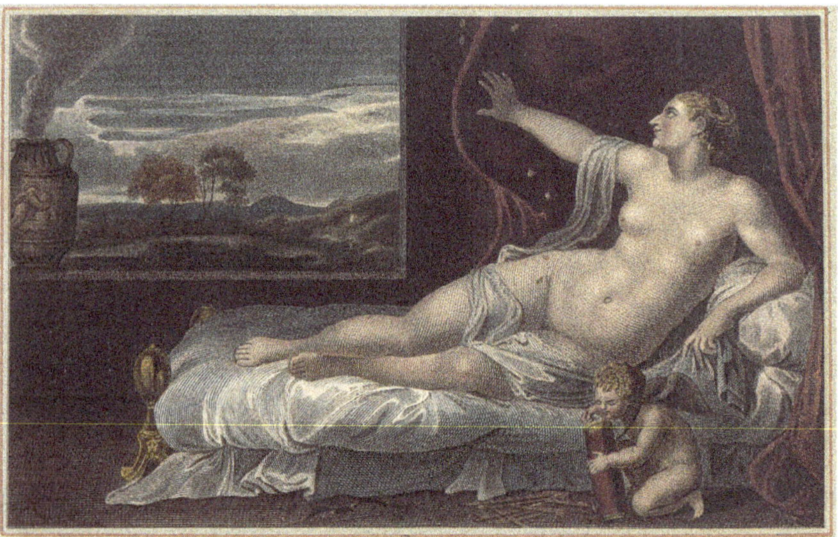

FIGURE 1.2 *Anon after Danaë by Annibale Carracci, in William Young Ottley,* Engravings of the Most Noble the Marquis of Stafford's collection of pictures in London, *London: Longman, Hurst, Rees, Orme, and Brown, 1818, engraving. Yale Center for British Art, Paul Mellon Collection.*

aesthetic principles of ancient Greece and Rome, suggesting a natural connection between the social practices of antiquity and those of contemporary London. Though no architectural drawings or correspondence between patron and architect have come to light, evidence drawn from Tatham's own writings and designs for other galleries reveals that his design for Cleveland House reflected a concerted effort to produce the very notion of a public art gallery, both in terms of how it should look and how it should be understood as a cultural space.

To 'reconstruct' Cleveland House, in terms of both its architectural and decorative elements and its social and cultural purpose, is to explore the vocabularies and meanings of classicism as they were constituted in early nineteenth-century Britain. The visual language of neoclassicism, inspired by avid study of antique buildings and objects, influenced every aspect of Cleveland House. Archaeologist and museum historian Susan Pearce has written that in Tatham's imagination the 'construction of aesthetic[s] is a part of constituent knowledge'.[1] For Tatham, creating an interior that could adequately accommodate a renowned collection of Old Masters and offer an appropriate setting for their study and contemplation was itself a question of aesthetics and design. There were many aesthetic modes available to architects and designers in the late Georgian period; to choose classicism was to make an argument for the gallery as a public space, even as it was cocooned within a private house. Surveying the fields of Georgian architecture and interior design, Hannah Greig and Giorgio Riello have written that 'the making of an interior was not simply about the adoption of the right elements within a certain vocabulary of taste that preferred, for example, columns to arches' but 'a historical construction, an association of terms, classifications and categories that have had a complex – and sometimes troubled – existence'.[2] Analysing surviving texts, images and objects allows us to excavate the historical realities of how art galleries evolved and functioned as well as construct the terms under which they could be understood. Moreover, the gallery's architecture, its decoration and the objects that filled its interior worked in concert to shape practices of displaying and looking at art in the context of a society where state and municipal galleries of art had not yet fully emerged.

'Sufficient for the dignity of a Princess': The Origins of the Gallery at Cleveland House

It is essential to begin by situating the gallery in the context of the life of its patron, George Leveson-Gower, Marquess of Stafford and the cultural milieu that prompted its construction. If not for a quirk of dynastic fate, the gallery at Cleveland House may never have been built at all. The enormously wealthy entrepreneur and art collector Francis Egerton, Third Duke of

Bridgewater ('Bridgewater') was a prominent figure, known primarily for the immense fortune he had accumulated building a major canal system in the northwest of England beginning in the 1750s. Bridgewater died on 8 March 1803; having no direct heirs he left the bulk of his estate to George Leveson-Gower, his nephew. Then styled Earl Gower, George would inherit the title of Marquess of Stafford upon the death of his own father in October of the same year. In 1833, very close to the end of his life, Stafford was created Duke of Sutherland. For the sake of clarity, this book will refer to him as 'Stafford' throughout, which was his primary title from 1803–1833 during the 30-year period he controlled the gallery at Cleveland House.

Stafford was born to an aristocratic Staffordshire family in 1758 (see Figure 1.3). In 1783 he married Elizabeth ('Lady Stafford'), who inherited the title of Countess of Sutherland in her own right as an infant (see Figure 1.4). The couple had four children born between 1786 and 1800, George, Charlotte, Elizabeth and Francis. After sitting as Member of Parliament for Newcastle-under-Lyme and Staffordshire respectively, Stafford was appointed Great Britain's ambassador to Paris, a plum diplomatic assignment that came at an uneasy moment only months after the fall of the Bastille. The family spent a few years in Paris during the waning days of the court of Louis XVI and Marie-Antoinette but, as the

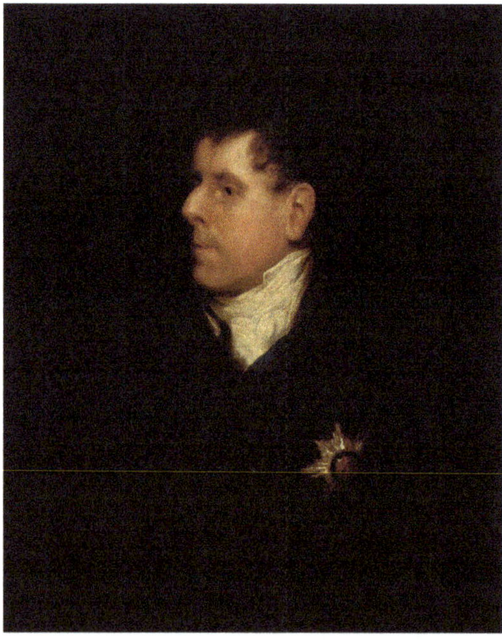

FIGURE 1.3 *Thomas Phillips,* George Granville Leveson-Gower, First Duke of Sutherland, *1805. ©National Portrait Gallery, London.*

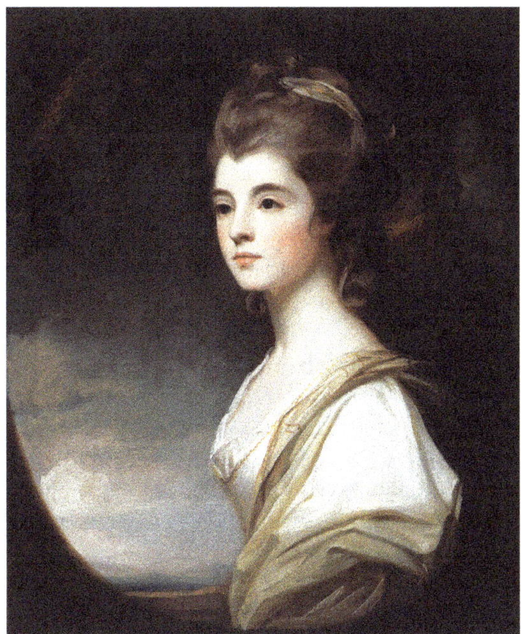

FIGURE 1.4 *George Romney,* Elizabeth, Countess of Sutherland, *1782. Cincinnati Art Museum, Ohio, USA© Cincinnati Art Museum/Given in honour of Mr and Mrs Charles F Williams by their children/Bridgeman Images.*

political situation deteriorated, the ambassadorship was recalled in August 1792. After returning from Paris, Lord and Lady Stafford took a house in Wimbledon, a suburb relatively removed from the political, social and cultural goings-on of aristocratic London, with which Stafford was not particularly involved during this period.

Stafford's profile on the London art scene increased dramatically in 1798 after he joined a consortium led by his uncle, Bridgewater, to purchase a large group of Italian and French paintings from the collection of the ducs d'Orléans. (The third member of the consortium was Frederick Howard, Fifth Earl of Carlisle ('Carlisle'), who was married to Stafford's sister, Margaret.) The ducs d'Orléans had assembled one of eighteenth-century Europe's most celebrated collections, rich in masterpieces by artists like Raphael, Titian, and Claude. The group of three men became known as the Bridgewater Consortium and the pictures known colloquially as the 'Orleans Collection' in English; both the Consortium itself and the market processes that brought the pictures to London have been the subject of extensive research.[3] The group of Italian and French paintings acquired by the Consortium in 1798 thus formed the core of the collection that the gallery at Cleveland House was built to display.

The fame of these pictures attracted enormous public interest. They were exhibited in London from December 1798 through early 1799 to large crowds and widespread acclaim.[4] Despite their significance, however, the Orléans pictures accounted for only about 15 per cent of those on display at Cleveland House when it opened in 1806. Bridgewater and Stafford assembled the rest of the collection through a sustained campaign of collecting and patronage about which Peter Humfrey has written in detail.[5] Bridgewater purchased continental paintings *en masse* during the period of opportunity presented by the revolution in France but did not neglect contemporary British painters, including Richard Wilson and JMW Turner, whose *Dutch Boats in a Gale* (1801), known colloquially as *The Bridgewater Sea-Piece*, became one of the collection's highlights (see Figure 2.5). Having never married, Bridgewater had no direct heir to continue his legacy in commerce or the arts, leaving open the question of who would inherit his enormous wealth. He ultimately decided to leave his most valuable business interests, property and possessions – the canal network, his London townhouse and the widely-admired collection of art held there – to Stafford, his nephew.

Bridgewater's death in early 1803 and the inheritance that followed marked an important turning point in Stafford's life. Several months later, Stafford's father died, giving him control of his own family's substantial estates in Staffordshire and elevating him from Earl Gower to Marquess of Stafford. The Bridgewater and Stafford fortunes combined amounted to an almost unbelievable fortune, even to its beneficiaries, and propelled the Marquess and Marchioness of Stafford into the uppermost tier of aristocratic London society. Shortly after learning of the inheritance, Lady Stafford dashed off a note to her longtime friend Frances, Lady Douglas. Tucked into another letter in the family's archive at the National Library of Scotland, it conjures the image of a woman with life-changing news she was eager to share: 'The D. of B has left L. G. a very large income . . . though there are 1000 entails & god knows what belonging to it. It is an immense thing, particularly to people who expected so little as we did – I will tell you all the particulars when we meet.' Yet, she outlines the contents of the bequest, which included the 'income of the navigation', referring to Bridgewater's Staffordshire canal system; Woolmers Park, Bridgewater's country estate in Hertfordshire and, almost as an aside, 'the house in Town', by which she meant Cleveland House. Summing up the significance of this inheritance Elizabeth wrote, 'I don't know what the income of this nav is, but it is something very large, sufficient for the dignity of a Princess'.[6]

Rumors about the value of the estate quickly circulated within London society. The Hon Caroline Howe, an elderly widow, wrote to one of her regular correspondents, diarist Mary Berry:

> Another very great death happened on Tuesday morning – that of the Duke of Bridgewater. What I am going to write will show what an immense property he has left behind him. . . . To Lord Gower he leaves

> the navigation, that is, the income of it; the management of the concern being put in trustees' hands; his house in town all strictly entailed (but to him for his life), the pictures, library, & c. as heir-looms, and then to his second and younger sons successively, and their sons, excluding whoever may be Marquis of Stafford; his intention being to make a new family, for whoever has it is to take the name of Egerton . . . The navigation is reckoned a clear 74,000l. a –year; the last year it produced 80,000l., and is supposed to be improving.[7]

Mrs Howe appears to have been extremely well informed. Eric Richards, the late economic historian who produced the definitive account of the family's finances, wrote that records suggest an income averaging about £75,000 per year from 1803 until the early 1830s.[8] While estimating how much this would represent in today's money is notoriously difficult, we might consider a figure of £7.5 million per year or more, keeping in mind that the buying power of this figure may have been even greater. The couple spent enormous sums on entertaining and travel while continuing to collect art. During the subsequent two decades, Stafford's income also permitted the expansion and refurbishment of the family's houses at Trentham and Lilleshall and of his wife's ancestral home, Dunrobin Castle, in the Scottish Highlands (see Figure 1.5, refer to Figure 4.1). Just before his death in 1833 Stafford was elevated to Duke of Sutherland. Calling him a 'leviathan of wealth', society memoirist Charles Greville wrote, 'I believe he is the richest individual who ever died, and I should like to know what his property amounts to, out of pure curiosity.'[9]

Cleveland House and the collection it contained were a source of wealth and prestige but, given high levels of public interest in the Orléans pictures, they also came with a pressing sense of civic responsibility. Within weeks of learning of Bridgewater's death, Stafford had hired architect Charles Heathcote Tatham to renovate Cleveland House's existing gallery and expand it substantially to accommodate the collection and permit the admission of the public. It was long assumed that the terms of Bridgewater's will obligated his nephew to make the gallery accessible but, as I have written elsewhere, this appears to be a misconception spread by a rumour beginning in the early nineteenth century.[10] Although Bridgewater's will did not explicitly mandate the display of the collection to the public, it did take pains to establish Cleveland House and its contents, including art, furniture, books and silver plate, as 'heirlooms' that demanded special consideration:

> the said pictures, paintings, library, books, manuscripts, and engravings shall be kept as one entire collection, and the same and the said furniture and plate shall from time to time be considered as in the nature of heir-looms, as far as the rules of law and equity will permit, and be kept at or in the said capital mansion house, and not be removed out of the same on any pretence whatsoever.[11]

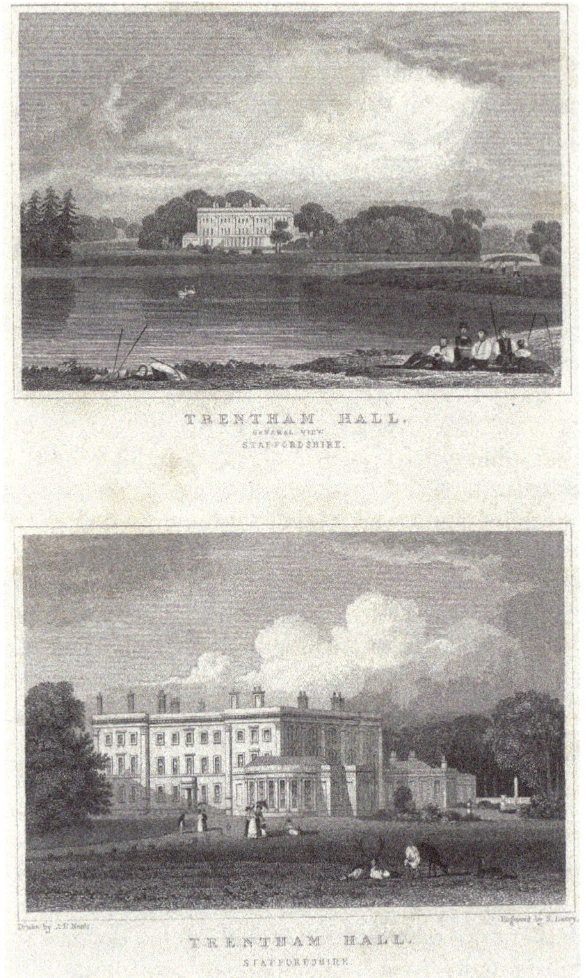

FIGURE 1.5 *S. Lacey after John Preston Neale (1780–1847), 'Trentham Hall' from* Jones' views of the seats, mansions, castles, etc. of noblemen and gentlemen, in England, *London: Jones and Co [1829–1831], engraving. Yale Center for British Art, Paul Mellon Collection.*

The will transformed a collection largely assembled during the course of a decade into an ancestral inheritance that would persist over the course of generations.[12]

Stafford's decision to use the combined Bridgewater and Stafford fortunes to renovate and expand the gallery at Cleveland House may be understood as a response to cultural pressures that had mounted over the previous century in favour of making private collections more easily accessible to artists and the general public. During the eighteenth century, spaces for the display and study of fine art had appeared in cities across Europe, including the Capitoline Museum in Rome, the Uffizi in Florence and the Belvedere in Vienna.[13] Of these the Belvedere Museum stood out as an early showcase for the idea of the public museum when it opened three days a week in 1776 under the auspices of Maria Theresa, as did the *Grand Galerie* at the *Palais-Royal* in Paris, designed by Jules Hardouin-Mansart for the duc d'Orléans.[14] The *Grand Galerie* housed d'Orléans' collection of nearly 500 pictures by sixteenth- and seventeenth-century masters, the very collection from which, after the French Revolution, the core of the collection on display at Cleveland House would be formed. The gallery at the *Palais-Royal* was freely accessible to polite visitors from the first half of the eighteenth century.[15] As these continental precedents accumulated, there was a growing sense that the lack of major collections in Britain – at least those that were open to the public – was an impediment to the training of young artists and the development of public taste.

Britain's perceived dearth of Old Master paintings had long been a point of contention amongst collectors and artists. Though not first to do so, in 1719 Jonathan Richardson lamented the scarcity of English connoisseurs as a form of national deficiency.[16] Without a native source of patronage, Richardson argued, England would never reach the first rank amongst European countries, nor would an English school of painting flourish. Richardson's assessment gained acceptance and, by the second half of the eighteenth century, the widespread view, given voice by Sir Joshua Reynolds, the first president of the Royal Academy, was that the improvement of the British school of art was predicated on improving artists' training by facilitating the regular study and emulation of the Old Masters.[17] But artist training alone would not fully solve the problem. Whetting the nation's appetite for the paintings and sculptures that would inevitably flow from the Royal Academy's regime would require that members of the general public be exposed to regular exhibitions of pictures by Old Masters to encourage a new generation of patrons. But what form could such exposure take? A few of the grandest country house collections, such as Petworth, Wilton and Burghley House, were accessible to tourists through the well-documented practice of country house tourism.[18] The country house tour involved presenting oneself at a house to request a tour from the housekeeper, preferably when its owners were absent. Jocelyn Anderson's recent work has demonstrated that the country house tour was better organized, more clearly defined and enjoyed broader participation at an earlier date than has generally been appreciated.[19] At the same time, the practice was available mainly to well-to-do travellers who enjoyed abundant free time and the resources to travel, not to mention the sophistication to navigate the social minefield that country house visiting represented.

The very remoteness of many country houses made access difficult and many prominent art world figures, including Reynolds, fretted that collections hidden away in country mansions could not adequately serve the needs of artists or the nation.[20] Britain's urban centres were conspicuously lacking public venues for the display of Old Master paintings. Britons could look to the Ashmolean Museum in Oxford or the British Museum in London, but these specialized in natural history.[21] Pictures by continental masters were sporadically available to view around the metropolis, but there was no consistent or easily-accessible venue and few London collectors experimented with opening their houses to visitors.[22] Invitations were extended on a case-by-case basis through the personal networks of the upper classes or, in the case of artists, by introductions from professors at the Royal Academy. A remarkable early example was the gallery at Richmond House, London, which the Duke of Richmond opened to painters in 1758; Iain Pears notes that the Duke's largesse created a 'stir' precisely because it was still so unusual.[23]

After the founding of the *Musée du Louvre* in 1793 and especially after many well-heeled British tourists first saw the Louvre in person during the Peace of Amiens of 1802–1803, discomfort with the status quo reached a crisis.[24] After this moment it seemed clear that if Britain were to have any hope of competing with France – its longtime rival in the realms of art, culture and industry with whom it was currently at war – developing equivalent spaces in Britain had become an urgent matter. Art collectors responded by seeking to create functionally equivalent spaces in London where artists and the general public could engage with works of fine art. By 1802, there were a few notable collectors of sculpture and antiquities, including Charles Townley and Thomas Hope, whose houses were accessible upon application (see Figures 1.6 and 1.18). Likewise, Bridgewater welcomed select friends and artists who could provide letters of introduction. Bridgewater's collection, rich with excellent examples of Italian and French painting, was precisely the type to which advocates of public and private galleries alike argued access was most needed.[25] Early on, Bridgewater followed the approach familiar from the country house tour; in general admission was granted based on personal connections and was not restricted to fixed days or times. In 1804, Hope upped the ante by opening his London house to members of the Royal Academy using a ticketing system. Hope's awkward attempt to issue tickets to Royal Academicians – as opposed to treating them like gentlemanly equals – created a minor scandal.[26] However, the design of his gallery represented an important precedent for Tatham's work at Cleveland House, as I will discuss in detail later in this chapter.

By the time John Britton's guidebook to Cleveland House was published in 1808, he was able to make the claim that Stafford was 'first in London' to admit 'the Public'.[27] While Britton's assertion was accurate in the strictest sense, it obscured the earlier efforts of Townley and Hope, among others. The process of gaining access to Cleveland House's Wednesday afternoon gallery openings was not as straightforward or transparent as Britton implies; in practice it depended on personal connections and social know-

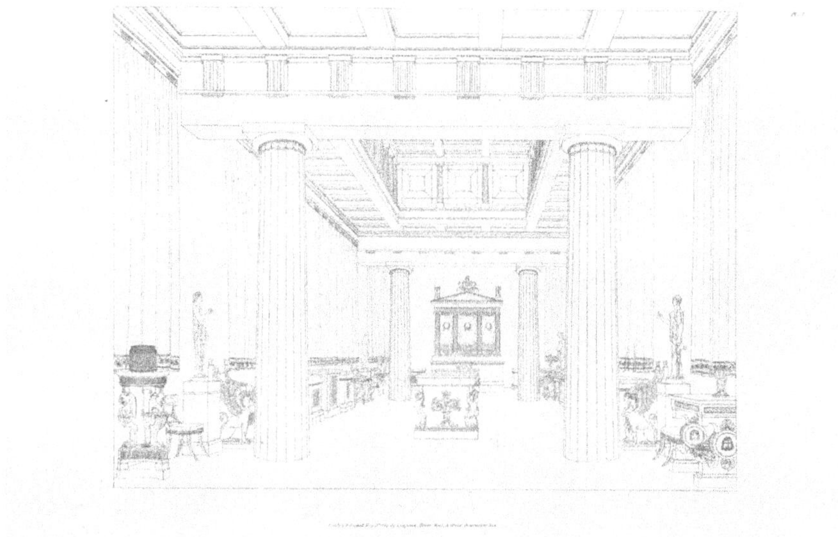

FIGURE 1.6 *'Picture Gallery' in Thomas Hope,* Household Furniture and Interior Decoration *(London: Longman, Hurst, Rees, and Orme, 1807). Getty Research Institute, Los Angeles (88-B10166).*

how. Even so, Britton's claim signalled Stafford's intention to position the gallery as a remedy for the general inaccessibility of important collections of art and to improve the state of British arts and design.

Several of the figures mentioned above were also instrumental in founding the British Institution for Promoting the Fine Arts in the United Kingdom in 1805. The purpose of the British Institution was to host loan exhibitions of pictures borrowed from private collections and make them easily accessible to members of the general public. It also mounted exhibitions of work by contemporary artists. The British Institution was the brainchild of a group of art patrons and collectors that included Stafford, Hope, Charles Long, Baron Farnborough, Sir George Beaumont and insurance mogul John Julius Angerstein (whose collection would form the nucleus of the National Gallery 20 years later). Although these men differed meaningfully in terms of social rank and wealth, they shared a commitment to using patronage and collecting practice to support the development of the British School.[28] Ann Pullan has argued that the British Institution functioned as a 'means by which patrician collectors were able to make their private possessions a public good'.[29] Her formulation suggests points of continuity between the impulses driving the British Institution and private galleries and why many of the same characters were active in both spheres of influence.

'A very complete business': The Design of the Gallery

Even as Stafford participated in founding the British Institution as one possible approach to making art from important private collections accessible to the public, construction on the new gallery at Cleveland House was already underway. Documentation of the design and construction phases of the project do not appear to have survived. However, barely more than a month after the Duke's death, the Hon Caroline Howe wrote again to Mary Berry outlining Stafford's intentions:

> Lord Gower sells his present habitation, and makes the late Duke of Bridgewater's his town residence; first building a fine drawing and eating-room, &c. to the park, raised to the height of the picture gallery and library, and moves the stables to Cleveland Court; then over the coach narrow way called Katharine-wheel Yard he throws a bridge, which leads to his garden in the Green Park; it will be a very complete business when finished.[30]

Again, Howe was very well informed. Her description of the scope of building works almost perfectly matches the finished structure that resulted three years later.

Stafford chose architect Charles Heathcote Tatham to lead the renovation and expansion of Cleveland House. The new space would need to balance the requirements of a private residence for a prominent family with those of accommodating the demands that admitting the public would inevitably bring; Tatham's career had prepared him to take on this challenge. In 1788, Tatham was hired as a clerk in an architectural office and within a few years had been accepted into the practice of fashionable architect Henry Holland.[31] Early in his career Holland had worked for Stafford's father on the renovation of Trentham Hall in Staffordshire (see Figure 1.5). His reputation grew thanks to several major projects, including Brooks's Club in St James's Street, and a series of speculative developments on the Chelsea estate in London, including Sloane Street, Sloane Square and Cadogan Place. These culminated in Holland being appointed to undertake a major remodelling of Carlton House, London, for the Prince of Wales.[32]

Entering Holland's office while work on Carlton House was ongoing allowed Tatham to gain valuable experience working on plans for prestigious clients. He became particularly known for his facility with 'ornamental decorations' – wall panels, friezes and fireplaces, for example – for both public and private spaces.[33] Tatham soon found himself mixing in rarefied circles. In 1794, with Holland's support, Tatham travelled to Rome to gather source material from classical antiquity.[34] Tatham spent several years in Italy, making drawings and circulating amongst prominent artists and collectors, including sculptor Antonio Canova, painters Angelica Kauffman and Richard Westmacott, diplomat and antiquarian Sir William Hamilton and his wife Emma, Lady Hamilton and, most significantly, the aforementioned Thomas Hope and Frederick Howard, Fifth Earl of Carlisle.

Both Hope and Carlisle, who had amassed distinguished collections by the end of the century, turned to Tatham to design galleries for their houses. Hope had spent years travelling around the Mediterranean collecting antiquities, including sculpture and vases.[35] In 1799, he acquired Clerk House at 1 Mansfield Street, London, which had been designed and built by Robert Adam in the late 1760s. Hope hired Tatham to design a new gallery and library, which became famous as a showcase for his idiosyncratic assemblage of antiquities and furniture; this house is often called Hope's 'Duchess Street mansion', which is how I will refer to it below.[36] Likewise, Carlisle was an avid collector of contemporary British and Old Master painting before joining the Bridgewater Consortium alongside Stafford (who was also his brother-in-law) in 1798.[37] In order to accommodate these acquisitions, Carlisle hired Tatham to finish the gallery at his family seat, Castle Howard, which had been left incomplete after the death of architect Sir Thomas Robinson in 1777. Tatham's brief at Castle Howard – a project which lasted from 1801–1812 and cost more than £4,000 – was to provide a grand setting for Carlisle's recently-acquired Orléans pictures, antique sculpture, busts of eighteenth-century political grandees and portraits.[38]

Tatham's facility with the vocabulary of neoclassical design, drawn directly from Greek and Roman sources, was evident in his work on both galleries. Tatham's involvement in Hope's gallery did not come to light until 2004, when late architectural historian and Hope biographer David Watkin published new drawings demonstrating that Hope had hired Tatham to carry out the design and construction of his influential house and gallery. While Hope made designs upon which Tatham's architectural drawings for the Duchess Street mansion were based, Watkin suggests that Hope purposely obscured Tatham's role in the project to claim sole credit.[39] The renovations enabled the display of antiquities and Old Master paintings, including a few Orléans pictures from the London sales, that were memorialized in a series of engravings published in Hope's landmark work of design history *Household Furniture and Interior Decoration* (1807) (see Figure 1.6).

Meanwhile, Carlisle hired Tatham to complete the gallery at Castle Howard. Unlike either Duchess Street or Cleveland House, Castle Howard's gallery survives. It has undergone only minor changes since the early nineteenth century and thus offers a rare opportunity to study one of Tatham's buildings in detail. A longitudinal section of the gallery published in 1811 indicates that Tatham adopted a stripped-down approach to its decoration (see Figure 1.7 refer to Figure 0.2). To this point, there was certainly no one rigid template for how galleries should be decorated or arranged, but there were generally accepted conventions. For example, one

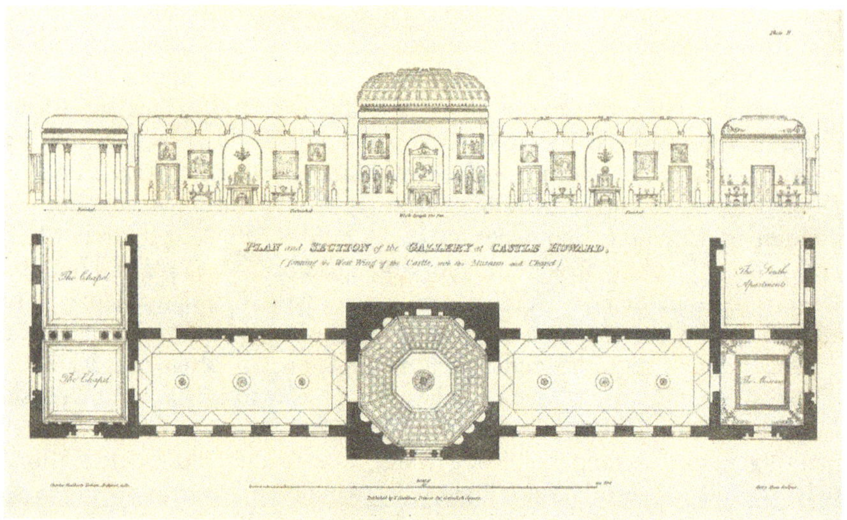

FIGURE 1.7 *Charles Heathcote Tatham, 'Plan and Section of the Gallery at Castle Howard' from* The Gallery at Castle Howard in Yorkshire *(London: T Gardiner, 1811). Avery Classics, Avery Architectural & Fine Arts Library, Columbia University.*

common practice was to cover the walls of galleries with rich green or red paint or fabric, considered a favourable background for oil paintings; likewise, pictures could be arranged on the walls according to a number of different systems of logic as I will discuss in Chapter Two.[40] Recent research has revealed that Tatham's design eschewed some of these expected practices, drawing inspiration from classical antiquity. The gallery walls were painted stone gray surmounted by coffered ceilings painted off-white.[41] Tatham placed an Egyptian-inspired fireplace at the centre of the interior wall, along which pictures were hung from rails. Pictures were hung so that each claimed its own distinct vertical segment of the wall. This arrangement was punctuated by pier tables, Roman Revival stools and several plinths displaying antique busts. Carlisle commissioned a portrait of himself and one of his sons standing in the gallery shortly after its completion; the resulting painting suggests that Carlisle hoped to promote the gallery as a space that prioritized looking at art over other concerns (see Figure 1.8). The gallery at Castle Howard was open to polite tourists under the principles generally in place for country house tourism and, in 1805, Carlisle published a guidebook which, as Jocelyn Anderson has pointed out, made an explicit claim for the country house owner (and art collector generally) as a 'guardian of culture'.[42]

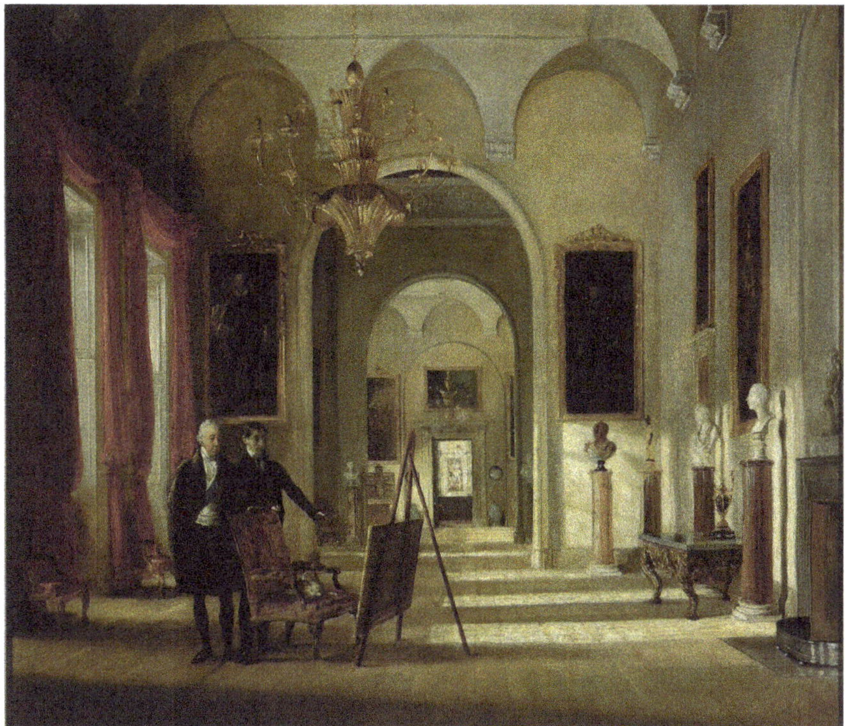

FIGURE 1.8 *John Jackson,* Portrait of the 5th Earl of Carlisle with his youngest son, in the Long Gallery at Castle Howard. *Oil on canvas painted c 1810. From the Castle Howard Collection. Reproduced by kind permission of the Howard family.*

Tatham's experiences working with Hope and Carlisle likely prompted Stafford to employ him to undertake the expansion and renovation of Cleveland House. Stafford would have encountered Hope regularly at such venues as the Royal Society of Arts and the British Institution, both of which Hope joined after completing Duchess Street in a bid to establish himself more securely in London society.[43] It is also probable that Stafford's wife had a hand in the decision to hire Tatham. Lady Stafford was a forceful character in her own right and a close friend of Carlisle's; they maintained extensive correspondence, some of which survives in archives.[44] Over time Lady Stafford became one of Tatham's staunchest supporters, even as his penchant for suing his well-connected clients alienated him from many.[45] *Designs for Ornamental Plate* (1806), one of several books Tatham published to promote his designs made after drawings from antiquity, was dedicated to her.

Though it does not survive, the expansion and renovation of Cleveland House should be understood as one of the most significant accomplishments of Tatham's career. What Caroline Howe had described as 'a very complete business' was, in fact, an enormous project that challenged the already-threadbare boundary between private aristocratic life and public beneficence. Portions of the existing building, including the Old Gallery and Library, formed one end of the gallery suite, to which Tatham added a Grand Staircase, New Gallery, Drawing Room and Dining Room, all of which were connected by a number of smaller anterooms and passages. Tatham's design facilitated the admission of ticketed visitors and members of the general public by incorporating a dedicated entrance from the street. This entrance opened directly onto the Grand Staircase, which in turn funnelled visitors to a first-floor landing from which they entered the gallery suite. In addition to the Grand Staircase, access to and from the gallery was facilitated by 'three lesser staircases' which were 'appropriated to the ingress and egress of the Company'.[46] The *London Courier and Evening Gazette* noted that when particularly large crowds gathered at Cleveland House, the 'entire suite of lower rooms' could be designated 'for the company while waiting for their carriages'.[47]

The very notion of the 'gallery' as a discrete space within the private house had begun to develop as far back as the sixteenth century, as Rosalys Coope argued in her two foundational articles on the subject.[48] Tatham's design comported with – but also elaborated and extended – the conventional definition of a 'gallery' as it was then understood. Galleries, also frequently called 'long galleries' in the sixteenth and seventeenth centuries, were first and foremost developed as spaces in which walking could be undertaken for exercise. Initially, galleries were long, narrow spaces situated along an exterior wall above ground level. Pierced with windows at regular intervals, they permitted views of gardens or parklands or of green squares in town. Opposite the windows were large, uninterrupted expanses of wall (save fireplaces and doorways) for the display of tapestries and other valuable objects, so the owners of these houses took advantage of these characteristics and located artworks there. Early on, portraits were likely to be situated in these rooms; visitors assembled there and were treated to views of the family's estates through windows on one side and to evidence of their lineage and political connections on the other. Galleries fulfilled a function quite different from 'cabinets', which were small rooms where precious objects were kept and shared with only the most privileged visitors.[49] Galleries were, even early in their evolution, more essentially public in nature than cabinets were ever intended to be, though the process through which they evolved from spaces dedicated primarily to social intercourse into ones dedicated to the display of art was slow.

Due to the inherently public nature of the gallery as a room type, over time a family's best paintings, furniture, sculpture and other *objets d'art* accumulated within, producing a palimpsest of family and social history.[50] Surviving evidence suggests that in the sixteenth and seventeenth centuries furnishings were sparse, in part to provide the unobstructed space necessary to accommodate exercise, but by the early nineteenth century these rooms had begun to fill up with furnishings designed to provide for a range of practical and social functions, such as tables for writing letters and playing cards or chairs for reading or conversing by the fire.[51] As a suite of rooms incorporating a full complement of room types, the gallery at Cleveland House served the gamut of functions an aristocratic townhouse was required to accommodate, ranging from displaying the collection to hosting thousands of guests and from the intimate to the necessarily impersonal. The dining room was for eating, the drawing room for drinking coffee and conversation and the library for storing books, the extra staircases, exits and waiting rooms for managing large crowds. The gallery in its entirety was to function as Cleveland House's public face, representing the intersection of family history and public duty.

Classical antiquity was the imaginative organizing principle informing the gallery's architecture and interior decorative scheme. Because Tatham's original drawings have not been preserved, any attempt to reconstruct the interior must rely on a handful of images, including Smith's view of the New Gallery (see Figure 1.1) and a laid-out floor plan of the same room made in 1818 (see Figure 1.9). The New Gallery's design emulated Roman temple architecture.[52] Smith's view and the laid-out plan depict long walls terminating in apses that highlighted points of egress from the room through simple columnar door casings. The lozenge-shaped coffering on the apses referred to the Temple of Venus and Rome as depicted in a sepia gouache by Lewis Vuillamy which, by the early nineteenth century, had become a familiar classical source (see Fig 1.10).[53] Tatham combined these ancient architectural references with influences drawn from public spaces for looking at art that developed in the seventeenth and eighteenth centuries. As the space designated for displaying many of the collection's most treasured Italian masterpieces, the New Gallery was the largest of the new rooms measuring 60 by 26 feet. Large expanses of wall were uninterrupted by the sorts of amenities typically found in domestic buildings, such as windows or fireplaces, enabling the display of very large pictures. It is certainly due to the dearth of fireplaces that the rooms were outfitted with three Moser's patent stoves, which one visitor said created the 'genial warmth of a summer's evening'.[54]

Both New and Old Galleries were fitted with skylights and picture rails, which functioned as architectural signs of the room's fitness for displaying and looking at art. Smith's view depicts a large rectangular skylight piercing the 20-foot-high ceiling, curtains drawn aside to reveal a clear day with only a hint of cloud. Skylights provided the brilliant natural light that close study of Italian religious and mythological pictures demanded. By specifying skylighting in key spaces in the gallery, Tatham was referencing institutional and commercial settings designed or adapted for the display of art in the eighteenth century such as the Royal Academy, Christie's auction room and artist's studios.[55] (Long-planned skylighting was installed at the Louvre

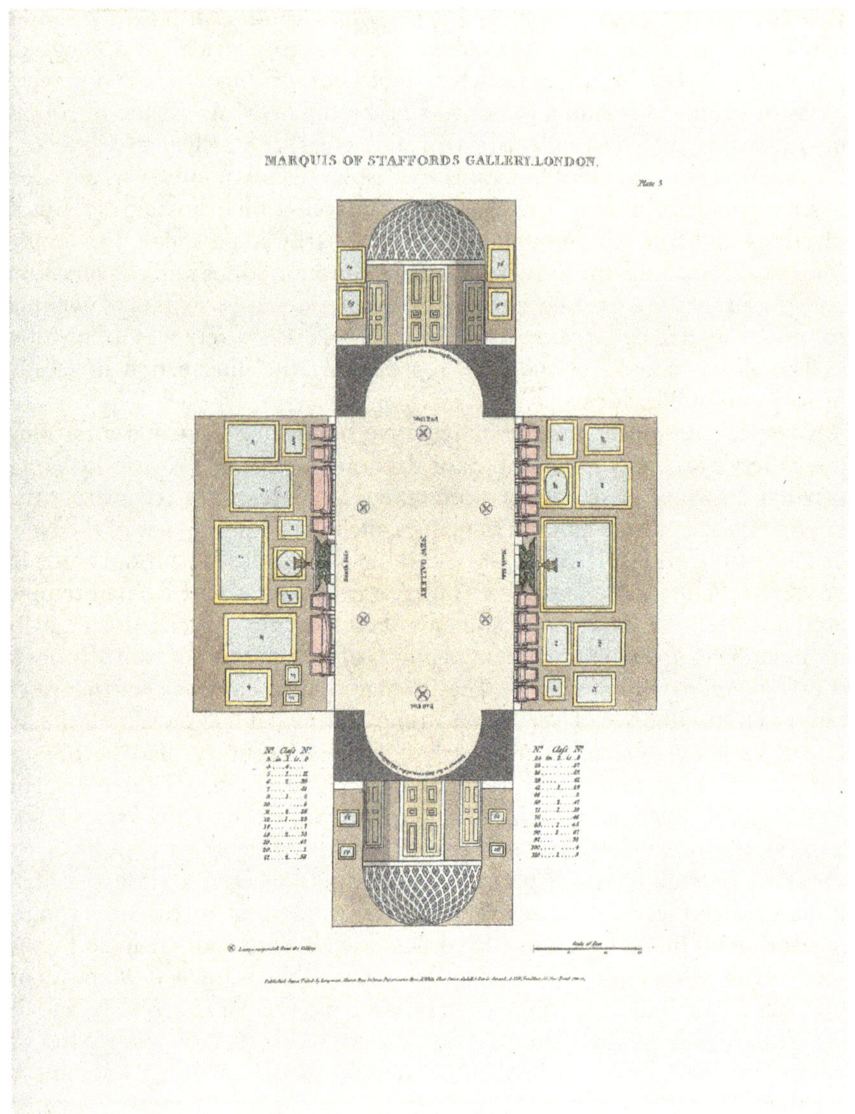

FIGURE 1.9 *[P.W. Tomkins, engr.] 'New Gallery' from William Young Ottley,* Engravings of the Most Noble the Marquis of Stafford's collection of pictures in London, *London: Longman, Hurst, Rees, Orme, and Brown, 1818, engraving. Yale Center for British Art, Paul Mellon Collection.*

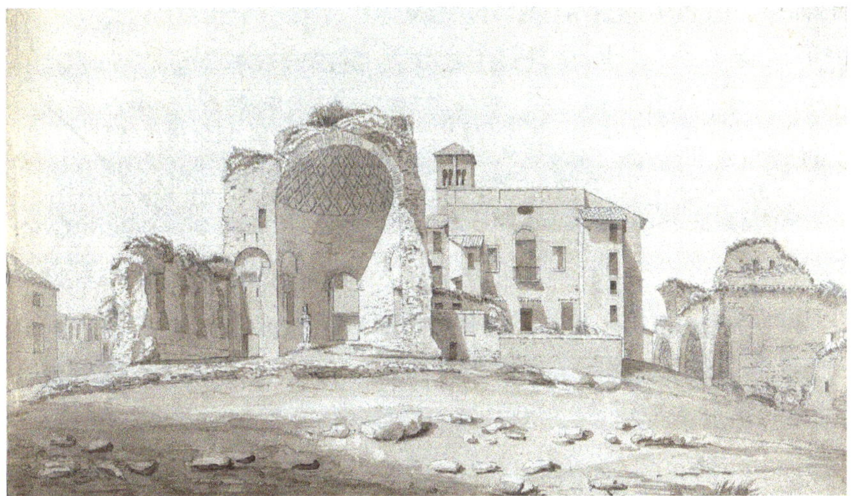

FIGURE 1.10 *Lewis Vulliamy,* Temple of Venus and Rome, Palatine, *between 1818 and 1822, Graphite and brown wash on slightly textured, thin, white laid paper, Yale Center for British Art, Paul Mellon Collection, B1975.2.749.*

while Cleveland House was under construction in 1805.[56]) Although the similarly large Old Gallery was also illuminated from above, smaller rooms in the gallery suite, notably the Dining and Drawing Rooms, were lit by large, floor-to-ceiling windows which provided views of the park. In all rooms, windows were augmented by mirrors, lamplight and oil chandeliers; one newspaper calculated that there were 263 oil lamps throughout the gallery suite, which would have cost a fortune to illuminate.[57] I will discuss the effects of lighting at Cleveland House in more detail in Chapter Two, so for the moment it should suffice to point out that the brilliance of the lighting at Cleveland House was one of its most oft-mentioned characteristics in periodical literature and personal accounts. Similarly, picture rails were becoming standard features in designated gallery spaces, allowing for the convenient movement of pictures when new acquisitions or other circumstances dictated their rearrangement. Picture rails were rods mounted a short distance below the coffered soffit encircling the room from which pictures were hung with visible chains; as one account of Cleveland House asserted, pictures were 'suspended to rods, which are fixed at the top of each room; so that any picture may be exchanged for another without injury'.[58] These chains, or 'lines', were covered in a fawn-coloured textile to match the walls.[59] Smith's view depicts both rail and chains, which engraver William Bond accentuates to visually emphasize that the gallery's design provided every modern facility for the display of pictures.

'Grecian simplicity and perfection': The Gallery's Interior

It is fitting that Tatham chose antiquity as an organizing principle for the New Gallery. It is difficult, if not impossible, to disentangle the development of the gallery as a room type from the vision of neoclassicism being promulgated in the influential circle of architects and patrons in which Tatham circulated. Previous generations had laid the groundwork for the austere interpretation of classicism that gained currency during Tatham's lifetime, which was further shaped by contemporary events and concerns.[60] As discussed above, Tatham worked closely with better-remembered practitioners of turn-of-the-century design, especially Henry Holland and Thomas Hope. Holland and Hope departed from the stylish, idiosyncratic approach to neo-classicism popularized in the second half of the eighteenth century by Scottish architect Robert Adam by attempting to follow historical sources closely, resulting in a more austere, less playful approach.[61] Architectural historians have credited Holland in particular with simplifying Adam's fanciful design vocabulary to create a more 'elegant' style, which he employed on projects for a roster of wealthy and influential clients, including extensive work at Carlton House for the Prince of Wales (see Figure 1.11).[62] Similarly Hope, who hired Tatham to help him transform his house in Holland Street into a Greek- and Egyptian-inspired temple to the arts, was attuned to the work of contemporary European architects working in a severe classical-revival style such as Friedrich Gilly and Claude-Nicolas Ledoux.[63]

Tatham's own publications played an instrumental role in disseminating the new approach to neoclassicism outlined above.[64] He produced an enormous number of drawings after antique architecture and ornament during his stay in Rome in the mid-1790s. These formed the foundational material for a book of designs titled *Etchings, Representing the Best Examples of Ancient Ornamental Architecture* published in 1799. Archaeologist Susan Pearce has written that 'Tatham's collecting and drawing activities are part of the sociocultural discourse of the 1790s which perceived the remains of the classical past to be a prestigious source of an ethic of style', which he was keen to bring to bear on designs for his elite clients.[65] Tatham's second book, *Designs for Ornamental Plate*, is dedicated to the Marchioness of Stafford, its preface dated April 1806, one month before the gallery at Cleveland House opened. The timing of this volume and its dedication suggest that Tatham's work designing fittings and furniture for the gallery were significant factors in its production. What seems clear from these publications is that Tatham believed passionately in the notion of rigorous fidelity to ancient sources as the basis for contemporary design. Biographers have suggested that because of his rigidity on this point, Tatham did not attract a wide patronage; those projects for which he was hired tended to be picture galleries and monuments.[66] (Tatham also designed a mausoleum for the grounds of Stafford's country seat, Trentham House.) Pearce and architectural historian Frank Salmon have published the

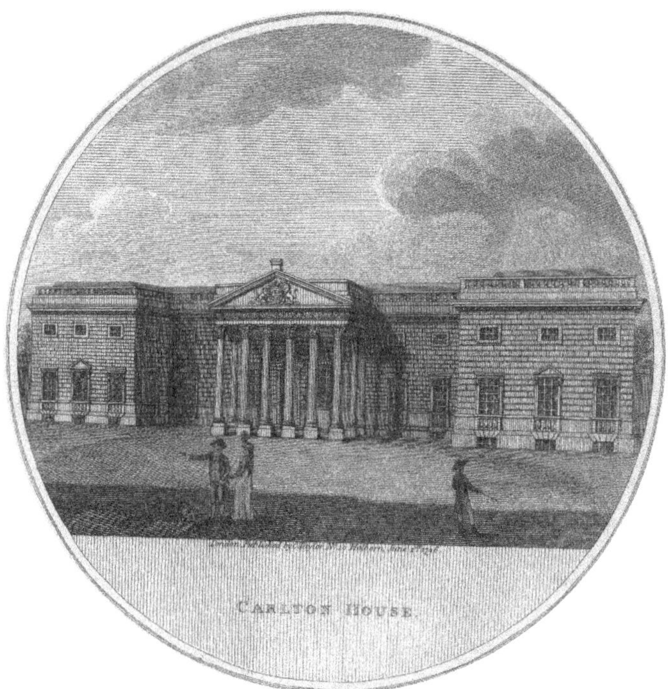

FIGURE 1.11 *View of Carlton House, from* The Temple of Taste. *Printed for C Taylor . . ., [1796] Yale Center for British Art, Paul Mellon Collection.*

definitive source on Tatham's writings, drawings and biography; most surviving materials date to the part of his career predating his work on Castle Howard, Duchess Street and Cleveland House as it is believed that his children burned most of his papers after his death.[67]

Tatham's books argued for bringing the aesthetics of classical antiquity to bear on the design of contemporary household objects. Previously, writers and designers had neglected interior decoration in favour of exterior elevations or floor plans of buildings, for example Colen Campbell's *Vitruvius Britannicus, or The British Architect* (1715), though there were important exceptions. Viccy Coltman has shown that Sir William Hamilton's publications of antiquities in the 1760s were mined and adapted by designers and manufacturers to produce a range of luxurious objects meant to adorn the elite interior during the second half of the eighteenth century.[68] But unlike many before him, Tatham specifically addressed the theoretical question of ornament. His introduction to *Etchings* explicitly expresses his ambition to introduce principles of 'Grecian simplicity and perfection' to British interiors.[69]

Etchings included examples of everything from patterns for mouldings to drawings of ancient lamps (which, with some ingenuity, could be transformed into modern oil-burning fixtures) to movable furnishings. Tatham writes that he intends to supply faithful translations of original sources from the antique to the public and to artists, declaring, 'the works of the Ancients are a MAP TO THE STUDY OF NATURE'.[70] One drawing in the volume depicts an 'Antique fragment of a table foot, executed in Greek marble' (see Figure 1.12). Tatham notes that he first encountered this fragment displayed as a *basso relievo* – as an object displayed as a work of art in its own right – in the Vatican Museum, however his caption prioritises its original function as a piece of furniture, the base of a table. In *Designs for Ornamental Plate*, Tatham includes several original designs for oil-burning lamps taking the form of sculptural metal stands supported by a variety of winged creatures, winningly animated with delicate plumes of smoke emanating from the burners that surmount them (see Figure 1.13). In this example, the lamp depicted at far right is labelled 'used by the Author, at Rome', the others are Tatham's own designs made 'after the manner of Italian lamps'. Tatham considers ancient ornament specifically as inspiration – though not a pattern to be copied – for the designers of contemporary interiors and cites his own experience having used one of the lamps depicted as evidence for the authenticity of his approach.

Because much documentation of Tatham's career has not survived, it has been difficult for historians to assess the significance of his work amongst early nineteenth-century practitioners of neoclassicism. Hope and Holland, both instrumental figures in the burgeoning field of interior design, were influenced by Tatham's publications, as was royal upholsterer George Smith, who supplied furniture for the Prince of Wales' Brighton Pavilion.

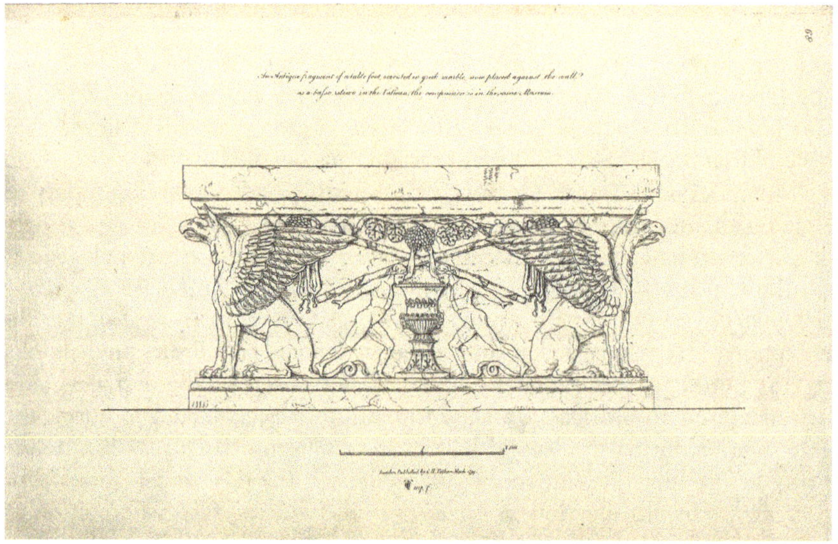

FIGURE 1.12 *Charles Heathcote Tatham, 'Antique Fragment of a Table Foot, Executed in Greek Marble' from* Etchings, Representing the Best Examples of Ancient Ornamental Architecture *(London: Printed for the author, 1799). Avery Classics, Avery Architectural & Fine Arts Library, Columbia University.*

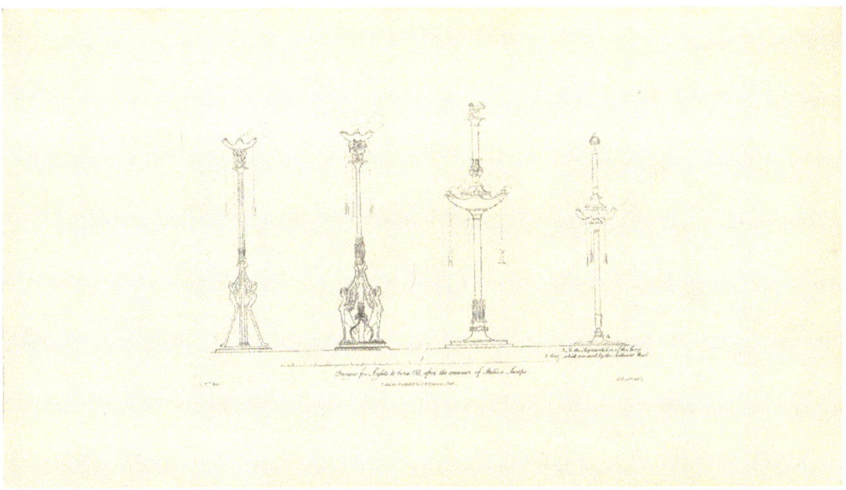

FIGURE 1.13 *Charles Heathcote Tatham, 'Designs for Lights to Burn Oil, after the Manner of Italian Lamps' from* Designs for Ornamental Plate *(London: T Gardiner, 1806). Avery Classics, Avery Architectural & Fine Arts Library, Columbia University.*

Hope's popular and influential *Household Furniture and Interior Decoration* (1807) included engravings depicting the interior of his Duchess Street house and gallery (see Figure 1.6). It is also known for being the first English-language publication to use the phrase 'interior decoration', Hope having developed the concept in parallel with Napoleon's architects, Charles Percier and Pierre Fontaine, who are generally given credit for coining the phrase in 1801.[71] *Household Furniture and Interior Decoration* – along with many of Hope's other publications – featured distinctive line engravings by Henry Moses, who showed elegant neoclassical furniture being used in domestic vignettes.[72] In *A Man, Two Women, a Child, and a Dog by a Fireplace*, Moses depicts an elegant grouping of figures, themselves reminiscent of antique sculpture in fashionable attire, warming themselves by a fireplace decorated with neoclassical motifs surmounted by a clock featuring winged griffons (see Figure 1.14). David Watkin has argued that the style of line engraving that has become closely associated with Hope and Moses' body of work was indebted to Tatham's *Etchings*; because the influence was not explicitly acknowledged at the time, it has been largely overlooked.[73]

Tatham's embrace of classical sources was symptomatic of a long evolution in British taste. An affinity for continental, and especially French, objects and design had been a clear marker of membership in the *beau monde* during the eighteenth century, as the phrase's origin suggests.[74] By 1800, French taste had become irretrievably associated with the *ancien régime* and in Britain had been long since displaced by a range of aesthetic modes, including Adam

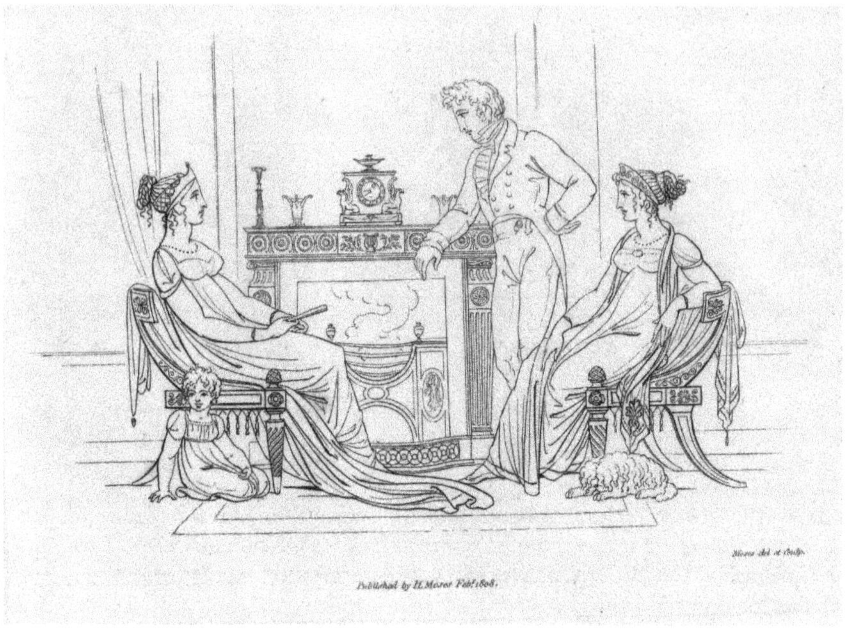

FIGURE 1.14 *Henry Moses, 'A Man, Two Women, a Child, and a Dog by a Fireplace' from* Sketches in Outline *(H Moses, 1808). Etching and engraving. The Metropolitan Museum of Art, New York, The Elisha Whittelsey Collection, The Elisha Whittelsey Fund, 2014.*

Style neoclassicism, 'Chinese' style, the picturesque and, in certain esoteric circles, a revived interest in English 'Gothick' style as implemented at Horace Walpole's Strawberry Hill and William Beckford's Fonthill Abbey.[75] As Britain became entrenched in war with France for the second time in less than a decade, looking to French sources for design was also impractical and undesirable. In 1805, Lady Bessborough wrote to Granville Leveson-Gower (the Marquess of Stafford's younger half-brother), that even a figure as influential as the Prince of Wales had turned away from French-inspired design for work at the Brighton Pavilion, since 'at the time there was such a cry against French things, &c., that he was afraid of his furniture being accus'd of jacobinism'.[76] The notion that one's choice of interior decoration might be regarded as a patriotic gesture could be seen as partly a nod to anti-French sentiment, but it was also an acknowledgement of the barriers to acquiring continental manufactures during a commercial embargo. Similar qualms infuse Hope's introduction to *Household Furniture and Interior Decoration*, which emphasizes 'patriotism' and 'virtue' in British interior design and disparages the 'repulsive and unpatriotic shape of expensive articles of foreign ingenuity and disadvantageous importation'.[77] Hope's text, written with an eye to the realities of wartime, relies heavily on Egyptian-inspired design, examples of which circulated widely after the publication of Dominique Vivant-Denon's *Voyages dans la Basse et la Haute Égypte* (1802). It didn't hurt that readers could claim a patriotic interest in Egyptian design thanks to Britain's victory over Napoleon at the Battle of the Nile.[78]

The influence of antique precedents outlined in Tatham's publications is evident in the few surviving examples of objects that are known to have furnished the gallery at Cleveland House. The New Gallery was fitted with six oil-burning chandeliers that provided supplemental light as indicated by the laid-out floor plan of the room published in 1818 (see Figure 1.9). The *London Courier and Evening Gazette* described these fixtures as 'magnificent circular lamps, suspended from the centre of the principal apartments by massy golden chains, each holding four burners'.[79] In addition, the gallery was supplied with a range of free-standing oil-burning lamps and fixtures.[80] Although Smith's view of the New Gallery does not depict chandeliers or light fixtures – indeed, eliminates all trace of them – the lamp designs included in *Designs for Ornamental Plate* must be very similar, if not identical, to those employed in the gallery.

Antique motifs also featured prominently in the best documented objects made for the gallery, a set of enormous pier tables Tatham designed in cooperation with his brother, cabinetmaker Thomas Tatham (see Figure 1.15). These tables, which anchored each of the New Gallery's long walls, are

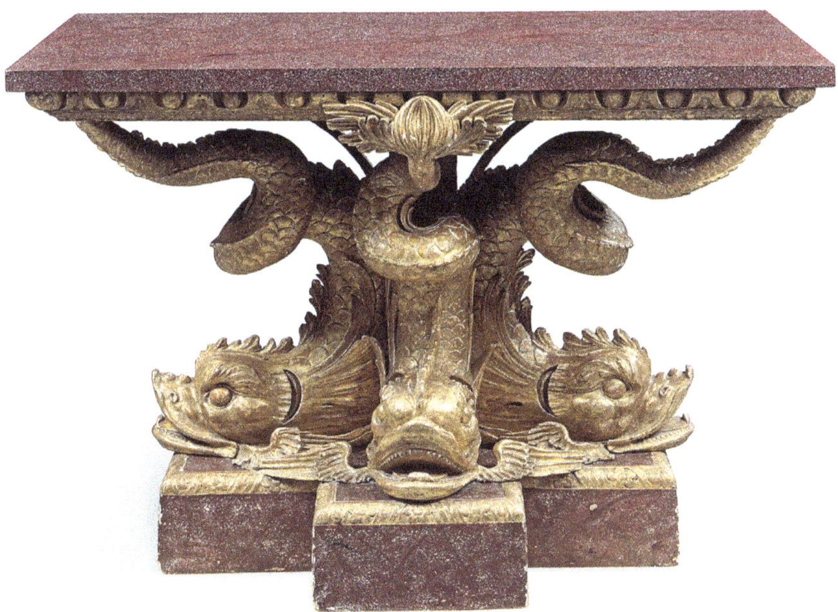

FIGURE 1.15 *Marsh & Tatham, Dolphin Pier Table made for Cleveland House c 1805–1806. Private Collection. Photo © Christie's Images/Bridgeman Images.*

clearly depicted in Smith's view.[81] Described in one newspaper as 'elegant marble slabs supported by groups of dolphins *en bronze*', the tables are reminiscent of examples Tatham included in *Etchings*, particularly the 'antique fragment of a table foot . . . in the Vatican . . . Museum' described above.[82] The visual rhyme between the Vatican example and the one designed for Cleveland House is clear, and although Tatham's design is similar in spirit, it is not a copy of the antique fragment. Tania Buckrell Pos identified a source drawing depicting a similar dolphin motif Tatham made in Rome in April 1795 from a fragment of the cornice of the Temple of Neptune (see Figure 1.16).[83] The inclusion of fanciful creatures – a pair of sphinx supporting the Vatican table and a pair of monstrous dolphins supporting Tatham's – allude both to the classical inspiration for the tables and their sculptural quality. (In *Etchings* Tatham mentions the 'SPHINXES, CHIMÆRAS, and other figures, which disgust in fable [but] please in Sculpture'.[84]) Annibale Carracci's *Danaë*, herself a time-traveller from ancient Greece by way of Baroque Rome, was hung over one of these tables, a tableau depicted in Smith's view (see Figures 1.1 and 1.2). The undulating curves of

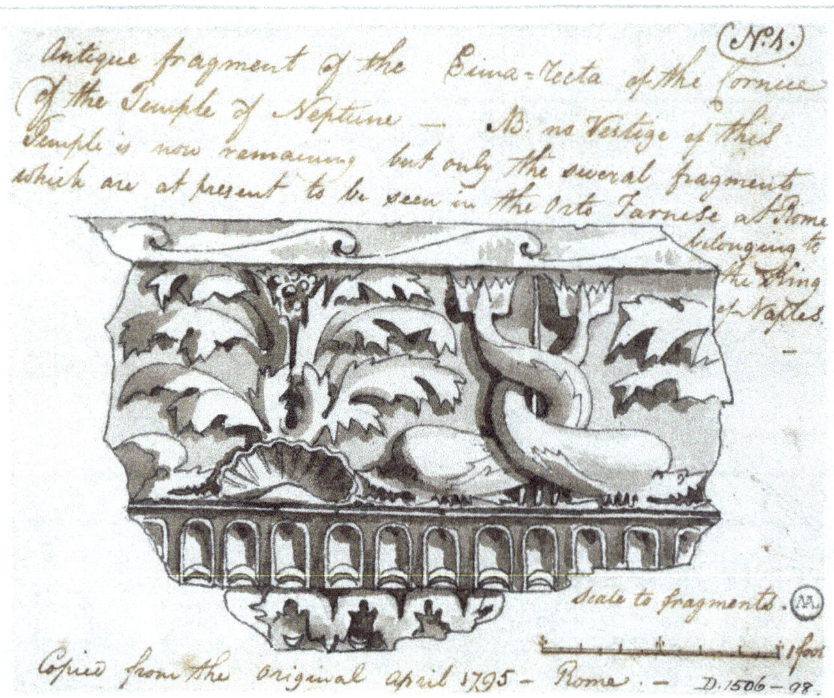

FIGURE 1.16 *Charles Heathcote Tatham, Drawing after an antique fragment from the cornice of the Temple of Neptune in Rome, pen on paper, 1795. Prints, Drawings & Paintings Collection © Victoria and Albert Museum, London.*

her body, drapery and plume of smoke at upper left are echoed in the curled tails of the sea creatures supporting the table below. Tatham's tables connect an antique fragment in the Vatican Museum to a contemporary piece of furniture and likewise connect the principle underpinning its design to the gallery's mission to display a collection of art.

The tables were probably the only objects in the gallery (except the paintings) that stayed in place at all times. This was partly for practical reasons. The tables were extraordinarily heavy, topped with marble slabs that Bridgewater was said to have acquired during his Grand Tour in the 1750s; certainly their presence gently discouraged visitors from approaching the art too closely. The evidence indicates that most other furniture and decorative objects were removed on open days. Examples of objects that likely came in and out according to the occasion include a set of bespoke carpets made for several of the rooms after drawings by the Marchioness of Stafford, described by the *London Courier and Evening Gazette* as 'truly nouvelle, representing a Roman tassilated pavement'.[85] Although they are not depicted in any views of the interior, they must have been similar to other carpets using mosaic patterns made in this period. Textile historian Sue Stern has written that such designs sprang from the inspiration provided by excavations in Herculaneum and Pompeii in the middle of the eighteenth century. Sir John Soane, who like the Staffords was a staunch supporter of Tatham's career, had an antique mosaic-pattern carpet produced for the Model Room in his house in Lincoln's Inn Fields. Stern points out that these carpets were often made for male patrons and placed in rooms with a scholarly purpose, like the Model Room where Soane instructed architectural students.[86] The selection of tessellated patterns for the carpets of Cleveland House could have resulted from a collaboration between Tatham and the Marchioness, whose 'taste in the knowledge of the best antique examples in the Egyptian, Etruscan, Greek, or Roman Stiles', the *London Courier* claimed, 'are well known to the lovers of the Arts'.[87] Evidence of this set of carpets is scant and no other documentation of them has come to light, yet they tantalizingly point to the personal involvement of the Marchioness in their design and to the intersection of personal impulses and public pressures in the bid to decorate a space that emblematized both public duty and private occupation.

Tatham's designs for Castle Howard and Cleveland House and, to a lesser extent, Hope's gallery at Duchess Street, made recourse to classical precedents in a way that may now seem like an entirely logical extension of the gallery's purpose as a public space. At the beginning of the nineteenth century, the association of neoclassical architecture with art galleries – pervasive by its end – was a relatively recent phenomenon. The princely galleries of eighteenth-century Europe were generally situated in buildings decorated with Baroque or Rococo motifs. For example, the *Grand Galerie* at the *Palais-Royal* in Paris, where the Orléans pictures were displayed for many decades before their sale around 1790, was an extravagant ducal residence decorated in the taste of the early eighteenth century. Philippe II, duc d'Orléans, commissioned architect Gilles-Marie Oppenord and painter Antoine Coypel to completely remake the *Grand Galerie* during the 1710s. This decorative scheme centered on Coypel's *trompe l'oeil* ceiling painting depicting the *Assembly of the Gods*, in particular the mythical hero Aeneas; this scheme, while based on the themes of classical literature, used the visual language of contemporary court culture to brilliant effect.[88] Similarly, galleries in British houses tended to exhibit the character of the buildings in which they were situated, such as the grand gallery at Northumberland House installed in the 1750s.[89] Given the opportunity to design and build an art gallery from scratch, Tatham chose the neoclassical idiom currently fashionable within elite circles; of course his own publications had helped disseminate and popularise this style.

Neoclassicism connected the project of the gallery – and by extension, the reputation of its owners – to the example set by ancient patrons of art and architecture. The tendency to allegorise contemporary patrons as the heirs to classical antiquity had been embraced by many founders of early public galleries and museums.[90] In making the comparison, early nineteenth-century Britons alluded to the widespread notion that London, presiding over an ever-expanding empire, could be considered a new Athens, an idea that was symbolically memorialised by events like the arrival of the Elgin Marbles in 1807.[91] Stafford himself was compared to 'Pericles', having launched a 'new epoch to the arts of his country', explicitly linking Cleveland House with the golden age of antiquity.[92] In 1808, caricaturist James Gillray gently satirised this notion in an image of Stafford making his way to an auction of '800 Capital PICTURES' at Christie's Auction Rooms. Easily recognizable to viewers thanks to his aquiline profile, Gillray dubbed Stafford 'Mæcenas' in reference to the renowned, ultra-wealthy Roman patron of the arts (see Figure 1.17).

Manifesting the principles of antiquity in contemporary architecture was understood to have moral as well as aesthetic significance.[93] The discourse of taste had evolved over the course of the previous century following the lead of writers like the Earl of Shaftesbury, who argued that gentlemen must reaffirm their commitment to classical antiquity and avoid elements that indulged the excesses of Baroque style.[94] 'One who aspires to the Character of a Man of Breeding and Politeness, is careful to form his Judgment of Arts and Sciences upon right Models of Perfection', wrote Shaftesbury in 1711. 'He takes particular care to turn his Eye from every thing which is gaudy, luscious, and of a false Taste'.[95] Shaftesbury's writings, while influential in the long term, were not immediately adopted by all, or even most, who continued to work with a wide range of stylistic modes from the 'Gothick' to the 'Chinese' and, of course, French, until the political winds described above narrowed the scope of acceptable style.[96] His severe attitude, however, went hand-in-hand with the Palladianism embraced by a small group of the wealthiest landowners building country and town residences during the

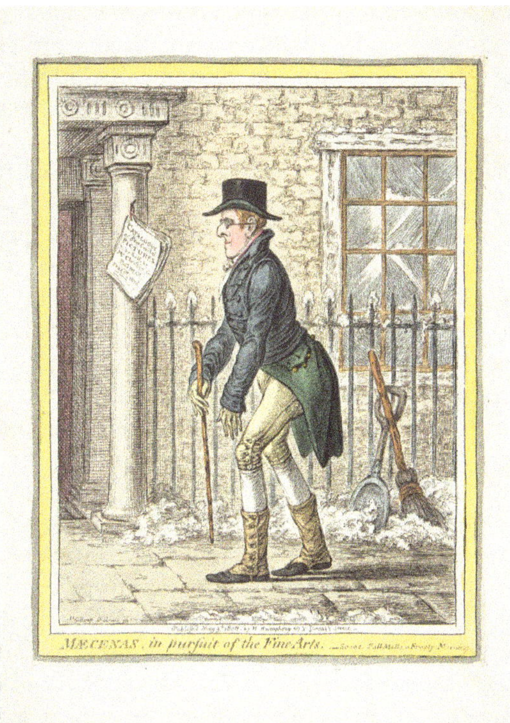

FIGURE 1.17 *James Gillray,* Maecenas, In Pursuit of the Fine Arts – Scene, Pall Mall; a Frosty Morning, *1808. Hand-coloured etching, The Metropolitan Museum of Art, New York, Gift of Georgiana W Sargent, in memory of John Osborne Sargent, 1924.*

first quarter of the eighteenth century. By 1800, writers across a range of publications were regularly using coded adjectives like 'chaste', 'simple', 'elegant' and 'tasteful' to describe the interiors of upper-class dwellings, terms that were underpinned by an assumption that classical forms were inherently imbued with aristocratic virtue.[97] Certainly, Cleveland House was described in similar terms. One newspaper reported that 'the suit of apartments are fitted up in the most elegant style and evince the taste and magnificence of the illustrious owner', eliding the elegance of the gallery's interior with its owners' apparent preference for antique forms.[98] The aesthetic and moral fitness betokened by the use of terms like 'elegance' worked their way into discourses of taste promulgated to wider audiences. Describing best practices for the 'construction of the domestic furniture of our dwellings' in 1814, the *Repository of Arts*, a periodical aimed at the ambitious middle classes, declared, 'To the credit of our higher classes who encourage, and of our manufacturing artists who produce, we now universally quit the overcharged magnificence of former ages, and seek the purer models of simplicity and tasteful ornament in every article of daily call'.[99]

The terms of gentlemanly taste, as defined by Shaftesbury and those who came after him, connected the morality and public-spiritedness of the owners of houses and collections of art and furniture to the Roman and Greek precedents upon which their designs were based. In *Etchings* Tatham wrote that 'we are certainly much indebted to Piranesi and LeRoy, and to our own countrymen Stuart and Revett, for having overturned that barbarous taste of Architecture and decoration which prevailed some time back, and establishing in its stead the true principles of Grecian simplicity and perfection'.[100] His language connected the evolution of contemporary neoclassical design – and his own efforts to continue this tradition in projects like the galleries for Castle Howard and Cleveland House – explicitly to the moral authority of classical antiquity and the eighteenth-century discourse of taste.

Tatham transformed classical precedents into contemporary interiors capable of accommodating the demands of modern life and responding to contemporary concerns. Susan Pearce has argued that Tatham's study of the material culture of antiquity, when considered in the context of his contemporary architectural and design practice, 'helped to produce a new aesthetic of experience, which . . . sustained new forms of exhibition and display'.[101] Tatham's commitment to classicism permitted him to use principles of decoration to connect the gallery he designed at Cleveland House to the very values that underpinned its opening to the public. Tatham worked in concert with men like Hope, Carlisle and Stafford to create spaces where they could display their collections for the benefit of the public, acts of magnanimity they understood as maintaining a tradition of public duty that called to mind ancient Greece and Rome. In other words, the gallery as an ideological construct helped to produce the language of neoclassicism developed to design and decorate it, but the neoclassical idea as expressed in Tatham's drawings also produced an ethos of antiquity that collectors were keen to embrace.

'To study domestic comfort': Gallery as Hybrid Space

The design of the gallery was embedded within an ethics of style that claimed neoclassicism as the appropriate framework for the public-spirited enterprise that the gallery embodied. Nowhere were the principles expressed in the gallery's architecture better articulated than in John Britton's *catalogue raisonné*-cum-guidebook published in 1808.[102] The guidebook's preface situates the gallery within the context of established practice for exhibiting art to the public both abroad and at home; over a scant two and a half pages, it unfolds into a perceptive meditation on the meanings and implications of opening a private house to the public. Britton frames Cleveland House first and foremost as a place that encouraged the 'expansion of human intellect' through 'cultivating the fine arts and polite literature'.[103] Reading Britton's preface alongside JC Smith's view of the New Gallery, which served as his book's frontispiece, reveals its subtle attempt to balance the exigencies of gentlemanly comfort and public benefit (see Figure 1.1).

As outlined earlier in this chapter, art world elites had long treasured the notion that both society and the fine arts might be improved by giving the public access to works of art. In keeping with this idea, Britton writes that the act of opening the gallery at Cleveland House will be 'ever memorable in the history of the fine arts in England', in direct contrast to the 'temporary notoriety' attaching to 'popular acts of party politics', asserting that the 'honourable' cultural work represented by the gallery is distinct from the self-interested work of the political field.[104] But in tangling with the question of access, and to whom and under what circumstances it may be properly granted, Britton makes an unexpected rhetorical leap. Justifying 'certain restrictions' on access, such as requiring visitors to provide letters of introduction or arrive in carriages, he writes:

> these, if properly constituted and regulated, are as useful and pleasant to the visitor, as to him who grants the favour. It should be recollected that private collections are generally formed for individual gratification, and that a private gentleman is naturally and rationally more disposed to study domestic comfort than to sacrifice it to public curiosity. Whenever, therefore, we are freely admitted to examine and study (without extravagant taxation) the valuable repositories of art, in the houses of opulent persons, we ought to be thankful.[105]

Specific details about restrictions and regulations and the process of granting entry to the gallery will be discussed in Chapter Two. For the moment, it should be sufficient to note that Britton frames the 'curiosity' of the public as a force that could, if unchecked, undermine the sanctity of the home. Its public face is necessarily intertwined with its status as a private dwelling.

What seems to be at stake for Britton – and we should assume, for his patron – is the notion that a grand London townhouse like Cleveland House might be thought a space of 'domestic comfort', a phrase that conjured a complicated set of assumptions and associations. Aristocratic townhouses (and their counterparts in the country) had long functioned as pseudo-public spaces, physical manifestations of political authority based in land ownership only a tiny number could claim. Adopting terms and phrases like 'private' and 'domestic comfort' to describe not just the building itself but its owner's state of mind, Britton evokes the pervasive cultural discourse within which they operated in the early nineteenth century. Domesticity is a remarkably capacious concept, involving a range of ideals and practices that elevated the centrality of the nuclear family to all aspects of private life and indexed the increasing separation of social, cultural and political spaces into 'public' and 'private' spheres over the course of the eighteenth and early nineteenth centuries.[106] To write of 'private' space was to evoke a sense of intimacy that had begun to attach to houses and their contents; likewise 'comfort' was shorthand for the trend toward informality in both interiors and personal interactions. These concepts were frequently deployed as coded language to describe a privileging of family and private concerns over those of community and public duty.[107]

During the late Georgian period, men and women from a range of class positions sought to marshal the practices and aesthetics of domesticity for a range of reasons. Amanda Vickery and Kate Retford have argued that interiors functioned as a locus of morality that in the early nineteenth century was not yet neatly aligned with notions of masculinity or femininity.[108] Britton aligns masculinity with domesticity using a formulation that expressed strength of moral character through decoration or care for the family home. This trope was expressed in a beloved episode in Jane Austen's *Pride and Prejudice* (1813), as Elizabeth Bennet's disdain for Mr Darcy transforms into love upon glimpsing his country house, Pemberley: 'The rooms were lofty and handsome, and their furniture suitable to the fortune of their proprietor', Elizabeth observed, 'with admiration of his taste, that it was neither gaudy nor uselessly fine'.[109] The word 'handsome' implies a quality of restraint that speaks volumes about the character of Pemberley's gentlemanly owner. Austen's affirmation of the stately country house as a bastion of solid, masculine taste took on a particular resonance during the Napoleonic period; as many British men were fighting and dying overseas, ever more lavish interiors were being installed into some of Britain's grandest houses. The opulent display of wealth during and after the war was often understood as a symbol of the continuing health of the nation, and thus as a marker of patriotic fervour.[110]

Austen's text points to the notion that the space of the house or gallery itself produced the conditions under which art could be viewed and understood, whether for better or worse. Images of art galleries in use, whether private or public, were relatively rare, but even so there are several instructive examples that suggest how space shaped viewing practices and the varying expectations for how men and women would engage in them. (I will discuss further examples of such views in Chapter Five.) William Chambers' view of Charles Townley's house in Park Street, made in 1794, depicts a trio of visitors studying Townley's renowned collection of antiquities (see Figure 1.18). One woman is deeply engrossed in her guidebook while a male companion leans back gently and peers through an eyeglass, his gesture implying intellectual engagement. The reserved body language exhibited by all three evokes a polite and educated public that proprietors of many spaces for looking at art in this period were eager to produce. In contrast Thomas Rowlandson's view of the 1808 Royal Academy exhibition imaginatively fills the Great Room at Somerset House with men and women of different ranks of society looking at the pictures, their guidebooks and each other. The RA was widely characterized as a space

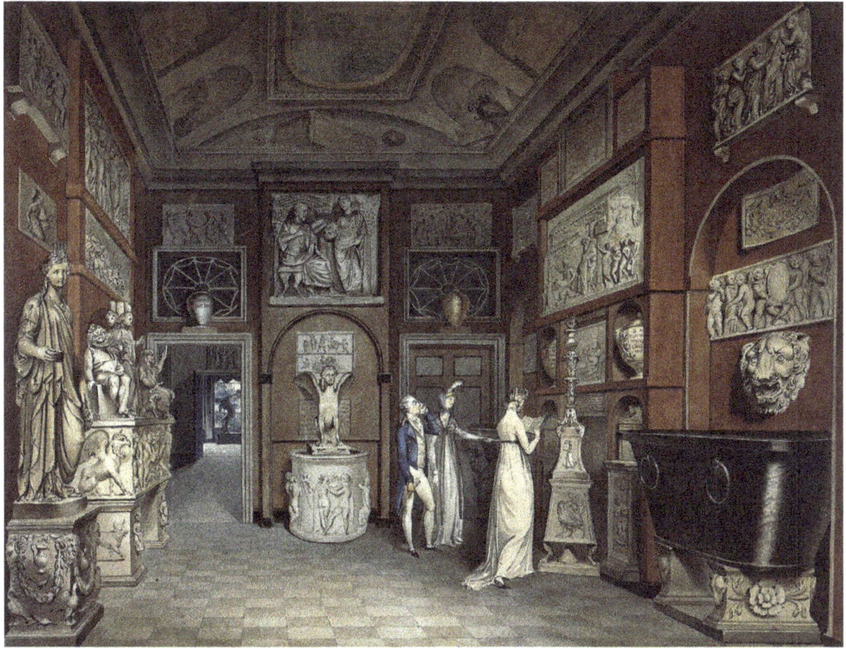

FIGURE 1.18 *William Chambers,* The Sculpture Collection of Charles Townley in the Entrance Hall of His House in Park Street, Westminster, *1794. Prints and Drawings, The British Museum 1995,0506.9. © Trustees of the British Museum.*

where the crowd was more fascinated by fashion than art and the risk of unexpected, awkward encounters loomed. Rowlandson's view implied a frivolous approach to connoisseurship encouraged by the Academy's exhibitions and lamented by critics (see Figure 5.8).[111]

Like Chambers' view, Smith's view of the New Gallery asserts the role of gentlemanly taste in affirming the private gallery as an idealised space for looking at art. Both images seem engineered to rebut any suggestion that gentlemen's galleries might share the failings of the Royal Academy. Britton's preface explicitly draws a contrast between Cleveland House and such boisterous 'public places':

> In England, where ignorance, vulgarity, or something worse, are the characteristics of the lower orders, and where frivolity, affectation, and insolence, are the leading traits in a class of lounging persons, who haunt most public places, it would be the excess of folly for gentlemen who possess valuable museums, to give unlimited admission to the public.[112]

If the same types of people who attended the Royal Academy exhibitions visited Cleveland House on Wednesday afternoons, their presence might turn the gallery into a similar space of sociability and spectacle. To readers well-versed in such stock critiques of the Royal Academy's boisterous atmosphere, the small and serious party inhabiting Smith's image rebukes any possible point of comparison. Embodying the seriousness with which Britton's preface exhorted visitors to approach the gallery, a single male figure, standing in for a member of the public, boldly approaches Raphael's *Holy Family with a Palm Tree* while studiously avoiding looking at the sensuous *Danaë*, hanging just above (see Figures 1.2 and 1.19). The man peers at Raphael's painting with intense concentration aided by a tiny guidebook – perhaps, in a self-referential gesture, the very one being held by the beholder of Smith's image – which is barely visible on the table to his right. While the male figure studies the art, at right his female companion

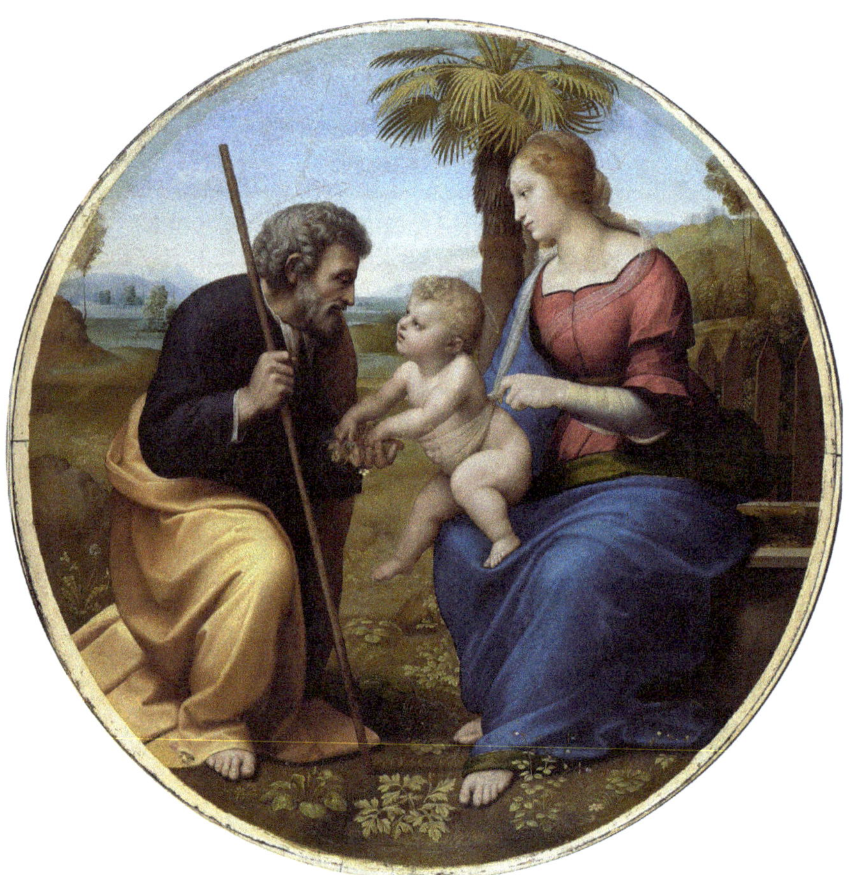

FIGURE 1.19 *Raphael,* The Holy Family with a Palm Tree, *oil and gold on canvas, transferred from panel, c 1506–1507. National Galleries of Scotland, Bridgewater Collection Loan, 1945.*

and a young boy hang back demurely, conducting themselves with restraint. Taken as a group, these visitors appear to be interested in nothing other than the pictures on display; given that there are no other figures present, this image suggests that the gallery's only function is as a repository of cultural artifacts and, as the child's presence makes clear, a nursery of taste.

That the gallery is shown populated by a family group instead of a large and diverse crowd of strangers invites the viewer to think of Cleveland House as an alternative to venues like the Royal Academy. At Cleveland House, visitors could be assured of the gentility of the crowd behaving themselves in a manner congruent with the expectations of domestic space. Smith's view, especially when considered in the context of Britton's guidebook, appears calculated to clarify that the gallery is designed to encourage the appreciation of Italian masterpieces in an ennobling, moral environment. It not only shapes such encounters, but its domestic scale and decoration alluding to antiquity demands them.

Britton's principal message is that what makes an English collection truly 'English' is its status as a public good wrapped up and made visible from within the collector's private realm. Public benefit is presented as a happy side effect of the gentleman's collecting but not its main goal, an argument that rests upon the conviction that a 'private gentleman' – in this case, the Marquess of Stafford – holds 'domestic comfort' and 'individual gratification' as the most 'natural' and 'rational' values. While this sentiment may appear to run counter to the prevailing notion that the defining feature of the gentleman was his sense of public duty it, in fact, is of a piece with the growing desire of the upper classes to conduct themselves according to the standards of an increasingly influential middle class.

Conclusion

A polite space was imbued with the moral authority of its patron and welcomed audiences exhibiting intellectual curiosity and decorous behavior. Fashion, commerce and the messier types of human interaction were amongst the incendiary characteristics of popular metropolitan venues that a private house was expected to neutralise. As Britton hints, some writers flirted with comparing private collections to 'museums'. One described Cleveland House as 'a National Museum rather than [a] private collection', while another suggestively dubbed it the '*Louvre* of London'.[113] Despite these allusions to affinities between private spaces and the burgeoning category of museums, the gentleman's art gallery occupied a specific terrain within the landscape of metropolitan art venues. The decorated interior and the objects it contained were never regarded as an immutable, generic backdrop to the display of pictures. Rooms were filled with a variety of smaller, often ephemeral, objects that enlivened them, and their decoration was in a constant state of flux as paintings were moved and furniture was rearranged to accommodate a variety of social occasions. Certainly, on Wednesday afternoons, many of the objects that filled the gallery might be swept away to create a space devoted solely to looking at art. During social events the gallery was brilliantly lit with oil lamps and chandeliers, festooned with drapery and filled with furniture.

Cleveland House's dual role as public venue for the arts and luxurious private dwelling were always understood to co-exist in a delicate balance. Even as it celebrated a tradition of art based on long-admired continental models, Cleveland House was in many ways a modern space, both in terms of its social mission and the architectural language it employed intermingling public and private modes of display. The man, woman and child occupying Smith's view may be read as a family group. Reminiscent of Raphael's *Holy Family* hanging nearby, their presence authorises the gallery's role as a civilising and refined space for looking at art that nurtures the private intimate unit of the family instead of catering to the crowd. At the same time, these figures embody the principle that the gallery fostered a 'new aesthetic of experience', transforming members of the public into connoisseurs of Old Master painting.[114] Smith presents the gallery as a space that was resolutely public, stripping it of many of the luxurious appointments that we know were present, not least the sumptuous furniture and fittings that greeted all who entered. The image's very bareness, the evacuation of so many of the objects and people which made the house one of London's most talked-about interiors, allows the viewer to imaginatively furnish and populate it in ways that may have surprised its original owners.

Fundamentally, galleries were rooms that provided essential gathering places for social and familial activities as well as for the display and viewing of artworks. The gallery at Cleveland House followed this pattern and included rooms that could serve myriad functions in addition to providing a space to look at art, such as dining, drinking tea and coffee, listening to music, reading and writing letters. The gallery was used for a variety of purposes on a scale ranging from the intimate to the very grand, including events such as dinners, musical evenings and balls. Tatham's architecture and décor created a stage set for a dynamic space where a wide range of social encounters were on display. In Chapter Two, I will explore the floor plan in detail, exploring how it conjures the gallery's public and private worlds. The gallery was not a proto-'museum', but a richly-layered social system in which different types of audiences circulated and negotiated expectations of class, taste and deference.[115]

2

'The high attraction of the spectacle': Displaying Sociability

In spring 1806, word spread that the building under construction at the intersection of Green Park and St James' Palace was nearly complete. On 7 May, the Marquess and Marchioness of Stafford hosted a ball to mark the occasion of the gallery's opening to the public, an event heralded in the periodical press. On opening day, artist and diarist Joseph Farington reported seeing artists in attendance, alongside 'Many Amateurs, & noble persons'.[1] The gallery proved an irresistible draw, a constant stream of gossip flowing through London's newspapers whetting the public's appetite with descriptions of its glamorous interior. Inundated by 'almost innumerable' applications, within weeks, Stafford established a system to manage admissions. Prospective visitors applied on Tuesdays to the Porter for tickets, which admitted them on the subsequent Wednesday between 12 and 5 pm.[2] After the ticket system was put into effect, the *Monthly Magazine* reported that access to these afternoon openings had been restricted to 'first rank' people, connoisseurs and artists due to the 'high attraction of the spectacle'.[3]

Chapter Two will use engraver John Roffe's detailed floor plan of the gallery at Cleveland House as a touchstone to consider the human activities and impulses that drove the social life of the gallery. The plan, like JC Smith's view of the New Gallery discussed in Chapter One, was made for inclusion in John Britton's guidebook and *catalogue raisonné*, and would have been used by visitors to navigate the gallery. While Smith's view presented an idealised image of the act of viewing art at Cleveland House, Roffe's plan is a relatively spare and functional image that would not appear to tell us much about a visitor's experience. Yet, as architectural historian Robin Evans has written, 'If anything is described by an architectural plan, it is the nature of human relationships'.[4] Because original drawings and plans for the building have not survived in any public archive, Roffe's plan is the only record of its spatial layout. Smith's frontispiece had focused on a single room, but the plan invites readers to consider the entire gallery suite as a system in which the viewing of art took place alongside other types of social interaction.

An important body of theoretical literature in the fields of history, philosophy and geography has encouraged scholars of historic spaces to think about social relations as being set into motion within spaces that shape and direct them.[5] Henri Lefebvre's seminal work, for example, argued that social spaces interpenetrate; so-called 'private' spaces such as the house or garden cannot be considered as completely distinct from 'public' ones like the city or the street.[6] Aristocratic dwellings had long been sites where distinctions between public and private life were tenuous at best, so to approach Cleveland House through the lens of such theoretical works permits thinking about the gallery as a space that was not a merely a stage, but produced the encounters between people, objects and paintings that unfolded within. These encounters shaped and moulded expectations for how people and objects circulated and functioned in the type of space that constitutes a 'gallery'.

The gallery's allure could be attributed as much to the Marquess and Marchioness of Stafford's aristocratic status and well-publicized lavish lifestyle as to the collection it contained. Private letters, diaries and periodicals describe Cleveland House as a glamorous centre for the *beau monde*, a once widely-used term that has been revitalized by historian Hannah Greig to describe the '"fashionable" urban culture' of eighteenth- and early nineteenth-century London and its 'associated systems of social prestige and exclusivity'.[7] As a 'spectacle', the gallery was essentially public-facing in nature, orientated toward entertaining and delighting visitors and guests.[8] Left ambiguous is the question of whether the 'spectacle' arose from the art collection, the sumptuousness of Cleveland House's interiors, the array of aristocrats and celebrities who frequented its rooms, or a combination of all of the above.[9] Contemporary accounts suggest that visitors experienced the gallery in a mode of visuality that embedded paintings within the magnificent spectacle of the spaces where they were displayed, as opposed to detached from social or material context.[10]

The gallery at Cleveland House was never intended to be encountered in only one way, or by one type of visitor or guest. Multiple levels of access governed who could and would be admitted. In addition to regular Wednesday afternoon openings, the gallery was used as a venue for Lady Stafford's famed concerts, assemblies and balls as well as for smaller-scale gatherings and dinners. Each subtly or dramatically changed the character of the space based on such factors as the number and type of guests, the time of day, or the furnishing of the rooms. Benjamin Heller has explored the 'topography of the domestic interior' to offer a road map for thinking about interiors while always bearing in mind their fluidity in terms of access and use.[11] Following sociologist Anthony Giddens and social geographer Allan Pred, Heller suggests that the meanings of spaces in the townhouse were in a continual state of flux, as the circumstances surrounding their use also shifted according to an array of possible variables.[12] Using the floor plan of the gallery as a form of material evidence, or trace, of the shape of past social encounters offers a path to thinking through the gallery in a new way – as a distinctive type of space in the metropolis. Considering the plan alongside diary accounts, letters and articles in the periodical press that memorialised the experiences of people who visited the gallery first hand permits us to appreciate the complicated intermingling of public, private and intimate space that the gallery exemplified, how the inside of the house related to the world outside and what this can tell us about the status of London's art world in the early nineteenth century.

'Arranged in a very judicious manner': Encountering Pictures at Cleveland House

In 1814, well-known author Priscilla Wakefield published a long description of the interior of Cleveland House. Her description – relayed second-hand through an acquaintance – is remarkable for the level of detail it provides about the gallery's interior. Wakefield does not dwell on the paintings, which she swiftly glosses as 'the productions of Raphael, Rubens, Claude, Vandyke and many other celebrated names'. Instead, she revels in the glamour and material comforts for which the gallery had become so widely celebrated during its first few years of operation. Cleveland House, she writes, 'is admired still more for the superb furniture within, than for its magnificence without'.[13]

Engraver John Roffe's plan, made after Charles Heathcote Tatham's original drawing and published in Britton's guidebook in 1808, is the best available representation of the gallery's layout (see Figure 2.1). It depicts the public rooms of the first floor of the house: two rooms designated as galleries, a dining room, drawing room, library, passages and anterooms, all of which together made up the gallery suite. Roffe delineates the original building in dark hatching and uses lighter hatching to depict Tatham's addition, which includes the New Gallery, Drawing Room and Dining Room. The plan also clearly depicts the curving profile of two large bow windows along the house's western façade, includes the dimensions of the rooms and suggests the presence of skylighting in the New and Old Galleries using faint dotted rectangles that encircle those rooms.

Roffe's plan overlays the functional organization of the space with a lettering system that imposes an art historical hierarchy over the entire suite. Each room is labelled with a letter from A to K, corresponding to the schools of art displayed in that room, beginning with the Italian schools of the sixteenth and seventeenth centuries through to those of Northern Europe. As Wakefield writes, 'the pictures, which are the chef d'oeuvres of the most

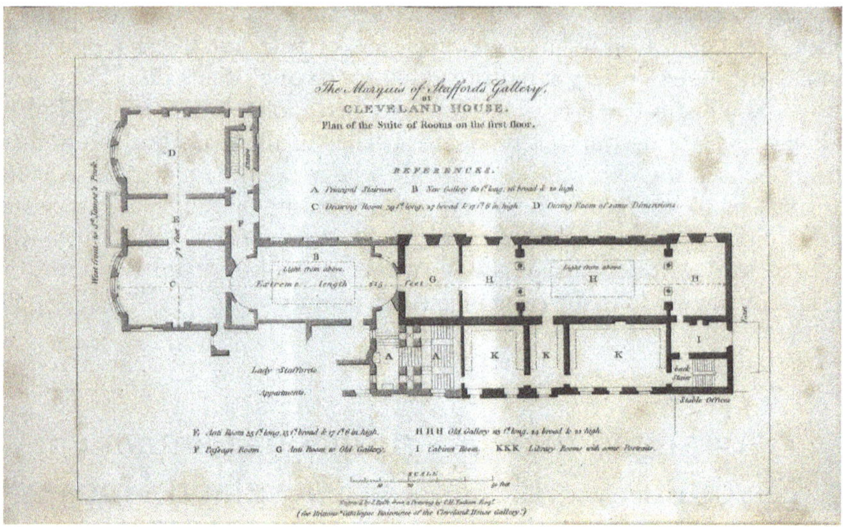

FIGURE 2.1 *John Roffe, engr. From a drawing by CH Tatham, 'Plan of the Suite of Rooms on the first floor' from John Britton,* Catalogue raisonné of the pictures belonging to the most honourable the Marquis of Stafford, in the gallery of Cleveland House *(London: Longman, Hurst, Rees, and Orme, 1808). Yale Center for British Art, Paul Mellon Collection.*

celebrated masters, are arranged in a very judicious manner. The various schools are displayed in the different rooms'.[14] Peter Humfrey has described the arrangement of the pictures in the rooms at Cleveland House in detail. Their organization followed the general trend of the late eighteenth and early nineteenth centuries toward sorting pictures both chronologically and according to national schools.[15] The publication of JJ Winckelmann's *History of Ancient Art* in 1764 marked the beginning of a move toward understanding artworks within an historical framework, a turn that itself had been invigorated by increased general interest in principles of science and classification.[16] These ideas were implemented at several of Europe's renowned princely galleries and early museums. For example, Christian von Mechel instituted a system of hanging that ingeniously built upon the differentiated spaces of the magnificently decorated Belvedere Palace to subdivide the collection into categories according to characteristics like regional school or date; as Michael Yonan argued, Mechel 'transformed a spatial scheme organized around courtly rank into one coordinated with artistic accomplishments'.[17] By the time the Louvre opened in 1793, arranged according to a historical succession of schools, this type of organization had become standard for serious connoisseurs and burgeoning state-owned art galleries.[18] By creating a sequence of rooms illuminating the work of different schools for the purpose of educating the viewer's eye, the gallery at Cleveland House encapsulated the ambition to approximate a 'public' collection in the context of a private house. Visitors were expected to follow an L-shaped route corresponding to the alphabetical sequence inscribed on the floor plan, encountering the artworks according to a hierarchical sequence in which the Italian schools came first and the Netherlandish and British Schools came last. The plan thus connects the catalogue's abstract representation of the collection, made via lists and textual descriptions, to the viewer's somatic experience of walking through the gallery.

Reading contemporary descriptions of the interior like Wakefield's alongside Roffe's plan it is possible to imaginatively recreate what early nineteenth-century visitors arriving at Cleveland House on a Wednesday afternoon might have seen and done. The experience of the gallery began, of course, before one had even arrived at its door. Visitors hoping to attend one of the Wednesday afternoon openings would have followed the instructions provided in Britton's catalogue to apply in writing on Tuesdays for tickets that would be issued for entry on the following day. A rare surviving example of one of these tickets is inscribed with the name of the bearer, Mr Willis and a note that he is entitled to three guests for the afternoon of 18 May 1825 (see Figure 2.2).[19] Tickets were issued by the Porter, a long-time family

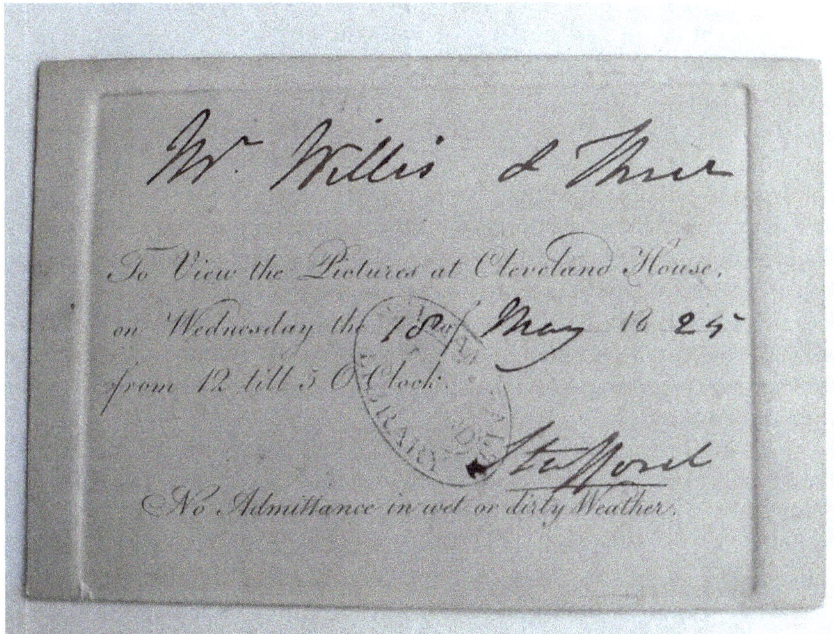

FIGURE 2.2 *Ticket for 'Mr Willis & Three' . . . .' To View the Pictures at Cleveland House. . .' dated 18 May 1825. William Salt Library S. MS. 592/8. The Trustees of the William Salt Library. Photo by author.*

employee named William Cantrill.[20] Ticketing was a process that promised openness and transparency, but as easily signified the possibility of exclusion. Joseph Farington recorded in his diary for 18 June 1806, that 'a written notice this day was placed on a table stating that after the last *Wednesday in August*, the gallery would be shut against *Tickets* for some months'.[21] The notice emphasizes the shutting of the gallery, a sign that its owner is reclaiming space to which some may have felt a right of access. At the same time, the placard's careful wording that the gallery is to be 'shut' against those who have '*Tickets*' implies it will remain open to those who obtain personal invitations.

Ticketed visitors were expected to arrive via carriage. This measure was imposed with the stated intention of preventing visitors from bringing dirt into the gallery, but of course also functioned as a marker of social class. Even as Cleveland House was opened to the public, it was also organized to transmit values of polite conduct in a gallery or museum space that were not well established. When he visited in 1811 Louis Simond reported that:

> it has been found necessary to exclude canes and umbrellas, for fear the pictures should be touched and spoiled; also the pickpockets might introduce themselves for the sake of the watches and handkerchiefs of the connoisseurs. I think a moveable balustrade might be placed, on shew-days, a few feet from the pictures; and as to pickpockets, numerous as they might be formerly, I have not met with any yet. . .[22]

It was only in the late eighteenth century that the assumption that museum or art objects were not to be touched was gaining currency. Constance Classen has written that until well into the nineteenth century, inviting visitors to touch objects at the Ashmolean Museum in Oxford, for example, was an 'expected mark of courtesy'.[23] Indeed, the dolphin tables described in Chapter One were in place in part to prevent injury to the paintings on display. As visitors became more numerous, the risk of damage to objects of course increased, but there seems also to be a general assumption that well-bred visitors could be relied upon to be gentle and restrained, an attitude that needed to be taught to people who might not have experience of rare and fragile objects.

At the door, visitors were admitted by Cantrill, who directed them to the Grand Staircase (marked 'A' on Roffe's plan). The Grand Staircase was elaborately ornamented and lit in order to build expectation as visitors mounted to the gallery above. One reported that 'the entrance from the grand Hall presents an elegant winding staircase; on the first landing are placed two beautiful figures, one representing Apollo of Belvedere and the other a Gladiator, in bronze, ornamented and illuminated with antique vases'.[24] (It also frames the gallery as a site of erudition in the tradition of classical antiquity, as discussed in Chapter One.) The *London Courier* noted that 'six antique Octagon vases' adorned the upper landing, where 'two immense plates of French glass, reflect[ed] the surrounding objects to an endless number' including Veronese's *Judgment of Solomon* which loomed overhead.[25]

After mounting this staircase, visitors finally entered the first room of the gallery suite, the 60-foot-long New Gallery ('B'), through a door at its far end. When the double doors on either end of the room were opened to allow circulation through to the Old Gallery on one end and Drawing Room on the other, the total combined length of the three spaces was 210 feet, a scale rivalling some of Europe's great princely galleries. Wakefield described the experience of stepping into this room and into the presence of works by the most illustrious names in European art as a *coup d'oeil*:

> On entering the great gallery, which is two hundred and ten feet in length, the eye is feasted with the productions of Raphael, Rubens, Claude, Vandyke and many other celebrated names. The coup d'oeil is completed by a most elegant curtain, at the end of the gallery, composed of light blue satin, bearing the appearance of an immense Turkish tent, the rich cornice of the room forming the dome.[26]

As the first and most prominent room on the gallery tour, the New Gallery was hung with the most treasured Italian masterpieces in the Marquess' collection, including an important selection of pictures that had come from the Orléans sale. (Pictures by Rubens and Van Dyck were hung in the Old Gallery ('G'–'H'), and were not immediately visible to a visitor on his or her first step into the gallery as Wakefield implies.) Wakefield's description is certainly based in fact. Other sources confirm the length of the gallery and the occasional presence of a tent-like drapery at its far end, but her description is also a fantasia, much like a Dutch *kunstkammer* painting in which the whole collection becomes visible at once. Seen through Wakefield's eyes, the New Gallery functions as synecdoche distilling the glamour of the gallery into a single moment of experience.

Descriptions of the rest of the gallery suite generally continue in a similar vein, following rooms in sequence after the New Gallery through the Drawing Room ('C'), Anti-Room/Poussin Room ('E'), Dining Room ('D') and finally returning to the Old Gallery ('G'–'H'). Each in turn is described according to the colour of drapery and upholstery, chimney pieces, lighting and occasionally with reference to the pictures displayed there. To accommodate a large number of pictures and permit maximum visibility even when the rooms were crowded, pictures were generally hung on two levels. Smaller paintings like Raphael's *Virgin and Child*, which rewarded detailed study, were displayed at eye level. Larger ones, like Carracci's *Danaë*, were hung closer to the ceiling where they would be visible above assembled crowds. This practice followed the pattern established in public spaces for art like the Royal Academy, with the caveat that pictures were hung much farther apart; the wall covering was visible behind them and the eye had something of an opportunity to rest.[27] As noted above, the pictures were arranged throughout the gallery suite by school. Britton's guidebook was organized by room and listed paintings in sequence from no 1 (Scarsellino da Ferrara's *Christ with his Disciples at Emmaus*) to no 252 (Paul Bril's *Nymphs and Fauns, in a Landscape*). The number assigned to each picture was recorded on a 'small ivory ticket(s)' attached to its frame and the numbering system corresponded to the order in which the pictures would be encountered as a visitor moved through the gallery. The numbers also corresponded with Britton's exegeses, 'rendering every necessary information' about them easily accessible.[28]

The pictures were organised according to new trends in classification to enhance connoisseurship, but were likewise arranged in patterns that had long been in use in private houses.[29] Since the seventeenth century, books and treatises had recommended that pictures be hung in rooms which correlated to their subject matter in size, function and prestige.[30] Spaces in the upper class house associated with the public face of the family, such as drawing rooms, dining rooms and galleries, were usually hung with religious or historical subjects alongside the portraits which were so essential to the public presentation of family identity. Pictures were likewise displayed in private houses according to their owners' idiosyncratic impulses and arranged to encourage a sense of discovery as the viewer's body moved through space. Organising the collection around national schools in order to conform to evolving standards for the display of art necessarily meant suppressing some of the strategies for displaying artworks that had previously prevailed in private interiors. However, the arrangement of pictures at Cleveland House left plenty of opportunity for whimsy, delight, surprise and contemplation. For example, the Dining Room featured two large mythological pictures by Titian, *Diana and Actaeon* and *Diana and Callisto*, which were considered two of the gallery's greatest treasures (see Figure 2.3). Both pictures depicted Diana surrounded by female attendants, all nude and striking a variety of alluring poses. As the paintings were hung flanking the door to the visitor's back as he or she entered, the surprise upon turning around would have provided a frisson of sensual delight, perhaps all the more appropriate to a room where dining and drinking took place. Certainly, a particular picture could be singled out for comment by visitors if it seemed to elicit reactions that were somehow inappropriate for the space where it was displayed. Philippa Simpson has argued that the presence of such erotic pictures in British private galleries frequently raised eyebrows during this period; for example, the Titian gallery at Blenheim Palace was open only to men while Britton's catalogue acknowledges the palpable physicality of pictures like *Diana and Callisto*, which invited viewers' attention through generous use of sensuous colour.[31]

Plentiful lighting permitting close study of the pictures on display was provided throughout the gallery. Proper lighting was critical to its educational mission and in descriptions lighting often functioned as a signifier of the

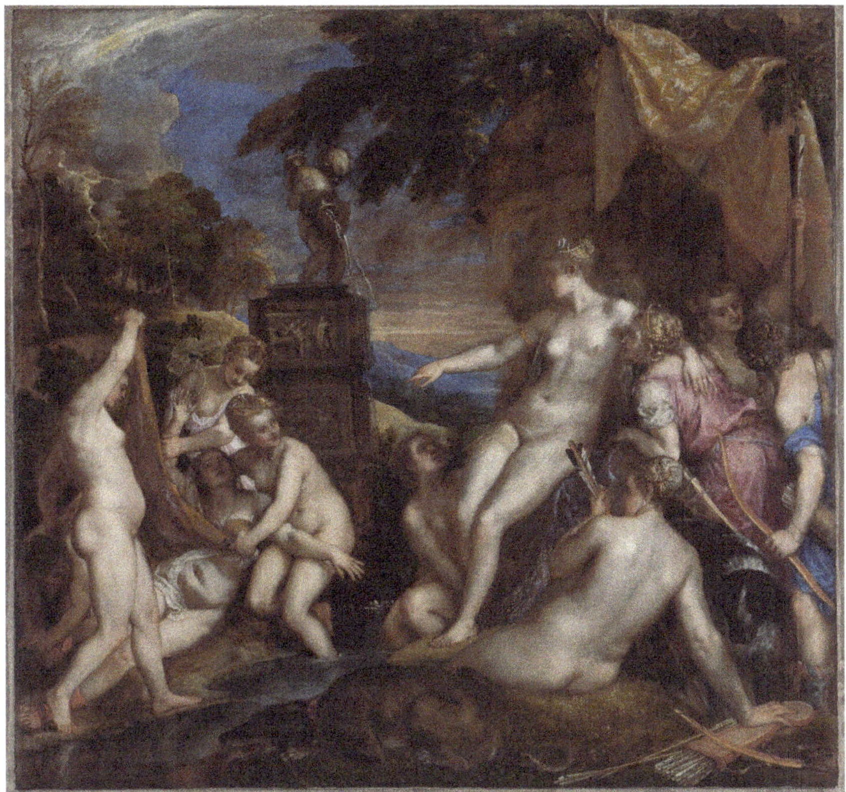

FIGURE 2.3 *Titian,* Diana and Callisto, *oil on canvas, 1556–1559. National Gallery and National Galleries of Scotland. Bought jointly by the National Gallery and National Galleries of Scotland with contributions from the National Lottery through the Heritage Lottery Fund, Art Fund (with a contribution from the Wolfson Foundation), The Monument Trust, J Paul Getty Jnr Charitable Trust, Mr and Mrs James Kirkman, Sarah and David Kowitz, Chris Rokos, The Rothschild Foundation, Sir Siegmund Warburg's Voluntary Settlement, and through private appeal and bequests, 2012 © The National Gallery, London.*

gallery's fitness as a space for looking at pictures. One writer remarked, 'The most minute and delicate touches of the painters were seen as if at noonday', another that the room's 'classic lamps' permitted the paintings to be displayed 'as clearly as in open day'.[32] Similarly American ambassador Richard Rush wrote on the occasion of one late-night assembly, 'the paintings commanded admiration. Under light judiciously disposed, they made a magnificent appearance'.[33] Although the New and Old Galleries were lit from above with skylights, other rooms, including the Drawing and Dining Rooms, relied on vertical, West-facing windows for illumination. Because London's weather patterns did not reliably provide full sun on gallery days, all rooms were also amply supplied with fixtures like chandeliers and lamps. As discussed in Chapter One, the gallery's architect, Charles Heathcote Tatham, designed both types of light fixture for the gallery based on antique examples (see Figure 1.13). Amongst the 263 lamps estimated by one observer were 'sixteen patent lamps, with double burners, standing upon the summits of sixteen elegant ebony columns, seven feet high, forming a double range of brilliant lights, shining through the most transparent lawn'.[34] To further augment both natural and man-made lighting throughout the gallery, a profusion of mirrors and gilded objects reflected light from other sources, including 'real bronze and *or moulu* tripods, candelabras, reflecting mirrors, side lights and every fanciful decoration that art can furnish'.[35] Mirrors were frequently used in the decoration of grand interiors to enhance the impression of lightness; mirrors also reflected light sources contributing to the room's splendour.[36] With light in abundance, visitors were able to experience the visual delight offered by the pictures under conditions available almost nowhere else in London.

The gallery's brightness could be – and was – interpreted not only as a sign of its fitness for the display of art, but also of its status as a dazzling aristocratic space appropriate for hosting Britain's elite. The generous use of candles, oil-burning lamps and chandeliers in the gallery was an easily understood index of Stafford's extraordinary wealth. Oil and candles were expensive resources and the more brightly lit a space was, the more it dazzlingly communicated the wealth and social position of its owners.[37] Such lighting also alluded to the mantle of cultural authority dating from antiquity that Stafford and other prominent collectors who installed skylights in domestic galleries were keen to don. As Alice Barnaby has written, the architectural lineage of sky- or toplighting can be traced to the Pantheon in Rome, which was the 'paradigmatic example of this lighting technique'.[38] It was adopted in such spaces as the Great Room at the Royal Academy and in other spaces constructed or adapted for the display of art, like Christie's Auction Room. Bringing skylighting into the private, domestic interior betokened the role of cultural leadership that private collectors assumed but also elided their houses with public spaces in a manner that they were not ready to fully embrace.

'The paintings of the masters hung all around us': Social Life in the Gallery

The '*coup d'oeil*' made by Cleveland House's indisputably glamorous interior was key to its allure amongst London society and the general public alike; as Richard Rush wrote succinctly, the 'rooms abounded in ornamental articles which wealth had amassed and taste arranged'.[39] The Marquess and Marchioness of Stafford were widely recognized as the richest, if not highest-ranking, couple in late Georgian Britain. Sir George Beaumont, another prominent collector, reportedly exclaimed that 'the stile of the Marquiss' living, His superb plate & table appearance & servants ... exceeded everything in this Country, no one could vie with it'.[40] The gallery, its architecture, the collection and its sumptuous arrangement all worked in concert to present the image of a family whose wealth and influence positioned them in the upper reaches of the *beau monde*.

The interplay of social class, gender, decoration and the layout and organization of the gallery were encoded in the various plans and images made of its interior. John Roffe's floor plan of the gallery memorializes the relationship between its public and private spaces and how circulation through it was contingent on layers of access permitted according to social position.[41] Following Robin Evans' observation that an architectural plan describes first and foremost 'the nature of human relationships,' Roffe's plan may be productively interrogated to reveal this interplay. On its face, Roffe's plan is a practical document. Its purpose, bound into Britton's guidebook facing Smith's view of the New Gallery, was to direct visitors through the gallery on Wednesday afternoons. The lettered spaces, corresponding to the *catalogue raisonné* the guidebook contains, allude to the presence of visitors in the space of the gallery, moving through its rooms in sequence, standing in front of paintings and reading Britton's exegeses on the pictures. A note in the 1815 edition of *The Picture of London* informed readers that 'Visitors will find Mr. Britton's Catalogue Raisonnee, published by permission of the Marquis, the best companion round the rooms, as not only the pictures are described, but it contains plans of the gallery and an historical and critical account of each picture'.[42] The notion of the guidebook as a 'companion' to the visitor suggests the interplay between reader, book and the somatic experience of the gallery that it was intended to mediate.

Of course the Wednesday afternoon openings, credited to Stafford's magnanimity, were only one of the organizing constructs shaping social life and human activity in the gallery. Lady Stafford was a renowned hostess in her own right who used the gallery as the setting for a busy schedule of balls, assemblies, concerts and private dinners. On these occasions the tidy organization of the gallery's spaces by letters of the alphabet did not apply and the rooms were transformed from the spare rectangles on Roffe's floor plan into sumptuous spaces animated by music, the scents of flowers and food and a glittering array of guests. The gallery appeared in a variety of guises, depending on the day of the week, the time of day and whether the space was being used by the family alone, by ticketed visitors, or for a ball with hundreds of guests. The notion that Cleveland House, or any kind of domestic or private space for that matter, was static in use or appearance flies in the face of available evidence from the period. Benjamin Heller has argued for a nuanced approach to thinking about the operation of social hierarchies in the nineteenth century interior, writing that 'the significance of locations within the home is created by a combination of time of day, activities undertaken, objects present and identities of people involved'.[43] This is just as true and perhaps more pronounced in the upper-class townhouse, which was designed for entertaining on both a grand and an intimate scale and to accommodate enormous numbers of guests alongside a small army of servants who attended their needs. Until the eighteenth century, it was common practice for rooms to be rearranged on a regular basis. When not in use, suites of chairs were arranged around the periphery of the room and were reconfigured as needed according to the type of social event and number of guests expected. By the end of the century, the notion of leaving rooms with furniture arranged in the centre, as if the family had just departed, became common. This phenomenon will be discussed in further detail in Chapter Three, but for the moment it is sufficient to point out that as a large house that was being used for both domestic purposes and a wide range of public and private social events, furniture and other decorative items at Cleveland House were themselves in a state of constant motion.

Because Smith's view of the New Gallery was made as a frontispiece for Britton's authorised guidebook, it portrays the gallery in its guise as a public space and reflects how its interior was arranged on Wednesday afternoons, as discussed in Chapter One. The floor is bare; all furniture except Tatham's massive pier tables, which kept visitors from approaching the pictures too closely, is absent. This relatively unadorned guise enabled the close viewing of works of art without forcing visitors to navigate around tables and chairs or subjecting carpets to constant heavy foot traffic. At other times, however, the room was filled with a wide range of furniture, textiles and decorative objects to accommodate a variety of purposes, including family use. Britton asserts that all of the rooms except the New and Old Galleries were 'fitted up and appropriated for domestic purposes', and though evidence of such use is frustratingly scant, he is reminding his readers that many diverse activities took place in the gallery, like reading, conversing and dining, at times when it was closed.[44]

The ball that took place on 7 May 1806 marking the gallery's completion and opening to the public is by far the best documented of the many social occasions that took place in its early years. Weeks in advance the *Morning Chronicle* predicted that it would become 'one of the most splendid fetes that has ever been remembered in London'.[45] The *Morning Post*, a popular newspaper that regularly reported on the comings-and-goings of the aristocracy, published a lengthy description of the event.

> About nine o'clock the company began to arrive, and before ten some hundreds were assembled. They were received in the great hall by twelve servants in the most superb State liveries, each of which cost the noble Marquis forty guineas; they consisted of a blue coat entirely covered with silver lace, and a scarlet waistcoat and breeches. On the coat there were no less than a hundred and twenty yards of lace. About double the

> number of attendants out of livery were arranged in order on the first flight of the grand staircase. The latter is built, and the dome above is supported, in the style of a Roman pavilion, having four pillars on each side to support the roof. In the interior of this beautiful structure, on the right and left, were placed two elegant Venetian lamps supported by groups of figures *à la Grec*. On this flight in the early part of the evening the Marquis stood, to conduct the company to the Marchioness, who was waiting to receive them in the Great Saloon.[46]

The *Morning Post*'s description paints a cohesive picture of the accretive layers of architectural and social convention through which visitors passed before entering the gallery itself. The gallery's literal and figurative separation from the street and the world outside marks it as private space, different in nature and kind from the Wednesday afternoon openings that were ostensibly aimed at the public. The ball is an occasion on which admission was granted by invitation only, but Wednesday afternoon visitors mounted the same staircase re-enacting the social ritual involved in being admitted to a grand aristocratic house. Stafford stands on the stairs, physically embodying the transition from public to private space and directing visitors to the 'Great Saloon' where their hostess awaited. (Presumably, the room the writer refers to is actually the New Gallery, but the author's misnomer using the word 'Saloon', a term generally associated with women's hospitality, seems a telling slip.)

The passage quoted above is typical of newspaper accounts of private houses in the period. It is preoccupied with specific, detailed descriptions of people and objects found in the gallery. The *London Courier and Evening Gazette* reported that 'the company will be conducted through the Entrance Hall to the grand *Escalier*, leading to the Principal Rooms, covered with rich Crimson Velvet Carpet'.[47] Continuing for several paragraphs in this vein, the *Courier* describes the staircase, the light fixtures, furniture, draperies, mirrors and other aspects of the gallery at Cleveland House that made its interior such a 'rich treat'. What the *Courier* barely mentions is the renowned collection hanging on the walls. After devoting the better part of seven paragraphs to cataloguing the décor, the *Courier* concludes: 'Our limits prevent us from enumerating the different Masters whose inimitable Works decorate and adorn the walls'.[48] Periodical accounts often subordinated the collection of masterpieces to the other innumerable luxuries in the interior and the roster of illustrious names present. The *Morning Post* concluded its description of the house by declaring that 'the magnificence of the spectacle can only be equaled by a similar exhibition at Carleton [sic] House,' which was the Prince of Wales' recently-renovated London residence (see Figure 1.11).[49] Such newspaper accounts permit their readers, the vast majority of whom would never have access to such spaces, to imaginatively experience them; a reader may be able to vicariously experience the sensation of mounting the enormous staircase at Cleveland House to enter the gallery hovering alluringly above.[50]

Periodical writers often attempted to quantify the luxury on display in the gallery, a quixotic enterprise given that the very nature of aristocratic prestige defied such easy or precise definition.[51] The *Morning Post* claimed that thirty-six servants were stationed on the Grand Stairs, each of whom wore a livery coat embellished with 120 yards of silver lace at a cost of forty guineas per coat. The servants themselves are regarded as little more than décor, their number and the decoration of their livery part of an accounting of Cleveland House's spectacle of wealth. Whether or not the figure of forty guineas per coat is precisely accurate, this (jaw-dropping) expenditure functions as shorthand for the overall sumptuousness of not just the house, but of its furniture, fittings and the human endeavour implicated in the creation of the spectacle. Objects in the gallery were described and valued with equal frankness. On a different occasion, the *Morning Post* reported that

> the noble gallery, the drawing-rooms, and anti-rooms were all thrown open about ten o'clock. The grand dining-room was appropriated for serving out refreshments in. A truly superb silver cistern was displayed on the sideboard, said to weigh one thousand five hundred ounces. The picture galleries had the finest effect imaginable, they were illuminated by a profusion of Grecian and patent lamps.[52]

The writer distinguishes the 'picture galleries' from other rooms in the gallery suite, though in practice important pictures were exhibited in every room. Paintings formed one of the most important elements of the visual spectacle that Cleveland House presented, yet at the same time is not considered distinct from the other pleasures the interior offers. Though the 'grand dining-room' mentioned was dominated by *Diana & Actaeon* and *Diana & Callisto*, the author focuses on the silver cistern on display nearby, leading a reader to conclude that the 1500 ounces of silver was even more impressive than Titian's sensual masterpieces. At a time when silver and copper were in short supply due to ongoing war on the continent, the cistern quantified wealth and its attendant forms of conspicuous consumption, in a way the Titians could not.[53]

Cleveland House was full of ephemeral and useful objects. The cistern symbolized enormous wealth while serving the practical function of holding bottles of wine, reminding us that a visitor's experience of the gallery and of the paintings was inflected by and interwoven with the range of sensory experiences that these objects activated. During the Georgian period elaborate temporary decorations at private parties and assemblies were extremely fashionable and as Melanie Doderer-Winkler has written, the range of such decorations ranged from floors chalked in ornate patterns to tablescapes composed of fruits and pastries.[54] While the archival record is necessarily incomplete, both periodical literature and household accounts suggest that

Lord and Lady Stafford were spending vast sums on accoutrements and supplies for the gallery during the season. Although Cleveland House was amply outfitted with oil lamps and chandeliers, additional light fixtures were hired in quantity for balls and other special events. The account books for Stafford's properties, kept by the house steward Mr Lilley, indicate regular expenditures in the range of £50 to £80 for lighting from the firm 'Smithurst' – certainly a reference to lamp-manufacturer and oil merchant James Smethurst, who regularly supplied the royal family and other rich clients with 'Lamps let out on hire for Balls, Routs, Illuminations, & c.'[55]

Moreover, account books record regular purchases of other consumable items used for entertaining like food, wine and flowers. The *London Courier* observed that the galleries were filled with 'jardinets, stocked with the choicest productions of the different nurseries around the metropolis, emitting the most delicious perfumes'; similarly Priscilla Wakefield wrote that 'fragrant odours scented the apartments, from the beautiful flowers displayed in the *jardiniers*, which gave winter the appearance of spring'.[56] A *jardinier* is a specialized piece of furniture designed for displaying plants. George Smith's *A Collection of Designs for Household Furniture and Interior Decoration*, published in 1808, features two examples 'well adapted for the ends of a long gallery or staircase', locations where such objects could have been placed at Cleveland House (see Figure 2.4). Accounts likewise show regular expenditures for flowers to fill these vessels; in July 1806, for example, Lilley paid a bill of £10/1/6 for flowers purchased at Covent Garden.[57] Even more elaborate decorations might be deployed on particularly important occasions, such as the May 1806 ball held to inaugurate the gallery, when the *London Courier* notes that 'at the extremity of the gallery, 210 feet in length, is a most elegant curtain, of light blue satin, combining the taste of modern drapery with the magnificence of Eastern grandeur, resembling an immense Turkish tent.'[58] It seems likely that this drapery, in the style of a 'tent room', was installed as a temporary decoration to create maximum possible magnificence. Tent rooms enjoyed a period of vogue around this time; a decade later Sir John Leicester's gallery in his townhouse in Hill Street, which I will discuss in Chapter Five, incorporated a tent room which he used as a setting for the display of *The Cottage Door* by Thomas Gainsborough, one of the prized British pictures in Leicester's collection.[59]

Music filled the rooms frequently. Lady Stafford was renowned for her Sunday evening concerts, which she hosted regularly even prior to moving into Cleveland House. In 1805 the Bishop of London spoke out against Lady Stafford's musical evenings. The practice of including secular works in these Sabbath-day concerts aroused suspicion, but despite the Bishop's interference, the concerts continued.[60] In April 1807 the Marchioness hosted an evening of songs by Madame Angelica Catalani, a famous Italian soprano.[61] A few weeks later, the same newspaper reported that an orchestra had been situated in the Old Gallery where the Flemish pictures were on display.[62] During concerts and

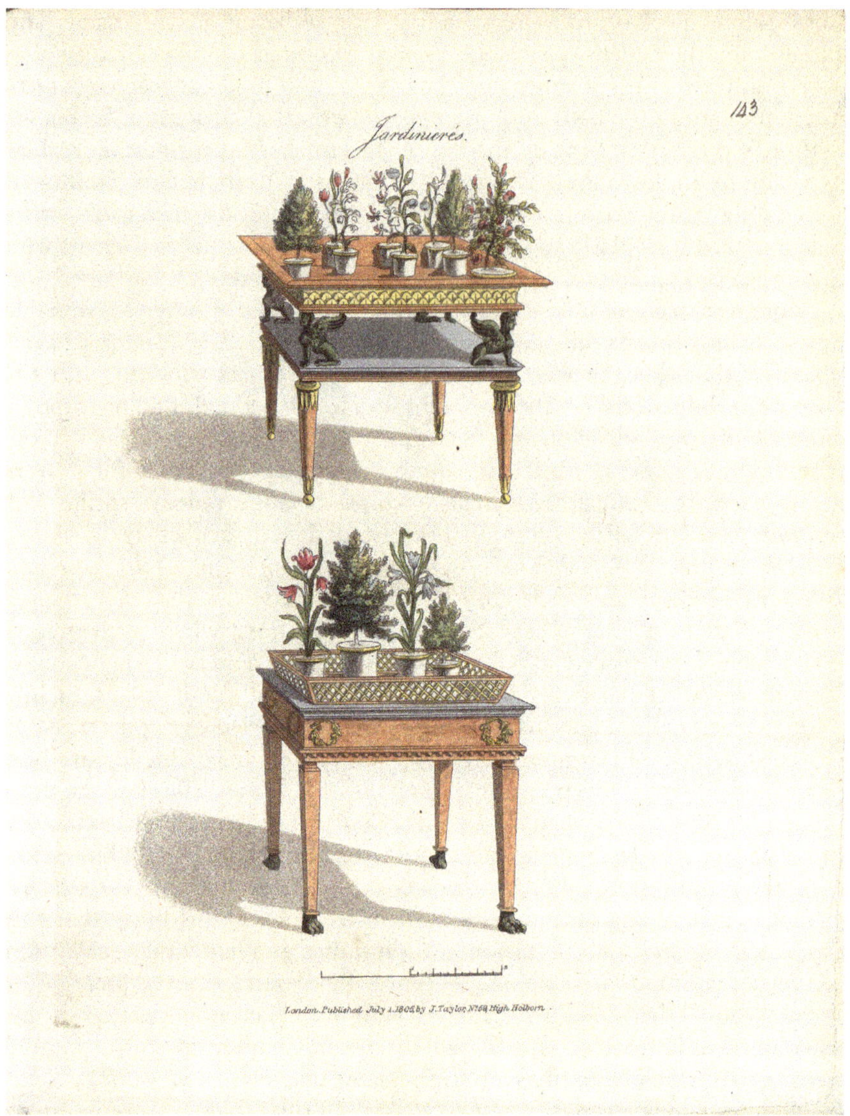

FIGURE 2.4 *'Jardinière' in George Smith,* Collection of Designs for Household Furniture and Interior Decoration *(London: J Taylor, 1808). Yale Center for British Art, Paul Mellon Collection.*

other assemblies, drinks and other refreshments were offered turning the gallery into a space for eating and drinking. During the orchestra performance mentioned above, the New Gallery accommodated 'a most sumptuous display of delicacies' which 'were set out upon a very long range of tables', illuminated by 'one of the most magnificent Grecian lamps ever seen in this country'.[63] In 1818, ambassador Richard Rush attended a dinner party at Cleveland House where such topics as 'the country life in England' and the 'literary publications of the day' were discussed, with 'the paintings of the masters hung all around us'.[64] In his memoir, Rush recorded that the table was set in the Dining Room and after dinner, the group retired to the Drawing Room, where Mocha coffee and black tea were served. He vividly recalled the Drawing Room windows having been opened to enjoy the June weather, writing: 'We had music from St. James's Park, into which the windows of Stafford [sic] house look. Its notes were the softer from the stillness of that scene, and the breeze of a charming summer night'.[65] Rush's memory of the pictures was interwoven with the sensory experiences with which Cleveland House was so richly layered. The scent of coffee, the sensation of the summer breeze and the sound of music all provided a framework within which he might better appreciate the collection and remember its highlights. Music, food and the scents of flowers, while frequently described in newspaper reports, were ephemeral aspects of the gallery that are difficult, if not impossible, to recover.

The reimagining of the social life of the interior sketched above is based on a range of sources including account books, diaries and newspaper reports. Yet they follow a pattern, one that an anthropological approach to material culture and luxury consumption illuminates.[66] Draperies, lamps, furniture and paintings worked in concert to create a space for appreciation of interiors and collections of art and use of luxury objects within the context of a social 'ritual activity' in which collector and visitors mutually participate.[67] The accounts cited above, drawn from a wide array of sources intended for a range of audiences, form a detailed record of processes by which wealth is made visible. The middle-class reader's understanding of the goings-on at Cleveland House would be wholly shaped by such journalistic accounts; those who had visited the gallery in person, or even attended a ball at Cleveland House, might read such descriptions quite differently. They could be understood as strictly descriptive, or as a lens through which to view the foibles of one's own class. Unlike clothing or carriages, interiors can only be appreciated when viewers are invited into the space for a dinner, a ball, or for a public opening. The objects that filled them, whether paintings, illuminated chandeliers, or jardinières full of flowers, had to be experienced in the presence of others in order to be fully understood and appreciated.

Catalogues taught visitors what to focus on in the gallery but, by a process of omission, what not to look at. Conventions of politeness dictated that if in the gallery as guests, visitors should focus their attention on the pictures. Newspaper accounts brought to life the aspects of the interior that manners did not permit visitors to openly stare at or remark upon like carpets, furniture, gilding, mirrors, signs of family life and oil-lit chandeliers.[68] Visitors would have been exquisitely aware of the delicate balance between public and private space that the gallery represented, attuned to the messages that Britton's text and Roffe's floor plan subtly communicated. Of course, many of the people reading Britton's catalogue at home in their own drawing rooms would never gain access to the gallery, lacking the social connections or wherewithal to acquire tickets. For them, Britton's catalogue operated as both their only means of access and a document justifying their exclusion. These viewers, no doubt conversant with the gallery's lavish interiors thanks to the many descriptions that circulated in periodical literature, could have used the plan as an imaginative point of entry into the spectacle of art, luxury and society that the house's interior held.

'Dazzling array of Duchesses Earls, Viscounts, Ladies & Sirs': Rank and Celebrity on Display

As the gallery at Cleveland House became a required stop on the London social circuit, acquiring tickets became a priority for people who wanted to be seen in the right places. The opening of the gallery presented an opportunity to cross the threshold of aristocratic space and participate in the rituals of the *beau monde*. Within weeks of the gallery's first opening in May 1806, the *Monthly Magazine* reported that tickets to the gallery were being limited to the 'first rank' persons and connoisseurs, but of course artists, one of the gallery's key audiences, were also given priority.[69] Priscilla Wakefield described the Marquess' gallery as 'a school of painting . . . the most extensive and valuable of any' then in the metropolis.[70] Nearly every artist working in London during the first quarter of the century visited – or attempted to visit – the gallery at one time or another. The regulations printed in Britton's guidebook state that artists were eligible for season tickets, but only if recommended by a member of the Royal Academy.[71] Amongst the better-known artists who are recorded as visiting the gallery are landscapists JMW Turner (whose *Bridgewater Sea-Piece* was the only work by a living British artist on display when it opened in 1806), John Constable, William Daniell, Thomas Hearne, William Gilpin, beleaguered history painter Benjamin Robert Haydon, society portraitist Thomas Lawrence and genre painter David Wilkie (see Figure 2.5).[72]

Cleveland House was a busy place and artists ultimately made up only a fraction of the people to be found there on any given Wednesday afternoon. The gallery's yearly opening coincided with the height of the London season and was positioned on the social calendar amongst other important events such as the Almack's Ball and the opening of the Royal Academy exhibition.[73] Open days were often packed with people of fashion, celebrities and well-connected foreign tourists. The gallery's first open afternoon in May 1806 was attended by 'Many Amateurs, & noble persons' and a preponderance of titled figures amongst the people sighted in the gallery suggests that the Wednesday openings remained a draw within the *beau monde*.[74] Farington records that such illustrious art-world figures as Sir George Beaumont, Sir

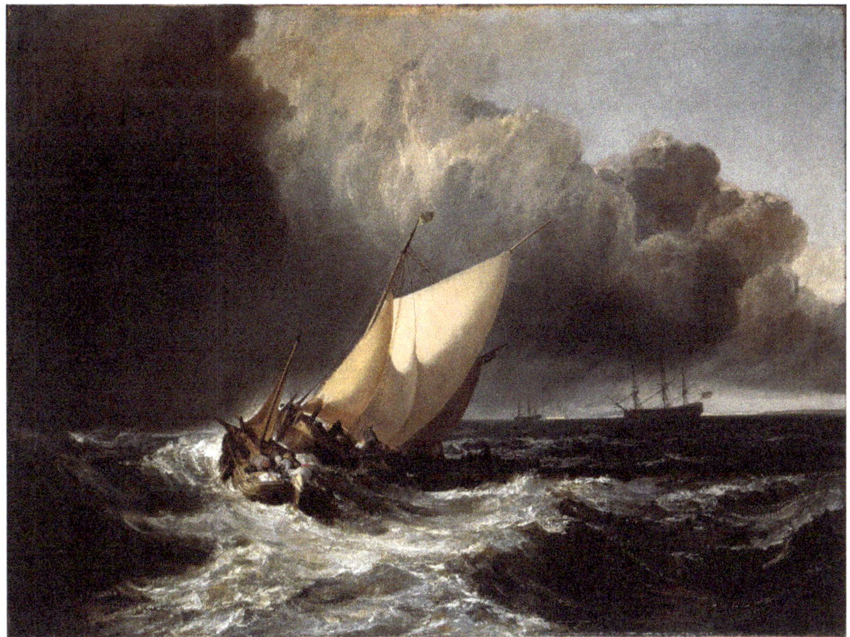

FIGURE 2.5 *JMW Turner,* Dutch Boats in a Gale ('The Bridgewater Sea-Piece), *1801. National Gallery, London. On loan from The Capricorn Foundation.*

Abraham Hume and Lord Grosvenor were present on opening day, all of whom followed the Marquess' example by opening their own houses to visitors within a few years.[75]

It is an accepted truism that the upper-class house acted as a lens through which to focus on the intricacies of social class; in 1807, Robert Southey wittily expressed this idea, writing: 'An Englishman delights to show his wealth; every thing in his house, therefore, is expensive'.[76] More recently than Southey and with great nuance, Hannah Greig has written about the ways in which the deployment of money in the pursuit of social and political prestige shaped elite metropolitan culture in this period.[77] The majority of written descriptions of Cleveland House catalogue the glittering roster of royalty, aristocrats, politicians and celebrities – 'a most brilliant assemblage of fashionables' – who filled its rooms during the many social events outlined above.[78] The notion that the townhouse functioned like a stage set for the performance of social status thus provides a useful frame for making sense of the myriad descriptions of the gallery that have been discussed above. The ability to see the gallery at times other than designated Wednesday afternoons was a mark of privileged status. In April 1822, Irish novelist Maria Edgeworth wrote that she was nearly turned away at the door of Cleveland House by a 'pimple faced red blotched door *holder*'. After this unfortunately described servant handed Edgeworth's card to another servant out of livery, 'he thought better of it and came forth to the carriage door saying "My lady is at home to you Ma'am". So out we jumped and up we went and Harriet for the first time saw the gallery &c.'[79] This unliveried servant may well have been porter William Cantrill, who had been entrusted by his employers to make spontaneous decisions about who did and didn't merit their attention. Edgeworth writes that once her party had entered the house, Lady Stafford herself greeted them and issued an invitation for dinner.

The picture of Cleveland House that emerges from the pages of periodical literature is of a place that was associated with the glittering ranks of British and European aristocracy as much as with the cerebral delights offered by the collection. Although members of the *beau monde* were consistently present on Wednesday afternoons, the society present at the Marquess and Marchioness of Stafford's many social events was more glamorous still. Guest lists were liberally sprinkled with prominent members of the aristocracy, diplomats and celebrities, described in one report as a 'dazzling array of Duchesses Earls, Viscounts, Ladies & Sirs'.[80] The greater the number of titled aristocracy in attendance, of course, the more exclusive the occasion and greater the glory reflected on Lady Stafford as hostess. Just as descriptive accounts had focused on quantifiable signifiers of wealth, such as the yards of lace in a coat or the ounces of silver in a cistern, many drew explicit attention to the number of guests present. One assembly held in April 1807 was reportedly attended 'by upwards of 200 fashionables' but by the standards of aristocratic London, this would have been a relatively modest affair.[81] While reports varied, the ball held in May 1806 to inaugurate the gallery was rumoured to have welcomed 'the largest Party ever collected at one time in any private house in London': 1,800 guests, amongst them notorious socialite the Prince of Wales.[82]

George Frederick Augustus, Prince of Wales until 1811 and Prince Regent until he succeeded his father as King George IV in 1820, was a frequent visitor to Cleveland House. The Prince wrote Lady Stafford a letter dated the day of the ball opening the gallery in 1806, asking for special accommodations for entry:

> As there will be no inconsiderable difficulty in approaching you this evening for all those who are anxious to pay their respects to you; will you have the goodness to order a servant of yours to be ready to give me admittance through the Park; he must let me in at the Gate [east] of the Mall, & afterwards through the Garden into the House, & if you are so good as to admit of this, I shall claim your permission to avail myself of the same mode of retreat.[83]

While it is impossible to know whether the Prince actually sneaked surreptitiously into and away from the ball through the garden that opened into Green Park, his presence that night was widely reported. The Prince visited the gallery on a number of other occasions. In May 1811, diarist Mary Berry wrote, 'Went to Lady Stafford's. We got into chairs in St. James's Street, the string of carriages was so long. 1,500 cards had been issued and yet it did not make a positive crowd in that great house, except near the circles where the Prince stood'.[84] In 1818, Richard Rush reported 'the rooms were full. The Prince Regent, royal family, many of the nobility and others, thronged them. It was past eleven when we arrived; yet fresh names were every moment announced'.[85] Mary Berry's astute description of the 'crowd' gathering near the Prince Regent indicates that the possibility of glimpsing high-ranking members of society in the gallery exercised a powerful allure and was perhaps at least as compelling as the collection itself.

The intense interest in the Prince's presence in the gallery points to his status as a leading light of the nascent celebrity culture of the period, which grew out of a fascination with people who were wealthy, famous, infamous, or well-connected.[86] Whether or not the Prince would have been understood as a 'celebrity' by the standards of the early nineteenth century, the presence of famous and notable figures in the gallery warranted mention in descriptions. In June 1806, 15-year-old Frances Waddington encountered renowned Shakespearean actress Sarah Siddons in the gallery:

> I stood very near Mrs Siddons for some time, to hear what she said. At length she picked out a painting of some Dutch fishwomen, the last thing upon earth you could call interesting, and 'what a sweet composition is that!' was pronounced in her deepest tragedy tones.[87]

Despite – or perhaps because of – her youth, Waddington proved a remarkably astute observer about the nature of the attraction the gallery posed. Siddons cannily used the gallery as a stage for the performance of her public persona; other visitors, like Waddington herself, surely treasured the opportunity to encounter the famed *tragedienne* up close. Unfortunately, records of specific personal encounters at Cleveland House are rare. Most accounts indicate that the space was generally experienced in a crush of visitors, all jockeying to see each other and the paintings. An evening concert of songs by Madame Catalani – herself an internationally recognised soprano – was reported to have attracted an especially glittering audience; the *Morning Post* reported that the guests included the Prince of Wales (again) and two of his brothers, the Dukes of Cambridge and Gloucester.[88] Also present was Louis Philippe d'Orléans, whose family's famed picture collection now hung on the gallery's walls. The *Morning Post*, a newspaper that habitually reflected the aristocratic point of view, referred to him as the 'Duke of Orléans', but officially he had been stripped of his titles after his father had been guillotined in 1793. By the time he visited Cleveland House in 1807, Louis-Philippe was living in exile in the London suburbs, where it is believed he taught geography and mathematics at the Great Ealing School to support himself and his family.[89] After the revolution of 1830, he would be crowned King Louis-Philippe I of France. As the *Morning Post* suggests, London's *beau monde* was well aware of the presence of a member of the beleaguered French royal family in their midst and he may have been a regular guest in many of their houses. We can only speculate as to Louis-Philippe's thoughts on seeing the renowned collection that had belonged to his own family hanging in a London townhouse being heralded as another nation's treasure.

'A display of matter, not mind': Pictures as Household Stuff

Cleveland House was the most prominent and well-documented example of a private art gallery in this period, but a similar dynamic played out in other aristocratic town houses. Another important example was Grosvenor House, which opened to the public in 1808.[90] Robert Grosvenor, Second Earl Grosvenor, hired surveyor and architect William Porden to undertake a renovation and redecoration of the building from 1806–1808. Fashionable cabinetmaker Richard Gillow was employed to supply furniture, but Porden dismissed Gillow's advice to create the effect of a lighter, brighter interior. As a result, the walls in several rooms were lined with crimson damask embellished with gold lace and tassel fringe.[91] Porden's insistence on using crimson followed the conventional view amongst connoisseurs that pictures were best viewed against a red ground and many visitors particularly noticed the colour's predominance in the interior. A dedicated picture gallery was added to Grosvenor House from 1817–1819.

The general effect of the decoration scheme is preserved in CR Leslie's family portrait of 1831, made in the gallery where the family's renowned group of paintings by Rubens was displayed (see Figure 2.6). Robert Grosvenor, seated at the centre of the composition, was created Marquess of Westminster in that year. Richard Grosvenor, who had likewise been elevated to the title Earl Grosvenor, stands at the centre of the composition, his wife, born Lady Elizabeth Leveson-Gower (who, as the younger daughter of Lord and Lady Stafford, had grown up at Cleveland House) at his left elbow. The pictures by Rubens, partially obscured by columns, sculptures and human bodies, are not the focus of the painter nor of any of the figures depicted. Instead, they listen and watch as female members of the family play the piano and harp at right while two of Earl and Countess Grosvenor's young daughters dance in the foreground. The interior is filled with a range of splendid objects, including the aforementioned musical instruments touched with gilt, an ornate birdcage for the children's parrot visible at left and a

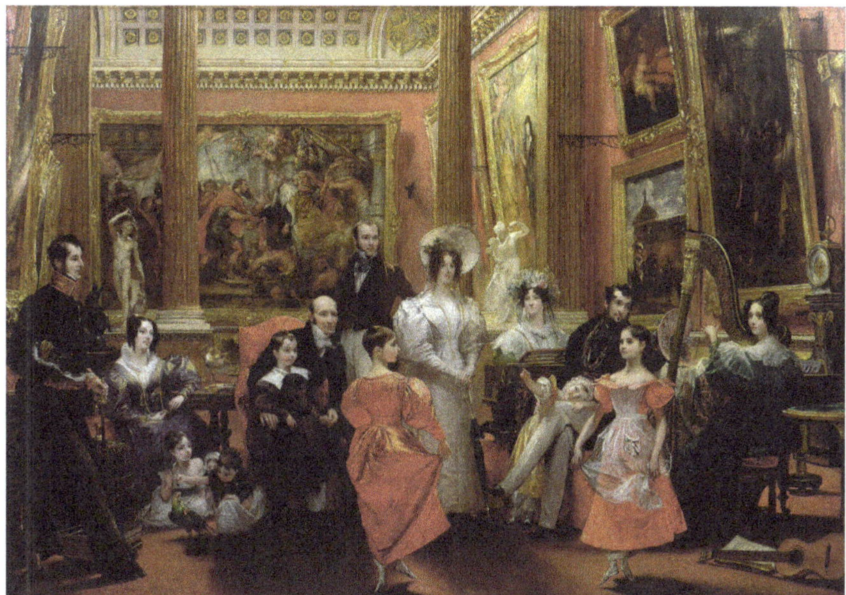

FIGURE 2.6 *CR Leslie,* The Grosvenor Family, *oil on canvas, c 1831. Private Collection/Bridgeman Images.*

baroque nautilus cup. Leslie's attention to the luxury objects in the interior prompted a few cutting reviews when the picture was exhibited at the Royal Academy. *The Examiner*'s reviewer acidly observed:

> Whatever else may be wanting, Mr. Leslie has not been sparing of his labour in the execution of this artificial composition. If unable to exercise his invention, fancy, and good taste, he has carefully represented every thing placed before him, – ladies, gentlemen, children, gowns, coats, bonnets, feathers, flounces, musical instruments, French clocks – in a word, all the household stuff, living and dead, usually collected in the principal apartment of a wealthy nobleman's residence. The work is consequently glittering, trim, polished, and unmeaning, – a display of matter, not mind, and, with an exception or two, possessing but little beauty of form or countenance.[92]

In the eyes of a contemporary art critic, Leslie's focus on the glittering array of expensive and rare objects found in the interior of Grosvenor House was an insurmountable defect which prioritised the inventory-like accounting of 'household stuff' over aesthetic concerns. However, it was this very household stuff that arrested the attention of many visitors. Louis Simond lingered over the 'red and sumptuous' cloth covering practically every surface and noted that 'the fringe of the draperies cost six guineas a yard'.[93]

In anticipation of the ball held upon the opening of Grosvenor House in June 1808, Sarah Spencer, Lady Lyttleton, wrote:

> To-night we are going to an assembly which is to outshine all past assemblies since the days of old-fashioned revelry as to splendour. Grosvenor House is to be thrown open to the world for the first time. It is said to be a mass of damask, velvet, gilding, statues, pictures, and magnificence of all sorts, beyond all powers of description or imagination, and has already, while only in prospect, the advantage of furnishing conversation in plenty to all the insipid misses and empty beaux I have seen for a long while.[94]

Spencer's keen observations neatly demonstrate how the social prestige bestowed by the prospect of admission to the houses of the elite became inextricably bound up with the work the gallery performed.

Grosvenor House simultaneously conjured an 'old-fashioned' world of splendour and, presumably, the unspoken understanding of rank and privilege it evoked. After the ball, she wrote:

> I ought to describe Grosvenor House to you, but really I have no room, and less strength of thumb left, to tell you of the vast quantity of beauties of it; for it really surpassed all my expectations. I derived great amusement from hearing every person in town, who has more than three rooms on a floor in their house, abuse and criticize that one, as if every one of their audience did not immediately guess at the nasty envy which dictated the observation.[95]

In place of a description of the interior, which she evokes solely by describing how much effort it would require to write, she judges its wonders by the level of 'nasty envy' expressed by the residents of somewhat smaller townhouses in response. This tension was endemic to fashionable urban culture in the period, reflected by the oft-repeated critique that the social spaces favoured by London's elite were frivolous in nature and, by implication, lacking intellectual weight or moral authority.[96]

Galleries decorated in such a sumptuous manner with 'damask, velvet, gilding, statues, pictures and magnificence of all sorts', in Sarah Spencer's words, created an environment in which pictures did not necessarily claim higher status than the objects of décor that surrounded them. In 1826 John Britton wrote of Grosvenor House in the *Original Picture of London*, an updated edition of a popular guidebook, that 'the pictures are so disposed as to appear in due subordination as ornaments to the apartments, and the apartments, without having any exhibitional character about them, are of handsome proportions and splendidly furnished'.[97] The apparent lack of 'exhibitional character' seems extraordinary in a house that had been designed with the display of art in mind, but suggests how important it was to the underpinning ideology of the private gallery that the public be frequently reminded of its domestic status. Similarly, Britton wrote of Devonshire House in Piccadilly, 'here, as in numerous other permanent London residences, the productions of refined art hold a subordinate place to the general uses of the apartments'.[98]

For the authors of guidebooks and descriptions of the interiors of houses, it went without saying that a Grosvenor House, Cleveland House, or Devonshire House contained a first-class collection. Their very inclusion in guidebooks was a mark of their status as places in which any curious or polite person was expected to have an interest. The trick was to remind the reader that these were not to be mistaken for venues to which the general public could expect some right of access. Britton's assertion that fine art held a 'subordinate place' at Devonshire House continued, 'although the inspection of them would unquestionably be highly gratifying to the public, the families are so habituated to regard them as connected with their domestic comfort, that any application from a stranger would, in all probability, excite at least surprise'.[99]

The 'spectacle' that Cleveland House presented to early nineteenth-century audiences was a heady cocktail of Old Master paintings, elite society, sumptuous décor and glamorous hospitality. From the outset, the impetus for the construction of the gallery had been to display Stafford's celebrated collection, especially the Orléans pictures, for the moral and intellectual improvement of the public and, by extension, the nation, but the spectacular mode of visual consumption that the gallery aroused in visitors made it difficult for many to focus on the art. French-American tourist Louis Simond wrote, 'It is amusing to sit in a corner and observe, as they pass, the countenances of the visitors in places of this kind, staring round with a total absence of all pleasure and all feeling. Nine-tenths of them know and care absolutely nothing about the pictures they look at, particularly the men'.[100] Similarly Frances Waddington wrote that 'the pictures are extremely fine, but it is quite ridiculous to observe out of the numbers that came into the room, how few thought it necessary even to look at them'.[101] Before the gallery had yet opened to the public, Lady Beaumont, the wife of patron Sir George Beaumont, reportedly said that 'the long succession of rooms, their spaciousness and loftiness had such an effect that people in [them] looked like Lilliputians, which produced one good effect, all awe of persons was done away for no one seemed of consequence enough to make any particular impression'.[102] Lady Beaumont mentioned the art only in passing, intuiting that the gallery's immense size was an index of its prestige, dwarfing the personalities of the aristocrats and celebrities who populated its rooms.

Cleveland House and Grosvenor House were vulnerable to the very critiques of crowded and fashionable London venues that they had been intended to deflect. If, as Dror Wahrman has written, 'fashion in the eighteenth century was about appearances alone – a play of surfaces without real substance, referent, or value', to combine the art gallery, a place that was supposed to encourage intellectual reflection, with social space was an inherently flawed model.[103] Cleveland House was supposed to offer real substance in the form of a collection of Old Masters. Despite John Britton's attempts to frame it as a place of serious study, in practice, visitors to Cleveland House and other notable town house galleries understood the gallery as a social venue and behaved accordingly.

Conclusion: 'Lady Stafford's Apartments'

Let us return to Roffe's floor plan, imagining a visitor navigating a path through the gallery. As our visitor toggles between book and room, the floor plan organizes an overpowering, somatic experience into a two-dimensional rendering that clarifies and makes sense of it. The gallery was a network of interlocking and interdependent spaces. Built with the admission of the public in mind from the start, it had a dedicated entrance and staircase. It forced circulation in an enclosed loop that did not interpenetrate with bedrooms, kitchens, or other spaces that visitors were never meant to see. Recalling the eighteenth-century technique of creating magnificence by connecting sequences of rooms *enfilade*, a visitor standing in the New Gallery ('B') could immediately apprehend the *coup d'oeil* represented by the gallery's full 210-foot length flowing through to the Drawing Room's bow windows to the west ('C') and through the Old Gallery and its Ante-Rooms to the east ('G'–'H').[104] At the same time, rooms within the gallery flowed logically from one to the next without recourse to corridors and the separation of rooms into independent, non-communicating spaces in a manner that would become accepted during the Victorian period.

As a document that records the organization and interrelationship of the rooms, the plan invites viewers to think about the gallery as a social space and to imagine the circulation of bodies within it. To return once more to Robin Evans' observation that what an architectural plan best describes is 'the nature of human relationships', we might also consider how the plan divides space.[105] Much is included within its embrace including the activities of looking at art, looking out of windows, listening to music, dancing, dining, drinking coffee and smelling flowers. The plan also invites its viewer to understand that there are parts of Cleveland House that will always be off limits. As much as boundaries between the interior and exterior of the house might be ambiguous, so much more so are the boundaries between the 'public' rooms of a town house, such as Drawing and Dining Rooms, and its 'private' spaces, such as bedrooms. As Henri Lefebvre wrote:

> *Social spaces interpenetrate one another and/or superimpose themselves upon one another* . . . Visible boundaries, such as walls or enclosures in general, give rise for their part to an appearance of separation between

spaces where in fact what exists is an ambiguous continuity. The space of a room, bedroom, house or garden may be cut off in a sense from social space by barriers and walls, by all the signs of private property, yet still remain fundamentally part of that space.[106]

Roffe's plan edits out much of Cleveland House's private space, focusing on the suite of rooms comprising the gallery on the first floor to implicitly proclaim its public status. Yet signs of the boundaries, as Lefebvre calls them, between the social space of the gallery and those of 'private property' – the back stairs, the Stable Office, the view to the Park – appear in the margins of the plan literally and figuratively, to alert the viewer that the gallery is subsumed within the larger social system of the aristocratic town house but is also contiguous with the street and city beyond.

Evans traced the development of domestic space from the Renaissance to the late nineteenth century through the gradual particularization of spaces within the domestic building type, which was brought into being with the use of the corridor and single entry-point rooms. He argued that the move toward highly demarcated spaces for individuals within a household was an index of and a catalyst for the development of a society which 'sees the body as a vessel of mind and spirit and in which privacy is habitual'.[107] This development also has class and gender implications, as this particularization gradually separated the members of households (men, women, children and staff of both sexes) into separate spheres of activity that interconnected as infrequently as possible. As Evans writes:

Dividing the house into two domains—an inner sanctuary of inhabited, sometimes disconnected rooms and an unoccupied circulation space . . . [made] it difficult to justify entering any room where you had no specific business. With this came a recognizably modern definition of privacy, not as the answer to a perennial problem of 'convenience', but quite possibly as a way of fostering a nascent psychology in which the self was, for the first time, felt to be not just at risk in the presence of others, but actually disfigured by them.[108]

Evans distinguishes this newly private space as 'an inner sanctuary', embracing the religious metaphor of domestic sphere as sanctuary that became predominant toward the end of the Georgian period.

The persistent association of domestic space with 'sanctuary' surely helped to foster the idea that the self is at risk when this space was violated. At the lower left corner of Roffe's plan, fragments of wall trail off before they can coalesce into distinguishable rooms. The plan identifies these ghostly, unfinished spaces as 'Lady Stafford's Apartments'. This part of the house was not open to ticket holders, nor to anyone without an explicit personal invitation. Acknowledging these inaccessible spaces, the plan subtly reinforces the sense of privilege conferred on those ticket holders, artists and guests who may examine both furnishings and paintings in the New Gallery with only a wall separating them from Lady Stafford's private world. In other words, the public status of the gallery is brought into focus by the privacy of the space on the other side of the wall – each defines the other. Labelling these spaces as 'Lady Stafford's Apartments' reinforces their private and feminine character and, by implication, confirms the gallery's identity as a space that is, first and foremost, public, patriotic and masculine.

The linking of sanctuary and home did not just reflect domestic ideology, but helped produce the conditions that fostered it. As domestic space became more frequently likened to a sanctuary, sanctuary became the ideal environment for looking at art. As many of the descriptions from diaries, letters and periodical literature cited in this chapter demonstrate, many visitors did not make a strong distinction between the masterpieces of European painting that hung on the gallery's walls and the extraordinary luxury of the interior as a whole. Visual and written depictions of the gallery gave rise to a new ideal for looking at art which rested on the assumption that the material signs of private ownership and elite sociability did not upend the gallery's public-facing mission, but rather were necessarily intertwined with it. These issues will be explored in detail in Chapter Three.

3

'The superb furniture within': Materiality and the Domestic Interior

One of the most extensive documents of any interior made in the nineteenth century is a sequence of 13 plans, each of which depicts one room in the gallery at Cleveland House. In 1818, the complete set was published in William Young Ottley's luxurious, fully illustrated four-volume *catalogue raisonné*, *Engravings of the Most Noble the Marquis of Stafford's Collection of Pictures in London*. The plans reproduce the entire gallery in miniature form, revelling in its Georgian splendour. The view of the Drawing Room, for example, draws viewers into its tiny world by reproducing every detail of its decoration, including frames indicating pictures on the walls, tiny bust on the fireplace mantel and view through blue silk curtains onto a verdant landscape beyond, the hint of a sunset in the western sky (see Figure 3.1).

Ottley's volume is an exceptionally exuberant example of the genre of the *catalogue raisonné*. *Catalogues raisonnés* did not merely reflect the contents of collections, but shaped expectations about how painting and sculpture related to the interiors of which they were a part. The floor plans, collected at the front of the first volume, function as its organizational framework, akin to a pictorial table of contents. They are immediately followed by individual engravings of nearly 300 pictures, printed three or four to a page, each of which was hanging in the gallery at the time of publication. Each engraving is in turn accompanied by a textual gloss documenting its title, dimensions and provenance and, occasionally, offering remarks on technique. By cross-referencing the numbers that appeared inside the blank frames on the plans with the illustrated catalogue of reproductions, an extremely patient and methodical reader could reconstruct the placement of every picture in the gallery at Cleveland House.[1]

The plans are, of course, an exceptional trove of information about the decoration of an interior that was dismantled long ago. They also offer an opportunity to understand the gallery as an architectural space, inviting us

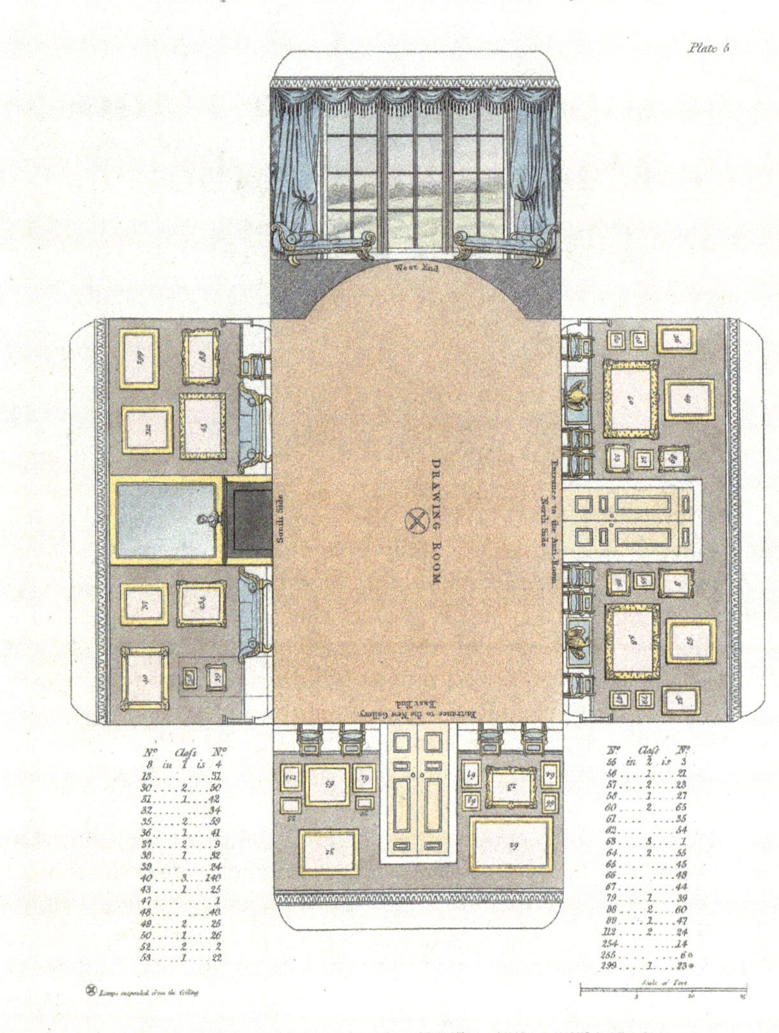

FIGURE 3.1 *[PW Tomkins, engr.] 'Drawing Room' from William Young Ottley,* Engravings of the Most Noble the Marquis of Stafford's collection of pictures in London, *London: Longman, Hurst, Rees, Orme, and Brown, 1818, engraving. Yale Center for British Art, Paul Mellon Collection.*

to consider people's lived experience of its interior and the objects it contained. The particular technique chosen to represent the interior, sometimes called the 'laid-out plan', permitted viewers to consider the objects it contained in association with the patterns of life that unfolded within. As architectural historian Robin Evans has written, laid-out plans record 'strong interactions between things visual and things social' and, as such, they offer a deep well for analysis.[2]

In this chapter, I will consider the plans' rich visual and social contexts to explore how the abundant materiality of the interior came to be understood as essential to – rather than a distraction from – appreciating the art collection it contained. The Ottley plans are in dialogue with a wide range of imagery that proliferated at the turn of the nineteenth century to depict interiors; these include bespoke architectural drawings as well as furniture pattern books distributed by influential cabinet makers and illustrated magazines disseminated amongst the middle classes, especially Rudolph Ackermann's *Repository of Arts*, published from 1809–1829. All visualized interiors in an accessible and aspirational mode intended to turn readers and viewers into consumers. To know how to inhabit a space like the Drawing Room – to know how to move through it and to appreciate the objects it contained – was to claim one's place in the social hierarchy. Ideologies of privacy and domesticity were mobilized in the early nineteenth century to signify the moral authority of the ruling class and became increasingly relevant to the decoration and organization of interior spaces. The technique of representation chosen for Ottley's catalogue, the laid-out plan, supported the ideological framing of the gallery as simultaneously private and public space and presented the pictures themselves as objects of décor as much as they were individual masterpieces. By cataloguing all the things that filled the gallery – paintings and window draperies and the many other objects that made the Regency interior an elegant and comfortable space – laid-out plans flattened distinctions between connoisseurship and consumerism and between aristocratic collectors and the aspiring middle classes.

Reading Tomkins' Plans: A Walk Through the Gallery

The plans were produced over the course of a decade before being published as a complete set in Ottley's *catalogue raisonné* in 1818. They are attributed to engraver Peltro William Tomkins who used a specialized technique called the laid-out interior drawing to reproduce the gallery's interiors in miniature. A view of the Dining Room was the first to appear in 1807 as the frontispiece to a slim catalogue of the gallery written by architect George Perry (see Figure 3.2). While this version of the plan of the Dining Room is not attributed to any particular engraver it is nearly identical to the one attributed to Tomkins in Ottley's catalogue and it seems likely that Tomkins was involved in the production of both. The 1807 image depicts the North wall hung with 13 small- to medium-sized paintings in a picturesque arrangement flanking the chimneypiece; by 1818, the image had been updated to reflect changes to its arrangement (see Figure 3.17). During the decade that separated the making of these two versions of the Dining Room, a laid-out interior plan was produced for each of the rooms and circulation spaces comprising the gallery.

Tomkins uses an unusual drawing technique that consists of an architectural plan in which four wall elevations are 'laid-out', or flattened radially, around a blank central space which is intended to be read as the floor of the room. There is no universally agreed-upon terminology to

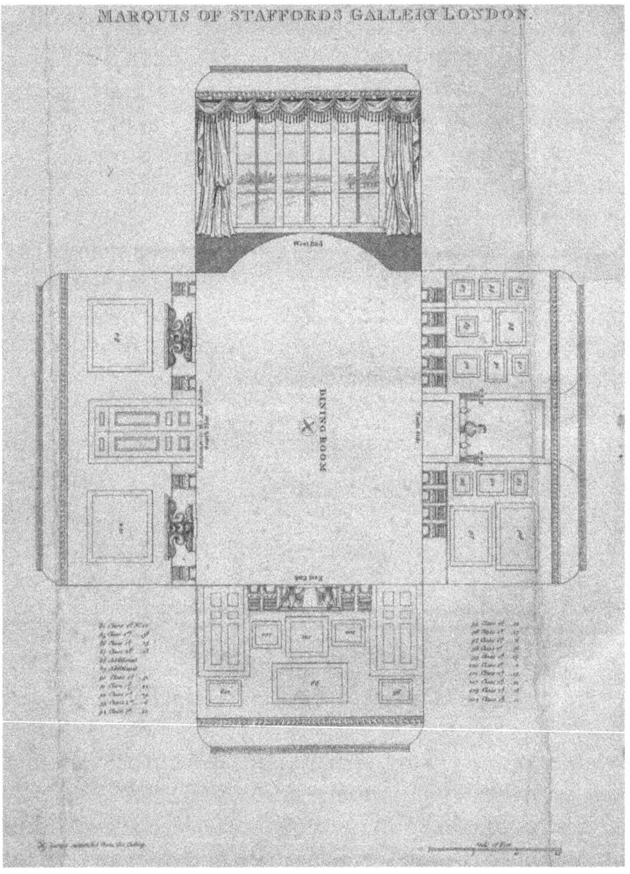

FIGURE 3.2 *'Dining Room' in George Perry,* A Descriptive Catalogue of the Pictures in the Collection of the Marquess of Stafford, in London *(London: J Walker, 1807). Frick Art Reference Library, New York, NY.*

describe this technique, which developed during the eighteenth century in the context of architectural drawing. The technique has been called both the 'laid-out interior drawing' and the 'developed surface interior'.[3] The view of the Dining Room consists of four wall elevations surrounding a void of white paper reflecting the dimensions and proportions of the room. In the centre of the space representing the floor, the engraving is inscribed with the words 'Dining Room', accompanied by an icon of a circle containing a cross which, as indicated by a legend at the bottom of the page, represents the position of a light fixture suspended from the ceiling. At the top of the page, the viewer sees an elevation of the West wall, where floor-to-ceiling windows surrounded by elaborate curtains frame a tiny landscape representing the view of Green Park visible from the West front of the house. Continuing to read the plan in a clockwise direction, the viewer encounters the North side, where a fireplace surmounted by a mirror and decorated with candelabras and a bust is flanked by two walls.[4] Each painting on these walls is represented by engraved rectangles indicating the size and shape of both the canvas and its frame, their arrangement describing the relationship of the pictures to the space of the wall and to each other. Moving clockwise again to the East wall, the plan indicates that doors give access at both sides. (According to the floor plan that appeared in Britton's guidebook, these doors opened onto one of two secondary stairwells, which likely facilitated servant access from the kitchen) (see Figure 2.1). Pictures are hung over a table in the form of two eagles supporting a stone slab. Finally, the viewer arrives at the South side (labelled as the entrance to the Anti-Room), where the doorway is flanked by large double rectangles indicating the placement of Titian's *Diana and Callisto* and *Diana and Actaeon*, each of which is positioned over one of Tatham's dolphin pier tables, which were discussed in Chapter One (see Figures 1.15, 2.3). Seventeen matching chairs are arranged along the three interior walls. Each of the four elevations is surmounted with a drawing of the classically inspired architectural moulding that connects wall to ceiling; the mouldings unify the elevations which are otherwise completely distinct.

The laid-out technique is applied to each of the plans in Ottley's *catalogue raisonné*. They are presented in the order a person visiting the gallery would encounter the rooms they depict, beginning with the Grand Stairs, a transitional space that conveyed visitors from the entrance on street level to the gallery suite on the first floor. (The sequence ends with plans of the Library and Reference Library, rooms added to the gallery tour in the mid-1810s; when the gallery opened in 1806, the Old Gallery was the final room on the visitor route.) The book's viewer imaginatively 'enters' the gallery via the Grand Stairs, in which only a few very large pictures were hung (see Figure 3.3). The plan juxtaposes stairs, doorways, wall elevations and a window in a dizzying circular arrangement. In the hand-coloured edition, blue skies have been painted into the window, suggesting a view unobstructed by trees or neighbouring buildings, though, in fact, the stairs were situated along the South side of the house facing the red-brick façade of St James's Palace where no such view was possible.

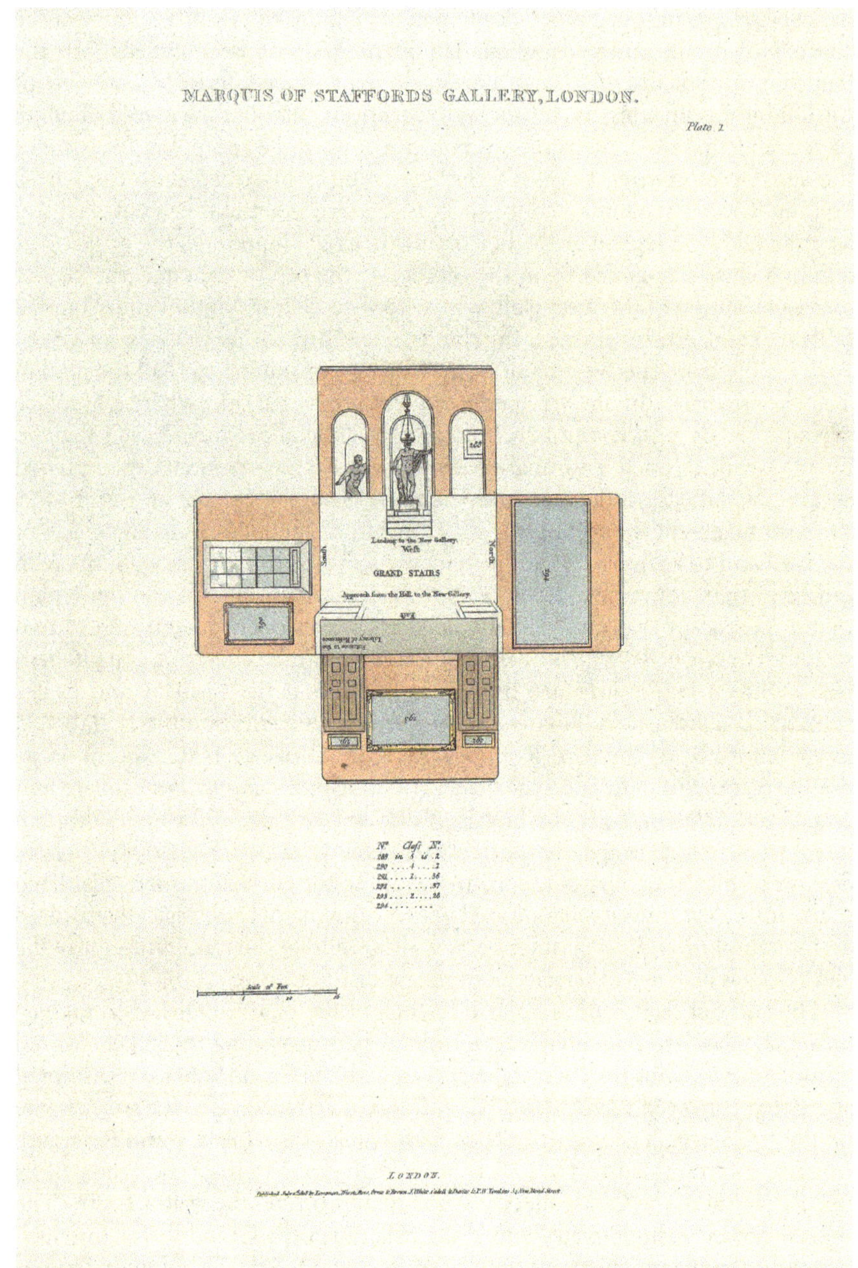

FIGURE 3.3 *[PW Tomkins, engr.] 'Grand Stairs' from William Young Ottley,* Engravings of the Most Noble the Marquis of Stafford's collection of pictures in London, *London: Longman, Hurst, Rees, Orme, and Brown, 1818, engraving. Yale Center for British Art, Paul Mellon Collection.*

Tiny print instructs the viewer as to how he or she might physically travel through the space. Looking at the book right-side up, the directions inscribed under a cast of the *Apollo Belvedere* read, 'Landing [. . .] to the New Gallery'. Upside-down and therefore more difficult to read, the words 'Entrance to the Library . . .' label a tiny door. The engraving awkwardly truncates the sculptures displayed in niches on the first-floor landing – the face of the *Apollo* is obscured by a chandelier hanging in the centre of the stairwell – giving the viewer a sense of how these objects might appear and disappear as his or her body travelled through space. Plate two, following directly from the first, depicts the small landing at the top of the stairs which functioned as the 'Entrance' into the first-floor gallery suite (see Figure 3.4). It is almost comically cramped, appearing on the page like an unfolded origami box, its sole purpose to funnel expectant visitors into the New Gallery where the most prestigious Italian Old Masters in the collection awaited. Yet, while care has been taken to depict the door frame, moulding and frieze that surmounted it, the partially-open door is drawn as a confusing triple screen, perhaps to reserve the '*coup d'oeil*' offered by the New Gallery for maximum dramatic impact.[5]

Turning one of the catalogue's immense pages, the viewer finally arrives in the New Gallery, the first in a series of four main rooms – the New and Old Galleries, Drawing Room and Dining Room, interspersed with passageways and anterooms – where the bulk of the collection was displayed (see Figures 0.7, 1.9, 3.1, 3.5, 3.6, 3.7, 3.8). These plans follow the same pattern as those described above. The walls are covered in arrangements of numbered rectangles representing frames; the reader may cross-reference these numbers with the illustrated catalogue of pictures using the indexing information provided at the bottom of the page. Architectural features, such as the apses located at both ends of the New Gallery, are attended to with the same care as the tiny reproductions of the sofas and chairs, tables and *objets d'art* the gallery contained. The generous lighting provided for the gallery, described at lower left as 'lamps suspended from the ceiling' is indicated with six encircled crosses.

The floor plans offer a view of the interior that unfolds from one space into the next, encouraging the viewer to imagine what it would be like to walk through and experience the interior spaces of the gallery, room-by-room, each unique in size, decoration and function. The relative importance of each room in the gallery and, by extension, the pictures it contained is represented by proxy, the size of each engraving on the page made in proportion to the size and importance of that space within the gallery suite. The New Gallery – which was the most important room because it displayed the collection's most famed Italian masterpieces – fills the paper on which it is printed. In contrast, the images of the Grand Stairs and the Entrance are both relatively small in terms of the swath of real estate they fill; each appears to float in the centre of its enormous white sheet of paper, like a specimen in a volume on natural history (see Figure 3.4).

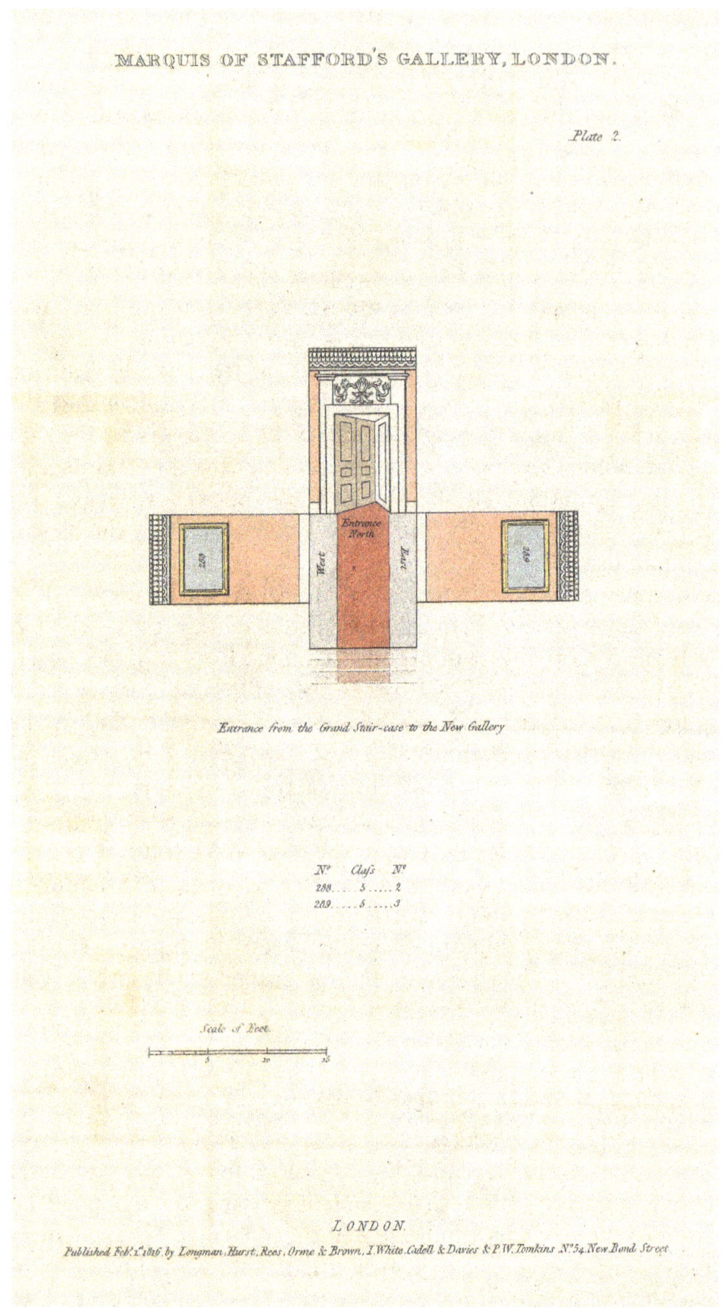

FIGURE 3.4 *[PW Tomkins, engr.] 'Grand Stairs' from William Young Ottley,* Engravings of the Most Noble the Marquis of Stafford's collection of pictures in London, *London: Longman, Hurst, Rees, Orme, and Brown, 1818, engraving. Yale Center for British Art, Paul Mellon Collection.*

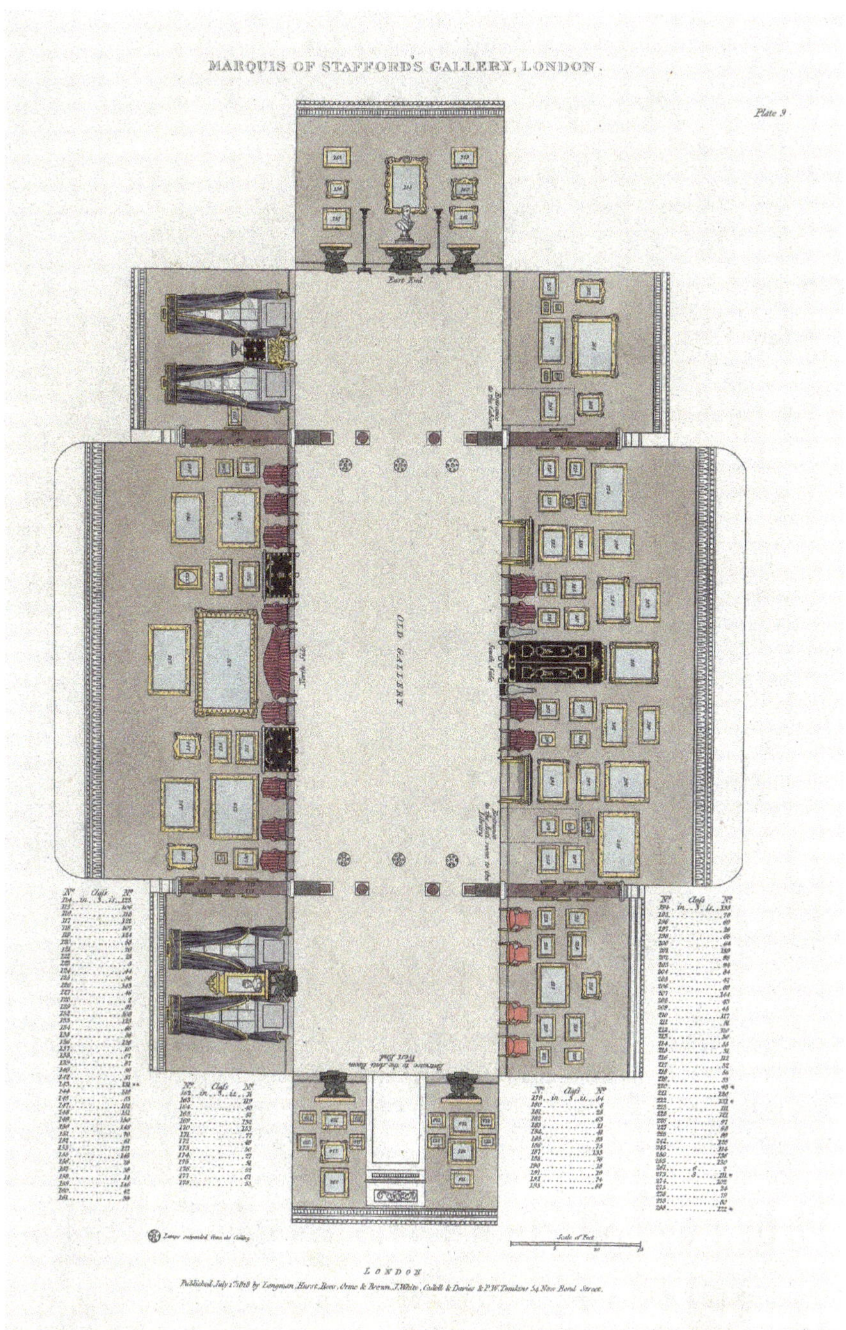

FIGURE 3.5 *[PW Tomkins, engr.] 'Old Gallery' from William Young Ottley,* Engravings of the Most Noble the Marquis of Stafford's collection of pictures in London, *London: Longman, Hurst, Rees, Orme, and Brown, 1818, engraving. Yale Center for British Art, Paul Mellon Collection.*

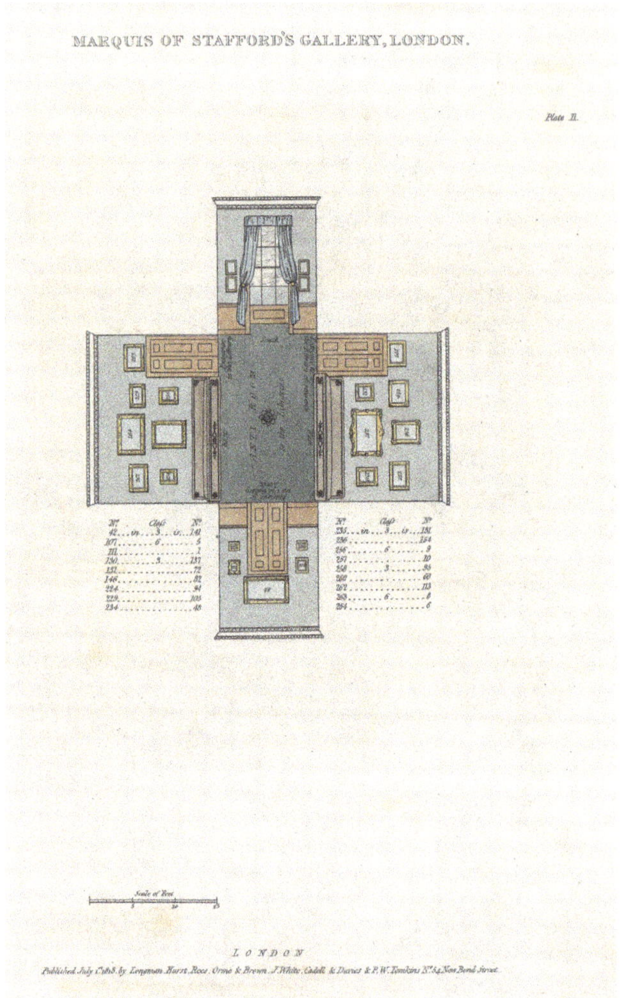

FIGURE 3.6 *[PW Tomkins, engr.] 'Anti-Room to the Libraries' from William Young Ottley,* Engravings of the Most Noble the Marquis of Stafford's collection of pictures in London, *London: Longman, Hurst, Rees, Orme, and Brown, 1818, engraving. Yale Center for British Art, Paul Mellon Collection.*

Picturing Collections: The *Catalogue Raisonné*

Tomkins' laid-out interior drawings are a remarkably complicated set of images that performed several functions simultaneously in the context of Ottley's *catalogue raisonné*. They convey basic information about the sequence and layout of rooms. They indicate to the reader how the pictures were distributed throughout the gallery while placing pictures specifically

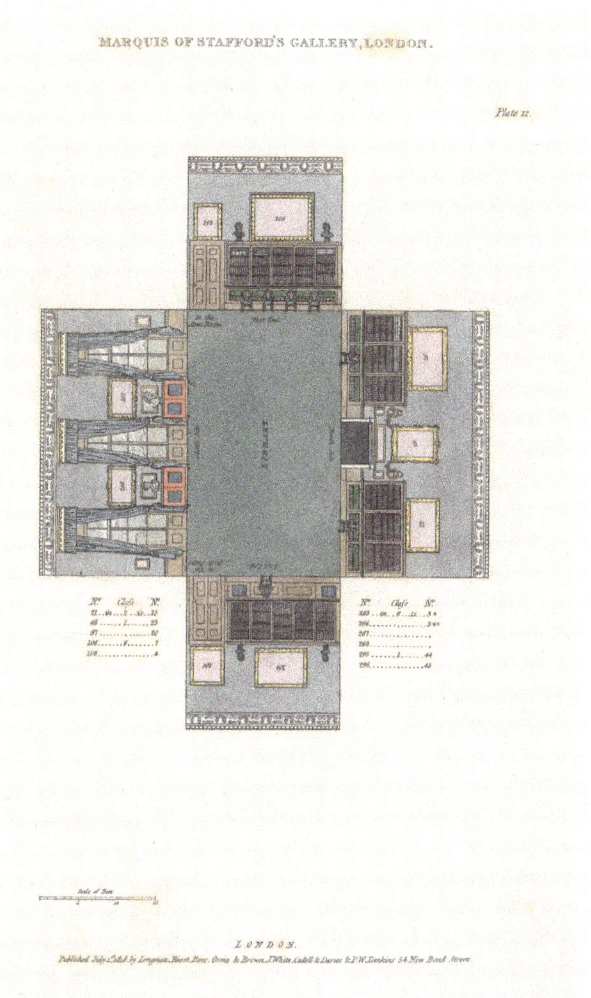

FIGURE 3.7 *[PW Tomkins, engr.] 'Library' from William Young Ottley,* Engravings of the Most Noble the Marquis of Stafford's collection of pictures in London, *London: Longman, Hurst, Rees, Orme, and Brown, 1818, engraving. Yale Center for British Art, Paul Mellon Collection.*

within the space of each of the individual rooms. They also attempt to recreate the interior of the house, its furnishings and lighting, fireplaces, mirrors, curtains and *objets d'art*. Finally, they allude to the position of the house within the wider landscape, views from its windows suggesting the park beyond. In order to convey such an enormous range of information within the context of a single image of each room, Tomkins' plans draw on and consolidate a variety of strategies and techniques for representing collections and interiors available by the early nineteenth century.

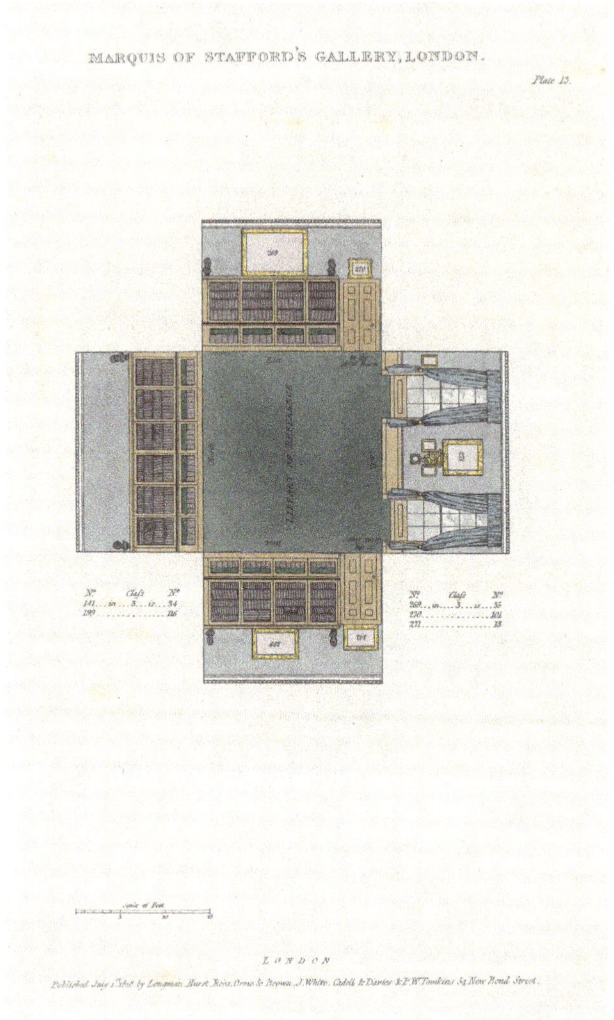

FIGURE 3.8 *[PW Tomkins, engr.] 'Library of Reference' from William Young Ottley,* Engravings of the Most Noble the Marquis of Stafford's collection of pictures in London, *London: Longman, Hurst, Rees, Orme, and Brown, 1818, engraving. Yale Center for British Art, Paul Mellon Collection.*

A conventional approach would have been to illustrate the interior with one or more perspectival views, which use the technique of three-point perspective to locate the viewer in or at the margin of the space. Perspectival views were widely used to represent the interiors of public and private buildings in guidebooks and periodical publications aimed at a range of audiences, allowing beholders to occupy the space from the same point-of-view that real visitors might take. Such views, of which JC Smith's view of the New Gallery (see Figure 1.1) may be understood as a typical example, could function as a means of providing access to spaces that were otherwise off-limits or invisible to most people. This idea was by no means new; as Katie Scott has written, views of early eighteenth-century French interiors 'extended entry to all, indiscriminately and, unlike the places they purported to represent, functioned to lend the readership a common identity and universal distinction'.[6] Eighteenth- and early nineteenth-century readers were becoming accustomed to having people, places and things that had once been invisible or unknowable made available for inspection in books. Medical treatises, volumes on natural history and archaeology and those recording the fashions, manners and customs of Europeans and non-Europeans alike were increasingly lavishly-illustrated and presented information that had once been available to only a few. Yet while such images of interiors and the books, catalogues and periodicals in which they appear do (to adopt Scott's phrasing) lend a 'common identity' to the readership and extend 'indiscriminate' entry, they also restrict access as surely as they widen it. The very fact of their existence implies a viewer who does not have access to the space itself. Whether impeded by social class, gender, physical distance or the passage of time, such viewers have only image and catalogue as a means of access.

Tomkins eschews the conventional approach to offer, both literally and figuratively, a different perspective. Resisting the impulse to represent the interior as a three-dimensional box into which the viewer is invited to peer, the laid-out interior drawing flattens it into two dimensions, laying it bare for the inspection of the audience. This choice was certainly made in part because the plans needed to fill an important documentary function, recording with precision the arrangement of pictures in the gallery at the moment the print was made, fixing it in time. The plans function as a visual index, allowing viewers to cross-reference the images with the catalogue to recreate the organization of the pictures, but they also assure the viewer that he or she is being given access to a view of the gallery as it really is at a given moment. The print is, of course, a static object. It could not be animated to show the regular small adjustments being made to the arrangement of pictures as Stafford continued to collect, but could be and, as noted above in the case of the Dining Room, was updated before reprinting to reflect the most up-to-date and accurate information.

By alluding to forms of illustration associated with natural history and antiquarianism, Tomkins' views attempt something akin to a visual manifestation of the impulses of the inventory or the *catalogue raisonné*. The inventory and the catalogue are two different, but related, types of document. Used to record collections of all kinds, they evolved from particular sets of motivations and precedents. Inventories, which are invaluable resources for scholars studying collecting history, were generally made for practical and – more or less, private – use by collectors and their circles. They were often drawn up in the context of wills or other legal documents where the sum of a person's possessions needed to be logged and documented. The medium of the *catalogue raisonné*, on the other hand, was intended to reach an audience. Its prospective viewership could be very narrowly defined as the immediate circle of the collector, or it could be intended for distribution amongst visitors to a particular collection or even the general public. *Catalogues raisonnés* were public-facing statements of a collector's achievement and taste and prioritized the objects in the collection, representing them by proxy with lists and, occasionally, engravings of objects they contained.

The most celebrated *catalogues raisonnés* produced in the eighteenth century reproduced individual pictures in engraving, often dedicating an entire page to each image. Important examples include the *Recueil Crozat*, published in France from 1729 to 1742 and the *Description des Tableaux du Palais Royal* published in 1727 which catalogued the Orléans collection – much of which later hung on the walls of Cleveland House – at the time of its creation.[7] Before the beginning of the nineteenth century, however, only rarely did catalogues include an image of the gallery's interior. Instead, they used the schematic strategy of subdividing the catalogue by the names of the rooms in which particular pictures appeared. Very elaborate catalogues, such as *Catalogue des Tableaux du Cabinet de M. Crozat*, published in 1755, describe each room by its name and then textually guide the reader through the rooms by locating

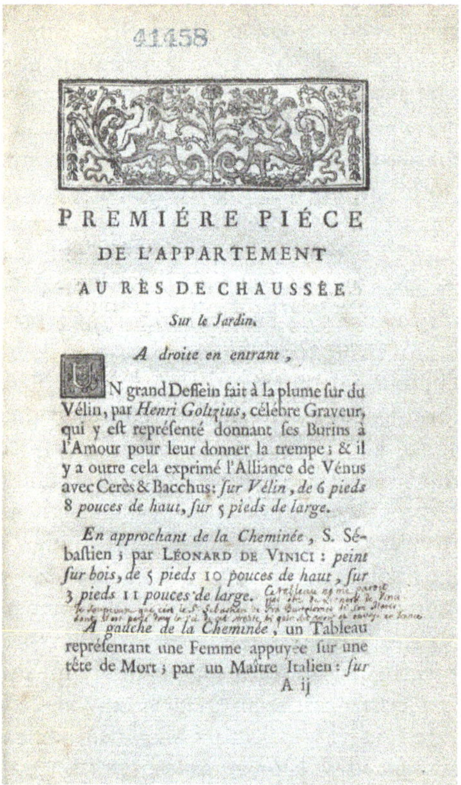

PREMIÉRE PIÉCE
DE L'APPARTEMENT
AU RÈS DE CHAUSSÉE
Sur le Jardin.

A droite en entrant,

UN grand Deſſein fait à la plume ſur du Vélin, par *Henri Goltzius*, célébre Graveur, qui y eſt repréſenté donnant ſes Burins à l'Amour pour leur donner la trempe; & il y a outre cela exprimé l'Alliance de Vénus avec Cerès & Bacchus: *ſur Vélin, de 6 pieds 8 pouces de haut, ſur 5 pieds de large.*

En approchant de la Cheminée, S. Sébaſtien; par LÉONARD DE VINICI: *peint ſur bois, de 5 pieds 10 pouces de haut, ſur 3 pieds 11 pouces de large.*

A gauche de la Cheminée, un Tableau repréſentant une Femme appuyée ſur une tête de Mort; par un Maître Italien: *ſur*

A ij

FIGURE 3.9 *Louis-Antoine Crozat,* Catalogue des tableaux du cabinet de M Crozat, baron de Thiers, *Paris: Chez de Bure l'Aîné, 1755. Frick Art Reference Library, New York, NY.*

pictures in relation to prominent architectural features such as doors and chimneypieces (see Figure 3.9). In this example, prefatory information tells us that expressions such as 'at left' or 'at right' are used in relation to the position of the person looking at the object. The reader/viewer is instructed, for example, that after entering the first room, which is described as located on the ground floor adjoining the garden, he or she is to turn right. If visitors have correctly followed the textual cues provided in the catalogue, they will find themselves encountering a large drawing in ink on vellum by Henri Goltzius.[8] Descriptions like these evoke the spatial layout of a room with great specificity but do not describe the style or decorative detail of the interior.

The textual approach to locating the collection in space described above was commonly deployed by the authors of eighteenth-century catalogues. Illustrations were reserved for only the most lavish projects cataloguing the most significant collections. Some of these included floor plans or even miniature wall elevations. An influential British example is the *Ædes Walpolianæ*, made by Horace Walpole in 1747, to catalogue the collection his

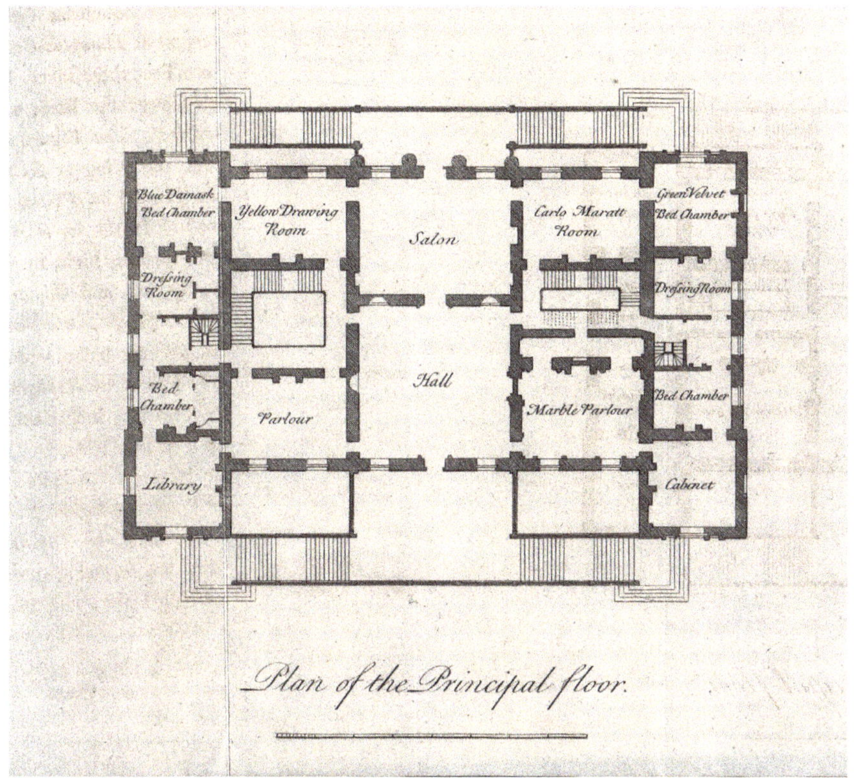

FIGURE 3.10 *'Plan of the Principal floor' in Horace Walpole,* Ædes Walpolianæ: or A Description of the Collection of Pictures at Houghton-Hall in Norfolk *(London: printed [by John Hughs], 1747). RB 106878, The Huntington Library, San Marino, California.*

father, Sir Robert Walpole, made at Houghton Hall.[9] Walpole combined detailed written descriptions of the arrangement of the pictures and the decoration of the rooms with exterior elevations and floor plans (see Figure 3.10). For example, describing the 'Common Parlour', where a variety of portraits and other assorted paintings were hung, he writes: 'Over the Chimney is some fine Pear-tree Carving, by *Gibbins* and in the Middle of it hangs a Portrait of him by Sir *Godfrey Kneller*. It is a Masterpiece and equal to any of *Vandyke*'s'.[10] Grinling Gibbons was an Anglo-Dutch woodcarver particularly known for the finely detailed, three-dimensional decorative woodcarvings he made in the early eighteenth century for English country houses and religious buildings. Walpole's text italicizes Gibbons' name alongside those of Godfrey Kneller and Anthony Van Dyck, suggesting that his decorative work was as noteworthy as that of painters understood as Old Masters. (Horace Walpole's personal extra-illustrated copy of *Ædes Walpolianæ*, now in the Metropolitan Museum of Art, includes laid-out floor plans made by the house's architect, Isaac Ware, with hand-written notations indicating the position of paintings on the walls.) Not long after, in 1756, French collector Jean de Jullienne produced an extraordinary, illustrated catalogue of his own collection, which Rochelle

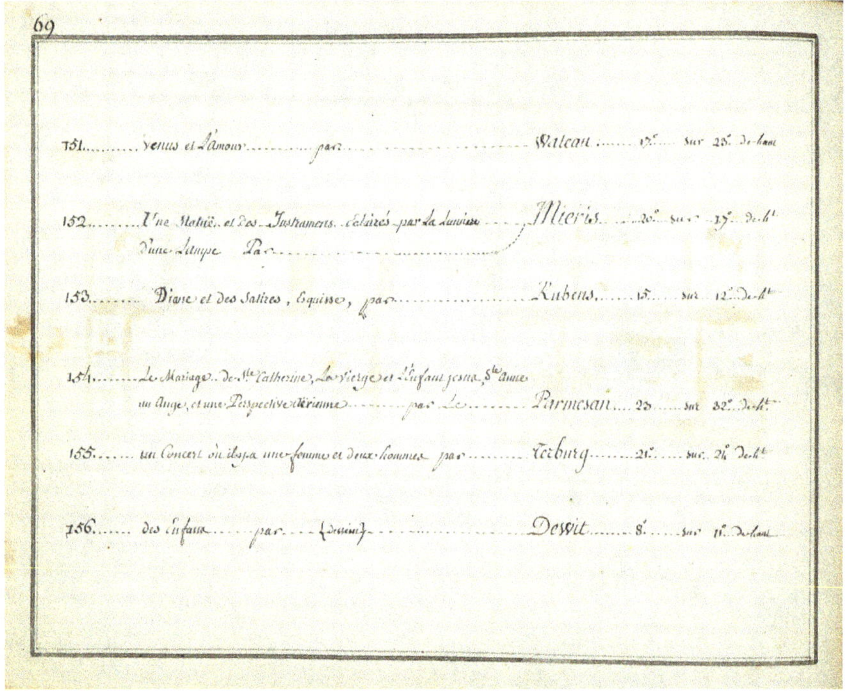

69

151........ Venus et l'Amour .... par .... Wateau ...... 17. ... sur 23. de haut

152........ Une Statuë et des Instruments éclairés par la lumiere d'une Lampe Par .... Mieris ...... 20. sur 17. de h.t

153........ Diane et des Satires, Esquisse, par .... Rubens...... 15. ... sur 12. de h.t

154........ Le Mariage de S.te Catherine, La Vierge et l'Enfant Jesus, S.te Anne un Ange, et une Perspective Aërienne .... par Le .... Parmesan.... 23 ..... sur 32. de h.t

155........ un Concert où il y a une femme et deux hommes par .... Terburg........ 21. .... sur 24. de h.t

156........ des Enfans ...... par ... {dessein} .... Dewit .... 8. ..... sur 11. de haut

FIGURE 3.11a *'Cabinet avant la Gallerie' from* Catalogue des tableaux de Mr de Jullienne, *Pen and black ink, gray wash, and watercolour, over preliminary indications in black chalk, on paper, Binding: 7 15/16 x 10 9/16 inches (202 x 268 mm); leaf: 7 ¾ x 10 ¼ inches (196 x 260 mm). The Morgan Library & Museum. 1966.8. Purchased as the gift of the Fellows.*

Ziskin suggests may have been influenced by Walpole's example. Jullienne's catalogue took the further step of representing paintings as miniature reproductions placed within wall elevations that evoke both the spatial and decorative context of the room by including details like doorways, windows and decorative mouldings (see Figure 3.11). As illustrated here, the wall elevations face pages where handwritten notations document each picture's artist, title and catalogue number.

Catalogues like Jullienne's were unique objects. They were handwritten, drawn and painted books that were not intended for distribution, but were certainly known amongst the collector's circle.[11] In their limited context, however, the catalogues served as models for other collectors in terms of the arrangement of pictures in the interior. In the process they set a precedent for later projects which sought to distribute images of picture hangs to a wider audience. A well-known example is Maria Cosway's *Gallery of the Louvre*, an ambitious project Cosway undertook in 1802 to represent the collection at the Louvre. Original plans for this project called for each wall section of the Louvre, 57 in total, to be reproduced as a hand-coloured etched plate. Each plate would, in turn, reproduce the individual pictures hanging on that wall and capture

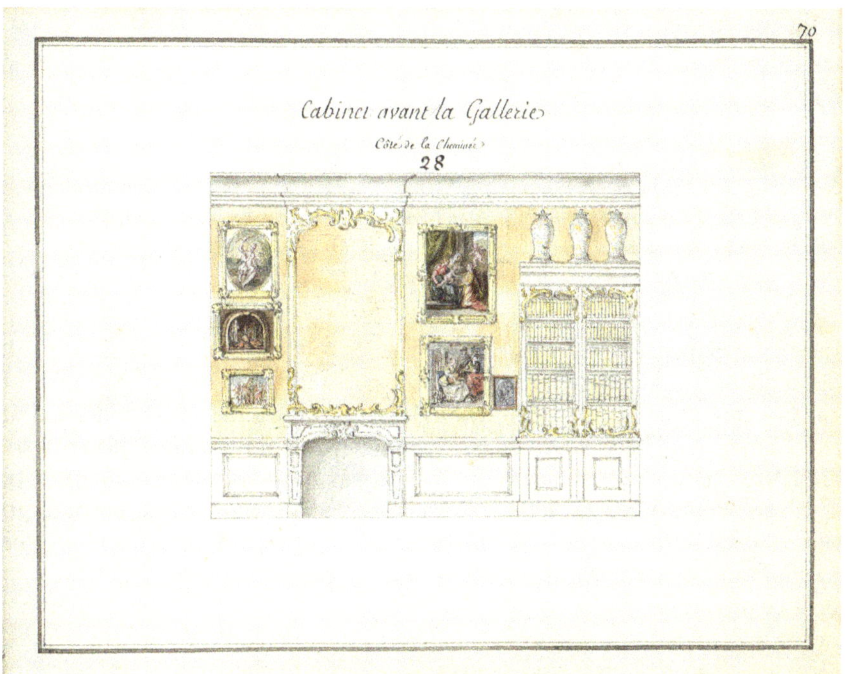

FIGURE 3.11b

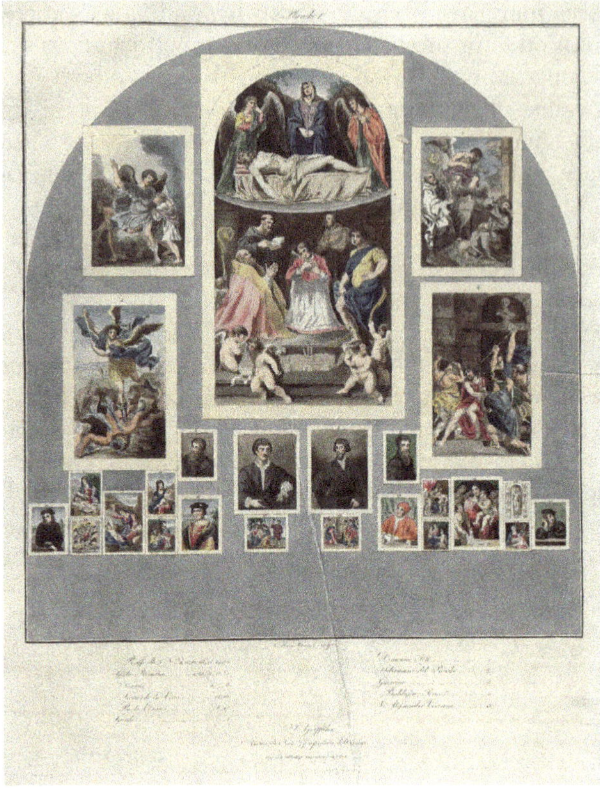

FIGURE 3.12 *Maria Cosway, Plate 1, from* Galerie du Louvre, répresentée par des gravures à l'eau forte exéctuées par Mme Maria Cosway *(Paris, J Griffiths, 1802). Hand-coloured etching on paper, 27 ¾ × 23 ¾ in. (70.4 × 60.4 cm). National Gallery of Art Library, Washington, DC.*

their arrangement and the spatial relationships between them (see Figure 3.12). Subscribers would receive two prints accompanied by historical accounts of each picture in every number of the subscription until the entire collection of the Louvre had been reproduced. (Only nine of the planned plates were completed, as Cosway's work in the Louvre was cut short by the resumption of the Napoleonic Wars in 1803.) The prospectus for this project encouraged potential subscribers to 'form a *Museum* within [their] own Apartments *on the plan of the Louvre*', prompting them to reimagine the Louvre on a scale that befitted private houses, using prints to recreate the effect of the Louvre's interiors in English '*Domestic Galleries or Drawing Rooms*'.[12] As I have argued elsewhere, the process of doing so might mitigate the sublime spectacle of violent social rupture upon which many visitors to the Louvre found themselves reflecting.[13] Cosway's project, focused on one of the first major art collections in Europe to be opened to the public in the guise of a 'museum', also served as a model – and a foil – for early nineteenth-century collectors, like Stafford, who were thinking of making their private collections available to the public.

Picturing Interiors: The Laid-Out Interior Drawing

Each example of the genre of the *catalogue raisonné* described above is exceptional in its own way. Until the end of the eighteenth century, visual representations of complete interiors were extremely unusual; those that did exist were generally architectural studies not intended to be seen by anyone apart from a patron and a small inner circle. In general, catalogues were abstract representations of collections as groups of objects floating free from the constraints of space, the exigencies of viewing them, or the decoration of the interiors they occupied. Instead, to express the vast amount of information that *catalogues raisonnés* contained in visual form, Tomkins looked to an ascendant drawing technique developed and nurtured in the fields of architecture and design during the early to mid-eighteenth century. Architectural historian Laura Jacobus associated the development of this technique, which she called the 'laid-out interior drawing', with the rise of the Palladian style in England, where it was used to particular advantage by architects including Isaac Ware and William Kent. The laid-out interior uses orthographic projection to allow the architect to visually express the proportions of wall elevations as opposed to using mathematical notation. This made it a particularly suitable technique for styles such as Palladianism in which proportional relationships are fundamental to the design.[14] Jacobus argued that the invention of this drawing technique can be tied to general developments in the way that architects conceived of interior space in the eighteenth century. The interior wall, once seen as an artifact of a building designed and built mostly to be looked at from its exterior, became a site to be decorated in and of itself. Jacobus writes, 'the laid-out interior drawing in its pure form expressed the values of the decorator by abstracting the wall surface from the mass of masonry behind it'.[15] The laid-out interior drawing brought 'decoration' to the fore, overlaying the representation of the building's fabric with two-dimensional decorative elements, such as grotesques and overdoors, as well as the other three-dimensional objects which turned 'architecture' into lived space.

As a result, laid-out interior plans could be particularly effective for presenting designs for domestic buildings to clients. Architect Robert Adam's drawing of a room designed for Headfort House in Ireland imagines a space richly decorated with neoclassical grotesques (see Figure 3.13). Notably, Cleveland House's architect, Charles Heathcote Tatham, also used this technique to present designs to clients. Tatham's drawing of the West Drawing Room for Stoke Edith House, for example, juxtaposes four walls, each of which shows in detail the type of furniture to be placed in the room and the use of paintings as overdoors (see Figure 3.14). In the centre of the paper, which represents the floor, visible outlines, labelled in the architect's handwriting, depict a number of sofas and small tables. Taking advantage of the bird's-eye view permitted by the technique, Tatham is able to depict both the items of furniture suggested for the space and their possible arrangement.

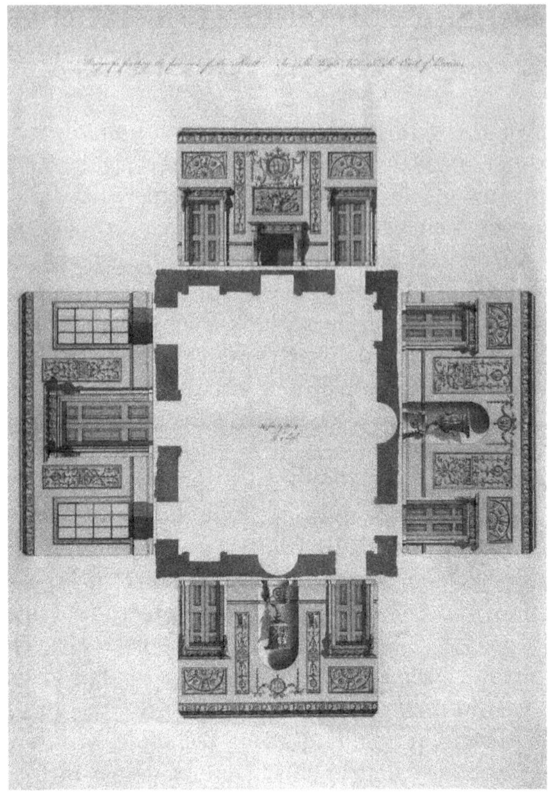

FIGURE 3.13 *Robert Adam, 1728–1792, British, Headfort House, Ireland: Elevations of the Front Hall, between 1771 and 1775, Pen with black ink and gray wash over graphite on moderately thick, moderately textured, cream laid paper mounted on canvas, B1975.2.786. Yale Center for British Art, Paul Mellon Collection.*

Prior to the late eighteenth century, furniture had typically been arranged against the walls when not in use; the arrangement shown by Tatham, known as a *dérangé* scheme, conjured an air of informality and was partially intended to make the rooms appear as if the family had just left.[16] The new emphasis on informality was just one of a network of responses to eighteenth-century theories about human interaction with nature. By the end of the century, it had become an important consideration in both the design and the use of the interior and new types and arrangements of furniture accompanied this change.[17] Though I have found no written documentation to confirm the idea, given Tatham's tendency to use this technique, it seems probable that Tomkins' laid-out plans for Ottley's catalogue were based on drawings Tatham made during the process of designing Cleveland House.

Combining architecture and furniture in one drawing allowed the client to understand the designer's complete vision at a glance. Furniture designers, including Thomas Sheraton and George Hepplewhite, also used laid-out plans

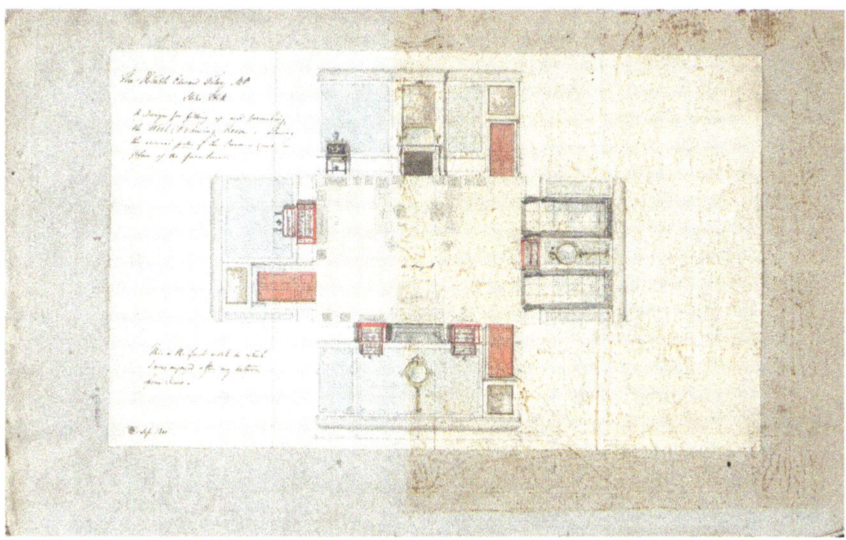

FIGURE 3.14 *Charles Heathcote Tatham, Plan for the West Drawing Room at Stoke Edith, 1800. Pen and ink and watercolour on paper. Prints, Drawings & Paintings Collection E.1311:8-2001 © Victoria and Albert Museum, London.*

to advertise their designs. Sheraton's comprehensive catalogue of drawings for furniture designs *The Cabinet-Maker and Upholsterer's Drawing-Book* (1791–1793), used laid-out interior drawings to situate furniture within elaborately designed interiors, as did the prominent fashionable furnishings manufacturer Gillows of Lancaster (see Figure 3.15 and 3.16). Given how effective this technique was for expressing the relationships between architecture, wall decorations and movable furniture, it is unsurprising that architects and designers alike embraced the laid-out interior drawing as an effective tool for marketing their services to potential customers. Holistically depicting rooms as they were intended to operate in daily use, the plans suggest the patterns of social life that might unfold within.

These trends in interior design and decoration were inextricably linked to developing notions of privacy and its corollary, domesticity. Architectural historian Robin Evans argued that the laid-out interior drawing (he called it the 'developed surface interior') was especially appropriate for representing domestic interiors from the 1770s through the 1790s because it allowed each room to be 'hermetically sealed' visually from the others.[18] In houses of this period, a circuit of rooms, each with its own unique self-enclosed design, created a panorama of different rooms for the person making the circuit, each room's design unfolding in its turn a surprising change from what had come before. The notion that each room is enclosed onto itself, inward looking rather than outward looking, more broadly conjures the development of notions of privacy and domesticity that had been developing during the course of the eighteenth century.

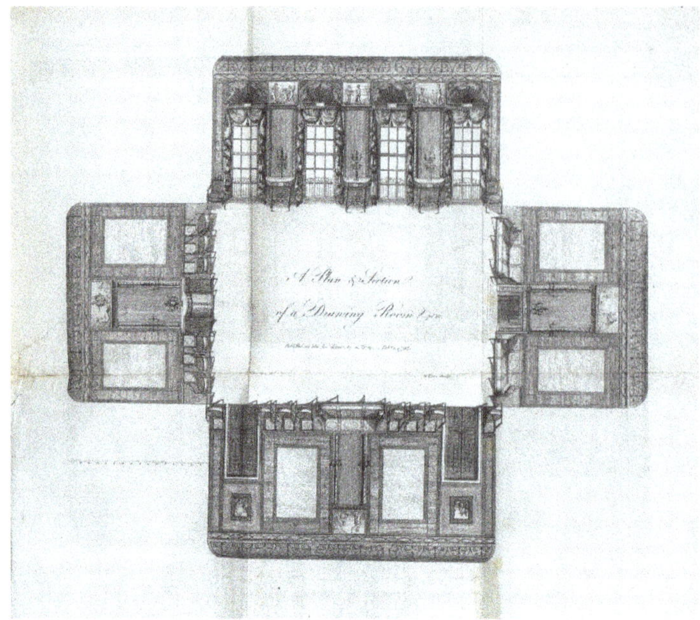

FIGURE 3.15 *'Plan and Section of a Drawing Room', Thomas Sheraton,* The Cabinet-Maker and Upholsterer's Drawing-Book *(W Baynes, 1802). The Metropolitan Museum of Art, New York, Rogers Fund, 1952.*

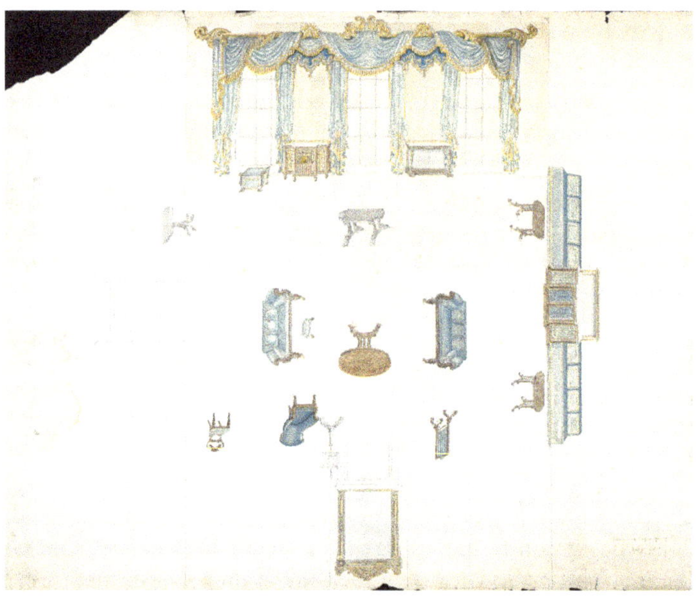

FIGURE 3.16 *Architectural drawing, early 19th century. Given by the Directors of Waring & Gillow Ltd. Department of Prints and Drawings E.355-1955 © Victoria and Albert Museum, London.*

By the early nineteenth century, domesticity had become associated with the English national character, a trait which crossed boundaries of class; a rich vocabulary arose with which to articulate the ideas and practices that flowed from it. As discussed in Chapter One, terms like 'privacy' and 'domesticity' were being used with increasing frequency to describe intangible associations of the private house with particular expectations of personal and family life. Alongside these, related words like 'comfort' and 'home' reflected the material and embodied experiences of these elusive ideals. The notion of 'comfort' in particular reflected changing ideas about the organization of domestic interiors during the second half of the eighteenth century, associated with a desire for greater informality in both domestic interiors and personal interactions. The rapid adoption of these terms marked the increasing prominence of the domestic sphere – and the single-family dwelling in particular – as a topic for public discourse.[19] Commentators embraced these terms to promote the cottage, house or manor as spaces that could accommodate the private lives of eighteenth-century Britons of all classes.[20] These themes resonated with readers during a period of seemingly endless war and rapidly expanding empire and were intimately connected with ideas associated with Romantic thought, such as exile and the importance of individual subjectivity.

The Marchioness of Stafford embraced fashionable concepts of domesticity and privacy. She was celebrated in *The Lady's Monthly Museum* in February 1808 as 'a pattern for her sex' in 'every domestic virtue'; that this language drew on formulaic ideas about femininity underscores the point that aristocratic women, who might previously have been exempted from such middle-class ideals, were being held up as exemplars for them.[21] In correspondence, Lady Stafford presented herself as a devoted mother in addition to her roles as a socialite and hostess. Her letters make regular loving mention of her four children and her desire to set up her household in the most comfortable manner possible. In 1793, shortly after returning from Paris, the family leased a house in Wimbledon while they considered how to reintegrate into London life. Lady Stafford wrote, 'we are now very comfortably settled here, building as usual, & ruining ourselves in the way of painting our walls, furnishing our rooms &c. &c. which will terminate at Christmas'.[22] They soon moved closer to the hub of aristocratic London centred on St James's and Mayfair, leasing a townhouse in Albemarle Street which would be their primary residence until moving to Cleveland House a decade later. Of life in Albemarle Street, the Marchioness wrote, 'I have been living a good deal at Home, there [are] no great inducements to go out, for except a few Casino Parties & the play there is absolutely nothing.'[23] As the second of these two passages suggests, her representation of herself as contentedly domestic did not preclude her involvement in the social and political life of the capital city, where she was an active and renowned hostess. (Lady Stafford was also a prominent Scottish landlady, about which I shall say more in Chapter Four.) As members of the aristocracy, the Marquess and Marchioness of Stafford's enormous political and social privilege demanded that they live in the public eye to a certain extent and the act of opening the gallery to the public was a visible manifestation of this tendency. But as the domestic interior became a theatre for political ambition, all factions of society had reason to claim this sphere as their own.[24]

Pictures and the Materiality of the Interior

The laid-out floor plan evolved as a particularly useful technique for depicting the domestic interior in parallel with the more general cultural trends described above. It emerged in the pages of William Young Ottley's *catalogue raisonné* as an especially apt strategy to represent the gallery at Cleveland House, emblematizing the slippage between private and public space that the gallery exemplified. The *catalogue raisonné* is by its nature intended to disseminate knowledge about objects and collections amongst the public; Ottley's ambitions to catalogue Stafford's collection resonated with the public-facing aspect of the gallery itself. He promoted his project as an enterprise that 'may truly be termed NATIONAL', sure to stir 'patriotic feelings' in all who encountered it.[25] Ottley planned for this catalogue to be the first in a series which would, when complete, comprise a national collection in book form at a moment when no National Gallery yet existed. The catalogue was framed as a benefit to the nation on much the same terms that the gallery's public days had originally been conceptualized. The stakes of Ottley's broader project will be more fully discussed in Chapter Five but, for the moment, it is sufficient to point out that the laid-out interior plans' indexical function supported Ottley's stated goal of documenting one of Britain's most important collections of art and making it visible in the public realm. Even as Ottley's book purported to present Cleveland House as a space of national, and by extension, political, significance, his choice to illustrate the interior using laid-out floor plans overlaid these conventional notions of public benefit with the aesthetic language of private sociability.

Tomkins' plans mark an important milestone in the development of a visual language to express upper-class domesticity in the context of the aristocratic dwelling. As we have already seen, Tomkins did not invent this language out of whole cloth, having adapted it from the genre of *catalogues raisonnés*, from architects' drawings and furniture-makers' source books and other sources that catered to aspirational middle and upper-middle class tastes. In addition to these, a category of fashionable periodicals aimed at female readers arrived on the scene in the early nineteenth century, of which Rudolph Ackermann's *Repository of Arts* (1809–1829) was the most significant example. The *Repository of Arts* was a monthly illustrated lifestyle magazine that circulated fashion plates and designs for cottages, follies and furniture to middle-class readers along with articles on literature, the arts and commerce.[26]

Tomkins' laid-out plan of the Dining Room at Cleveland House presents an opportunity to explore points of contact between the plans and the visual language of domesticity promulgated in these publications (see Figure 3.17). The Dining Room was hung with several of the collection's greatest treasures, amongst them Titian's large mythological pictures, *Diana and Actaeon* and *Diana and Callisto*, represented on the plan by frames depicted on the South wall labelled 84 and 104 (see Figure 2.3). Examples of wall elevations discussed earlier in this chapter, such as those made by Maria Cosway in the Louvre or by Tatham at Stoke Edith, reproduced paintings in miniature, inviting the viewer to peer closely at them. Tomkins does not follow this precedent instead depicting them as blank rectangles, encouraging the viewer's eye to roam over the many other furnishings that the room contained and the plan detailed. These include a chimneypiece of 'rich dove colour marble, ornamented in ormoulu' upon which a bust of the Duchess of Beaufort (the Marquess of Stafford's half-sister) by the fashionable neoclassical sculptor Joseph Nollekens was displayed and seating furniture upholstered with 'the most rich and costly damask'. Two of the set of elaborate pier tables designed by architect Tatham for the gallery are clearly visible on the South wall, flanking the doorway and anchoring the blank, numbered spaces that stand in for Titian's pictures. All is illuminated by a 'lamp of the Grecian order, which for beauty cannot be surpassed'.[27] This large chandelier fitted with patent burners, indicated by a cross inscribed within a circle on the plan, would have been positioned over the dining table in the centre of the room and was not primarily intended to light pictures to their best advantage.

The profusion of decorative objects covering each of the plan's four walls reminds viewers that the gallery was not a 'museum', as conceptualized in the austere designs of an Étienne-Louis Boullée or John Soane (whose design for the Dulwich Picture Gallery was constructed in 1811), but a suite in a private house designed to accommodate domestic life and private entertaining.[28] In addition, the orientation of the plan on the page, with the window elevation at the top, implicitly prioritizes the representation of the room's spatial layout and decoration over the easy use of the index for identifying the pictures in the space. Because of the book's enormous size, to closely view the South and North walls – where the majority of the pictures were displayed – the viewer must either turn the book, physically walk around the table, or uncomfortably contort his or her neck. The effect is that the large, floor-to-ceiling windows at the top of the page are given priority in the visual field and invite the viewer to examine them closely. The tripartite bow window is framed by voluminous floor length draperies adorned with tassels; written descriptions of the interior note that these were 'composed of the richest purple velvet, superbly embroidered with gold'.[29] Tomkins depicts the curtains drawn open to reveal a landscape that stands in for what would have been the view from these windows, a small private garden adjacent to the house just below and Green Park beyond.

Tomkins' strategy for depicting the window, curtains and view echo designs that appeared regularly in periodicals such as the *Repository of Arts*. One example depicts a series of tall arched windows dressed in

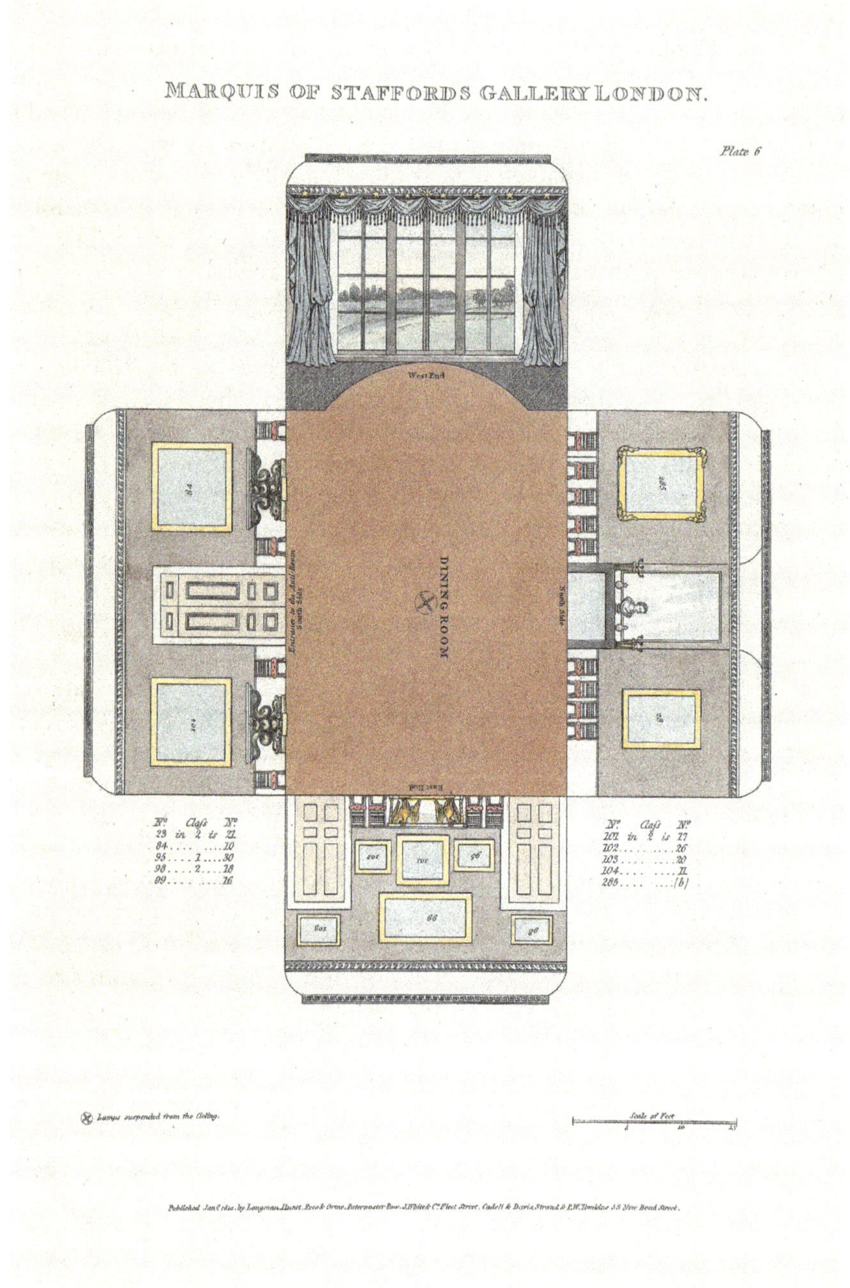

FIGURE 3.17 *PW Tomkins (engr.), 'Dining Room' from William Young Ottley,* Engravings of the Most Noble the Marquis of Stafford's collection of pictures in London, *London: Longman, Hurst, Rees, Orme, and Brown, 1818, engraving. Yale Center for British Art, Paul Mellon Collection.*

swags of golden fabric bordering a tripartite view of verdant landscape (see Figure 3.18). Such designs frequently framed uninhabited landscapes, as if the interior itself were not complete without a natural vista outside. Miniature landscapes were also brought into interiors by way of decorated transparent blinds which became popular in this period. A rare surviving example in the collection of the V&A Museum was painted in oils on linen and depicts a stone bridge crossing a stream under an Italianate tree and a deep blue sky (see Figure 3.19). Edward Orme's *An Essay on Transparent Prints*, which appeared in 1807, offered advice on the successful deployment of these blinds, which were considered especially useful in urban places where the views from windows might not be ideal. Many offered views of picturesque, classical, or even gothic landscapes to cater to the tastes of designers or their patrons. An example from Nathaniel Whittock's *Decorative Painters' and Glaziers' Guide* (1827) features a view onto the unlikely scene of ancient Roman philosophers holding forth in front of a landscape that seems to have been engineered by renowned eighteenth-century garden designer Capability Brown (see Figure 3.20).

The depiction of window, curtains and view in Tomkins' plan of the Dining Room invites viewers to imaginatively project themselves into its space, experiencing the collection not as a mere list of paintings but as objects contained within a social interior and subject to the serendipitous

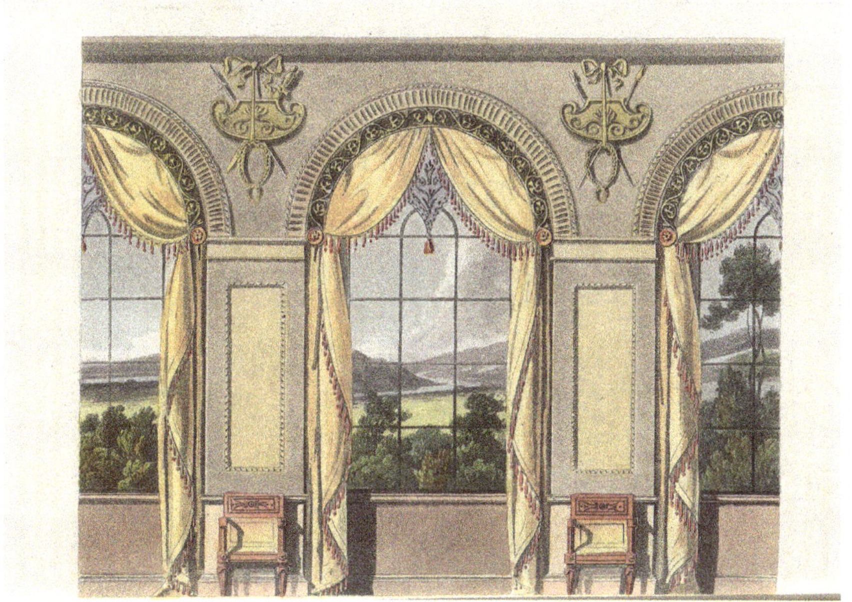

FIGURE 3.18 *'Dining-Room Window-Curtains' from* Repository of Arts, Literature, Fashions, &c *(London: Published by R. Ackermann, August 1816), hand-coloured aquatint. Yale Center for British Art, Paul Mellon Collection.*

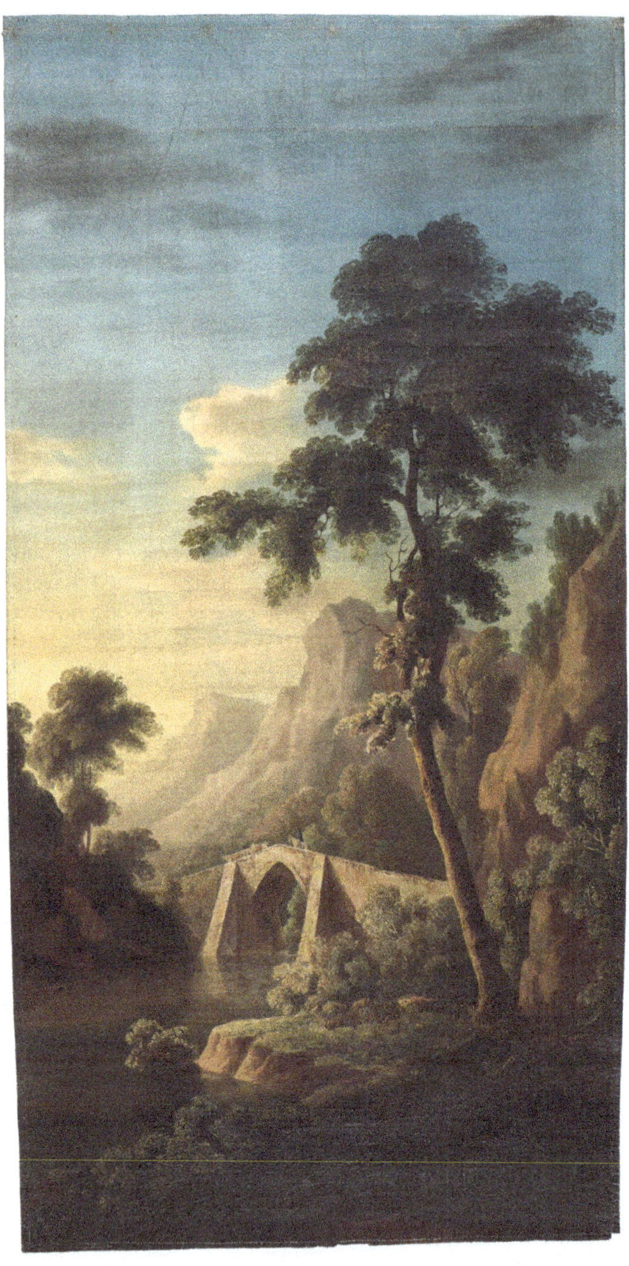

FIGURE 3.19 *Unknown, Window blind, Great Britain, 1800–1825, linen painted in oils and hemmed with hand stitching. Textiles and Fashion Collection, T.37-2008 © Victoria and Albert Museum, London.*

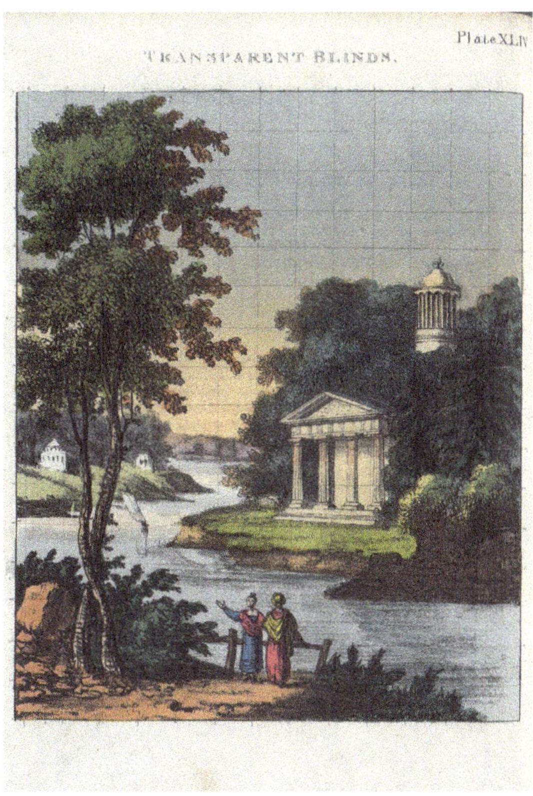

FIGURE 3.20 *Nathaniel Whittock (1791–1860), Plate XLIV,* The Decorative Painters' and Glaziers' Guide *(London: G. Virtue, 1827), hand-coloured lithograph. Yale Center for British Art, Paul Mellon Collection.*

connections and associations that the act of looking often made. If a visitor were physically present in the gallery, these windows offered a view from Cleveland House onto the verdant landscape outside. As noted above Cleveland House was oriented with its West façade facing Green Park so that both Drawing and Dining Rooms had views over this landscape; after French-American traveller Louis Simond toured the gallery in 1811, he described the park as 'delightfully fresh and luxuriant at this season of the year'.[30] Buckingham House, which had not yet undergone its 1825–1830 transformation into a palace by architect John Nash, would have been only just visible through the trees. Townhouses were often designed to capture the views of adjacent landscape and, as Todd Longstaffe-Gowan has observed, in this period it was the 'expansive view' over large urban parks that was the most desirable of all. Until 1820 when it was landscaped (also by Nash), Green Park was a relatively wild space, bringing the effect of a rural idyll into the most elite neighbourhood in the city.[31]

Visitors in the Drawing Room experienced this view of Green Park while encountering some of the Marquess of Stafford's most distinguished landscape paintings, including examples by Claude Lorrain and Nicholas Poussin, interspersed with smaller religious pictures such as Guido Reni's *Infant Jesus sleeping on a Cross*.[32] Tomkins' laid-out plan of the Drawing Room (see Figure 3.1) depicts the window bearing what appear to be identical draperies to those found in the Dining Room, adding a chaise longue in front of the window on both sides; these again draw the viewer's attention to the furnishing of the space. (It also offers additional hints as to the room's functionality; the swing door permitting discreet servant access is depicted in outline on the South wall. Frames number 38 and 39 hang on it.) Hanging adjacent to these windows were Claude's *Appulus Changed into a Wild Olive Tree* and *God Appearing to Moses in the Burning Bush*, archetypal examples of Italianate landscape (see Figure 3.21). The perceptive viewer was prompted to compare the landscape of classical Italy with that of modern-day London. Likewise, Britton's guidebook, which many visitors would have had in hand, contained an extended exegesis of Claude's *Appulus*. Recounting the fable of the ill-fated shepherd, Britton writes that having approached 'five female figures . . . dancing

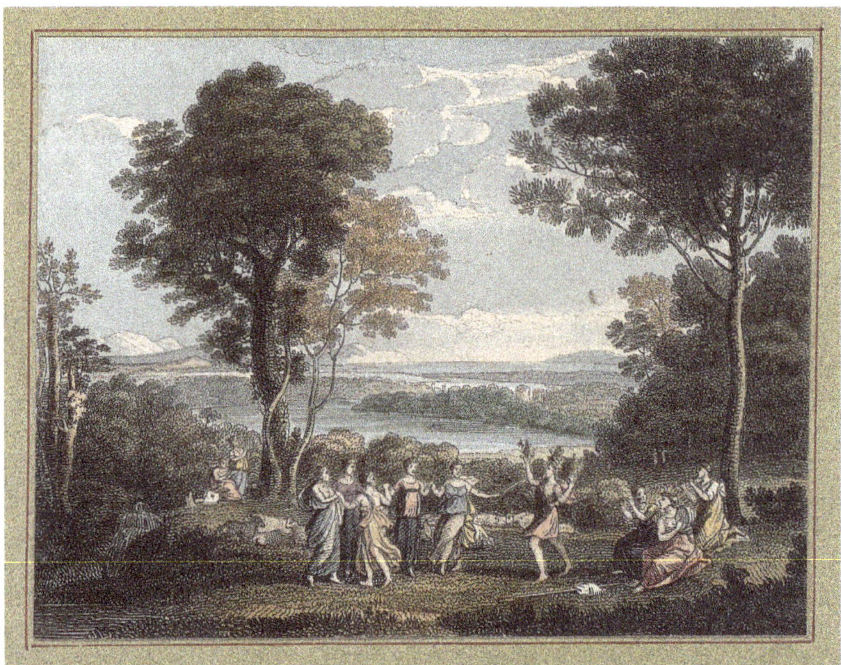

FIGURE 3.21 *After Claude Lorrain, 'Appulus Changed into a Wild Olive Tree' from William Young Ottley,* Engravings of the Most Noble the Marquis of Stafford's Collection of Pictures in London, *London: Longman, Hurst, Rees, Orme, and Brown, 1818, engraving. Yale Center for British Art, Paul Mellon Collection.*

on the green turf to the inspiring sounds of musical instruments', he 'is punished for his imprudent intrusion, by being transformed into a tree'.[33] Britton's next, somewhat unexpected, observation relates these events to contemporary social ills: 'If the impudence and criminal advances of all modern coxcombs were doomed to meet a similar punishment, we should not have cause to lament such frequent trials for *crim. con.* or hear of so many instances of the shameless prostitution which conspire to disgrace the present age.'[34] The viewer in the gallery looking at the view from the window in juxtaposition with this painting could have easily made the connection between its theme and the untamed areas of these large urban parks, which were frequented by all ranks of society and gave cover to a wide variety of illicit activities.

Tomkins' plans invite the viewer to imaginatively animate the space with the practices of private life that ostensibly took place within, suggesting that the social life of the interior was intertwined with the objects it contained. Mirrors reflected light, furniture provided seating and doors allowed for entrance to and egress from the room. Curtains offered privacy from the busy goings-on in the park outside but also protected people and objects inside the house – some of which were sensitive to light like pictures and upholstered furniture – from the sun on bright days. As a complete set Tomkins' plans, illustrated in sequence and with attention to the relative size and importance of each room, permit each room in the gallery to be represented with its individual idiosyncrasies intact, each room one stop on a picturesque journey through the gallery providing a different set of pictures, references and associations for the viewer. Moreover, these associations and ideas extend to the pictures in the collection; pictures are part of the décor and social meaning of the interior, they are not exempt from them. The adaptation of the visual signifiers of decoration emphasized the values of privacy and domesticity associated with the private interior over those more commonly associated with public spaces.

Ottley's catalogue explodes the eighteenth-century country house guidebook, with its economical lists of paintings and rooms, into a visual feast of pictures, interiors and furnishings. Wide open, flattened wall elevations make the pictures that made the Stafford collection so influential—along with the spaces and decorative interiors that framed it—available for public scrutiny. From this perspective, Ottley's catalogue offered radical transparency on Stafford's part, a true gesture toward the wide public access that the gallery had been theoretically designed to accommodate. On the other hand, the visual language of the laid-out floor plan expresses the gallery's essential hybridity. When pictures are represented as blank, numbered rectangles they are understood within the logic of the laid-out interior plan as patterns on the wall and not as pictures by Titian and Raphael. Depicted as movable objects in the context of the material abundance expressed by Tomkins' plans, the continental masterpieces that underpinned the prestige of the collection and the house were also understood as objects of interior décor. The catalogue was poised between asserting the house's contents as personal possessions which could and should be best enjoyed and understood within the context of the private interior and declaring them as public, even national, property.

Conclusion

In 1816 the *Repository of Arts* featured an engraving of 'Grecian Furniture', which suggests how pictures might have appeared when surrounded by the sofas, light fixtures and drapery of the chic Regency interior or, rather, how pictures could function as a backdrop for luxurious items of interior décor. It evokes the contemporary taste for setting pictures within a richly furnished space filled with an abundance of decorative objects (see Figure 3.22). The painting on the wall is a generic classical landscape, yet it is hardly the focal

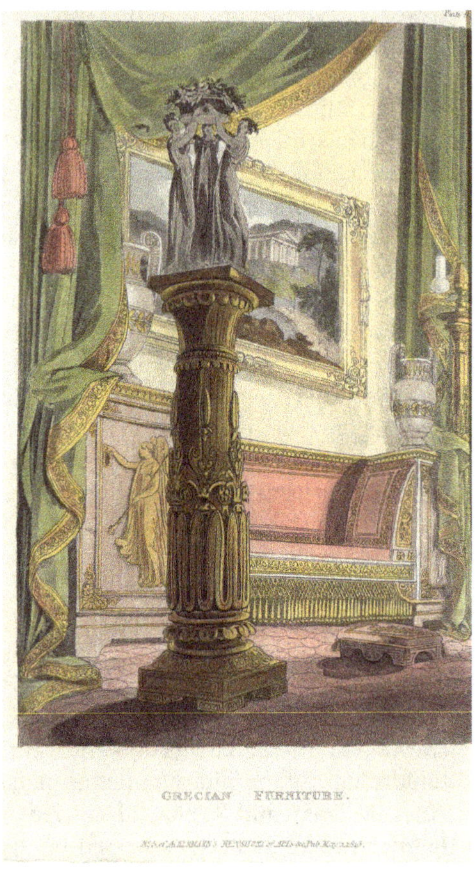

FIGURE 3.22 *'Grecian Furniture' from* Repository of Arts, Literature, Fashions, &c *(London: Published by R Ackermann, May 1816), hand-coloured aquatint. Yale Center for British Art, Paul Mellon Collection.*

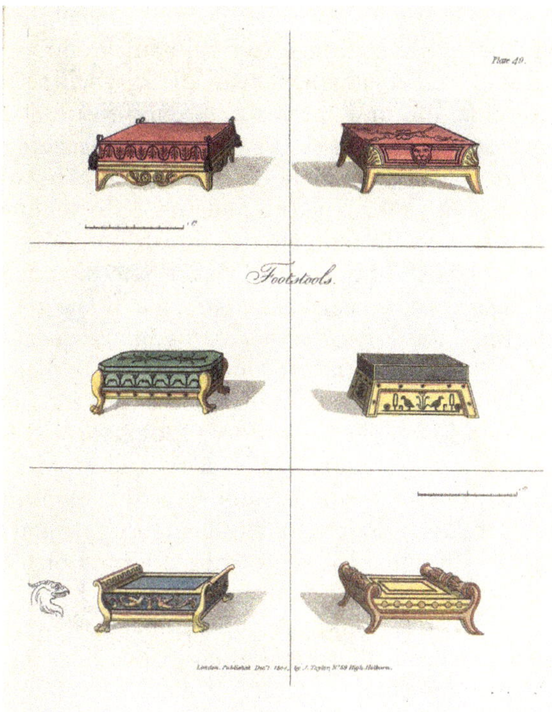

FIGURE 3.23 *'Footstools' in George Smith,* Collection of Designs for Household Furniture and Interior Decoration *(London: J Taylor, 1808), hand-coloured aquatint. Yale Center for British Art, Paul Mellon Collection.*

point of the image, partially obscured by an elaborate stand supporting a sculpture of the Three Graces, in turn flanked by amphorae atop a sofa and enveloped by immense green curtains embroidered with gold. A forlorn footstool, situated toward the bottom right of the composition, functions as a nod to human comfort in a fantasy interior that otherwise appears more akin to a stage set. The accompanying text exhorts the reader to see the vignette as one that presents a holistic interior, in which architecture, pictures and furniture combine to create a form of 'Art': 'Art indeed it may properly be called, when the designs of this species of embellishment embrace the combinations of form, composition, light, shade, and colour, and are as classically united agreeably to the laws of fitness and truth, as they are found to be in the works of masters eminent in the walks of pictorial beauty'.[35] While readers of the *Repository of Arts* could not hope to hang a genuine Claude in their interiors, the image offers a recipe by which the grandeur of a Cleveland House might be translated to more modest dwellings (see Figure 3.23).

By the late eighteenth century, a notion of personal privacy had emerged in the aristocratic imagination but its development was always in tension with the aristocracy's commitment to a dependent public. The trappings of domesticity were embraced widely across people of many social ranks; as a result, the domestic sphere became a cultural battleground where political authority could be won. Though this state of affairs would seem to represent a retreat from public life into the realm of the private, it paradoxically exposed domestic space to the instabilities of the political arena. In Chapter Four, I will explore how Lord and Lady Stafford's embrace of a controversial land management policy threatened to undermine the reputational benefit the gallery had bestowed. To mitigate this threat, Lord and Lady Stafford relied upon the public benefit the gallery was seen to offer as proof of their commitment to their own dependents and to the national good.

At the same time, the *Repository of Arts*'s image depicting a fantasy interior filled with 'Grecian Furniture' offers a reminder that any elision of the interiors of Cleveland House with the middle-class interiors featured in its pages can only go so far. The *Repository*'s genius was to re-package elite culture in a form accessible to its middle-class readers. Moreover, as Ann Pullan has argued, women were understood to be the *Repository*'s principal readership and its focus on designs for clothing, furniture and garden follies encompassed under an umbrella of generalized aspirational consumerism, was associated with femininity and stereotypically female pursuits like shopping.[36] Indeed, the text accompanying the image of 'Grecian Furniture' makes explicit that what is illustrated is not a real interior, rather it is a vignette taken from cabinet maker George Bullock's furniture showroom at 4 Tenterden Street, London.[37] Within the context of eighteenth-century debates over luxury and refinement, the domestic interior was in danger of being contaminated by the very consumer comforts and luxuries that bred effeminacy and threatened the public good. To introduce the commercial drives that underpinned the *Repository* into a private gallery like Cleveland House risked undermining its status as a space for the knowledgeable appreciation of fine art.

Cleveland House's promoters like Britton and Ottley worked to hold it apart from such middlebrow enterprises by emphasizing the public-spirited nature of its mission and the masculine nobility of its owner.[38] Visual and written representations of the gallery worked in concert to characterize the gallery as a private and domestic space, but one which always retained the moral authority and fitness for cultural (and, implicitly, political) leadership that domesticity connoted. As the fascination with the interior decoration and social scene in a house like Cleveland House grew, critics writing about the London art scene were increasingly concerned to ensure that art exhibitions and galleries would be understood as spaces of polite masculinity, to avoid falling into the trap of acquisitive desire that middle-class consumerism represented. These rhetorical moves imply that the very notion of domesticity could still be claimed by elite men, who adapted the decoration and use of their interiors to gentlemanly pursuits, bolstering their reputations as men fit to rule not only Britain, but its growing empire. I will explore these ideas in detail in Chapter Five.

4

'We have lately been much attacked': Exhibiting Morality

The opening of Cleveland House in May 1806 presented the very picture of patriotic aristocratic benevolence. A splendid stage for hospitality and diplomacy, it was transformed on Wednesday afternoons into a polite and intellectual venue for the improvement of the British public. However, the glamorous image Cleveland House projected within elite London circles formed a stark contrast to the small, poorly-maintained cottages occupied by the Marquess and Marchioness of Stafford's tenants on Lady Stafford's ancestral estate in Scotland. Before she was two years old, Lady Stafford had inherited the title of Countess of Sutherland (with the ancient title Great Lady of Sutherland – in Gaelic, *Ban mhorair Chataibh*), her family's seat Dunrobin Castle which overlooked the North Sea (see Figure 4.1) and hundreds of thousands of acres of inhospitable, mountainous terrain in Northern Scotland. To improve the productivity of this land and the prospects of the people living there, in 1806 – the very year Cleveland House opened to the public – Lord and Lady Stafford began to reorganize the estate using a process called 'enclosure'. These alterations formed part of a widespread campaign of agricultural improvement in Scotland that proved enormously controversial and, in the long term, damaging to their family's reputation.

The practice of 'enclosure' was central to the process of improvement and refers to the consolidation that took place as large landlords increased their acreage and smaller farms were absorbed into larger ones in a bid to increase the productivity and profitability of land.[1] While enclosure was used widely throughout Britain in the eighteenth century, in Scotland this decades-long campaign of agricultural improvement has come to be known as the Highland Clearances and is now viewed as a period of traumatic rupture in Scottish history. Whether one viewed Clearance as a social good or ill depended substantially on class position. In theory, these campaigns were intended to improve the rocky landscape by converting small subsistence farms into large grazing areas for sheep and moving impoverished tenants to the coast, where they could pursue more profitable occupations such as fishing. In practice,

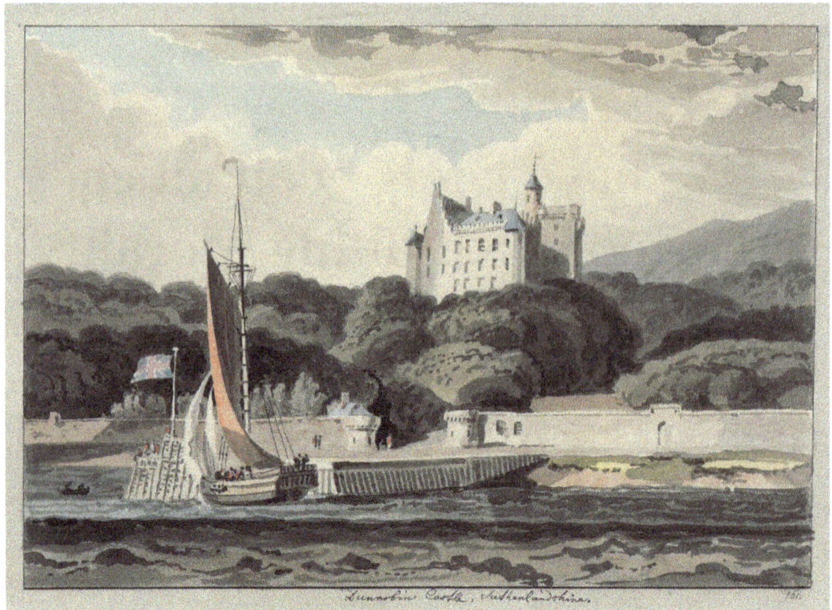

FIGURE 4.1 *Unknown artist,* Dunrobin Castle, Sutherlandshire, *recto, cropped to image, after 1814, Watercolour with pen and black ink on medium, smooth, cream wove paper, Yale Center for British Art, Paul Mellon Collection, B1975.3.394.*

many Highlanders violently resisted the removal of their homes and villages, a process which was frequently contentious. Tenants who did not accept their landlords' plans emigrated to Australia, Canada and the United States of America and, as a result, much of the worldwide Scottish diaspora today may be traced to these events. The controversy surrounding Clearance persisted through the nineteenth century – Karl Marx invoked the Highland Clearances as an example *par excellence* of the triumph of 'capitalistic agriculture' – and was revived in 1963 with the publication of John Prebble's popular history *The Highland Clearances*.[2] Prebble's polemical account of the Clearances portrays a greedy aristocracy with a near-genocidal mania to replace their human tenants with sheep. More recently, economic historian Eric Richards, whose work is essential to understanding the phenomenon of Clearance, has published numerous books detailing Lord and Lady Stafford's complicated finances and demonstrating the subtle inter-relationships between the family's canal and railroad holdings and the Highland properties as sources and sinks of wealth.[3]

These events may seem to have nothing to do with the gallery at Cleveland House. As heir to the Duke of Bridgewater's house, picture collection and fortune as well as an influential patron and collector in his own right,

Stafford was indisputably a leader in metropolitan art circles. He was lauded during his lifetime for his 'noble and patriotic' efforts in support of the arts and this is primarily how he has been remembered in the art historical record.[4] At the same time, historians of economics and land management have long recognized Lord and Lady Stafford's deep involvement in Clearance. The waves of scandal and controversy that accompanied it troubled the family's reputation even as the gallery was being fêted in contemporary media. This chapter will draw together these histories, which have heretofore been largely separate, through in-depth analysis of a series of commissions from the 1810s that shed light on the fraught relationship between the Staffords, their Scottish tenantry and critics of the practice of Clearance. The first example is a privately printed catalogue, *Etchings from Original Pictures in the Cleveland-House Gallery*, which circulated amongst the Staffords' friends and family in 1812, at the height of Clearances on their Scottish estates. A few years later, Stafford asked renowned Scottish painter David Wilkie to paint a scene of domestic life for the gallery.

Neither commission was explicitly linked with events in Scotland at the time. However, the circumstances surrounding each commission suggests that its appearance was prompted by the undesirable publicity Clearance generated. Close analysis of these commissions reveals the role that collecting and displaying art could play in alleviating points of friction that arose as landowning families navigated the political and cultural landscape of the early nineteenth century. Clearance was a manifestation of the cultural gulf that had opened up between London and the rest of Britain as industrialization and improvement ensured more Britons were living in the metropolis than at any time in the nation's history. This chapter will re-intertwine the histories of the gallery and of the Clearances to examine how the understanding of each reflected the other.

Englishness, Scottishness and the Nation

In 1807, an architect named George Perry published a catalogue that included descriptions of approximately 50 of the 'most prominent excellencies' of the gallery at Cleveland House. (It was in Perry's catalogue that a laid-out plan of the Dining Room, discussed in Chapter Three, appeared for the first time; refer to Fig. 3.2.) A year later, John Britton's catalogue would highlight the collection's richness in Italian and French Old Master painting and Stafford's intent to exhibit them to the public, but Perry's frames Cleveland House as a 'lasting Monument of English Taste and Liberality'.[5] Perry begins his imaginative tour of the collection in a small room, the anteroom to the Old Gallery, which was dedicated to the few English pictures on display at Cleveland House. Perry's catalogue bestows special attention upon *Niobe* by Richard Wilson, praising the artist as the 'English Claude' and comparing him favourably to other painters whose work was on display nearby including Claude Lorrain, Nicolas Poussin and Albert Cuyp.[6]

The prospect that pictures by British artists would one day be able to hold their own alongside works by established Old Masters had been one of the gallery's founding principles. Stafford purchased and commissioned work from a wide range of contemporary British artists, in keeping with his role as a leader of taste and as a founding member of the British Institution, including Edward Bird, James Northcote and Augustus Wall Callcott.[7] Especially in the early years, however, few British pictures were displayed at Cleveland House. The vast majority were kept at the family seat, Trentham Hall, in Staffordshire. Britton's text highlights their absence from Cleveland House; to reassure readers that Stafford had not been neglecting his duty to collect British paintings he wrote, 'it is but justice to state that the noble Marquis has made a considerable collection of these, which are deposited at Trentham Hall, Staffordshire'.[8] The British pictures that were selected for display at Cleveland House demonstrated the artist's absorption of European painting traditions that promoters of the British School were keen for young artists to emulate. They included Wilson's *Niobe*, JMW Turner's *Dutch Boats in a Gale*, *A Head of Charles I* by William Dobson (Dobson had been a pupil of Van Dyck), *The Boa Serpent* by James Ward and a view of cattle by Thomas Gainsborough. The small selection of works by British artists on display at Cleveland House – and really, they were English artists, with the exception of the Welsh Wilson – could have been understood to present visitors with a capsule history of British art as it then stood.

Niobe had been one of Bridgewater's earliest acquisitions, bought during the 1750s while he was on the Grand Tour with his tutor, Robert Wood (see Figure 4.2). Wood commissioned works to ensure that his youthful charge amassed pictures to display upon his return to England to properly commemorate his Italian education.[9] When hung in the gallery at Cleveland House, *Niobe*, a sophisticated merging of landscape and history following the example of Claude Lorrain, represented the ennobling effect on English art when young British artists studied and absorbed the lessons of Europe's great painters. Likewise, Bridgewater had commissioned Turner's *Dutch Boats in a Gale*, now known as *The Bridgewater Sea-Piece,* in 1801 as a companion to Willem Van de Velde's *A Rising Gale* (1672), which he had recently acquired (refer to Figure 2.5). *Dutch Boats in a Gale* was admired by Turner's contemporaries for its wholesale absorption and bravura reinvention of the Netherlandish seascape tradition. Royal Academy President Benjamin West favourably compared it to the work of Rembrandt.[10] Yet despite these nods to highlights of recent British painting, Cleveland House remained resolutely devoted to the display of pictures by continental masters, many of which had been acquired *en masse* following the Bridgewater Consortium's purchase of pictures from the Orléans Collection,

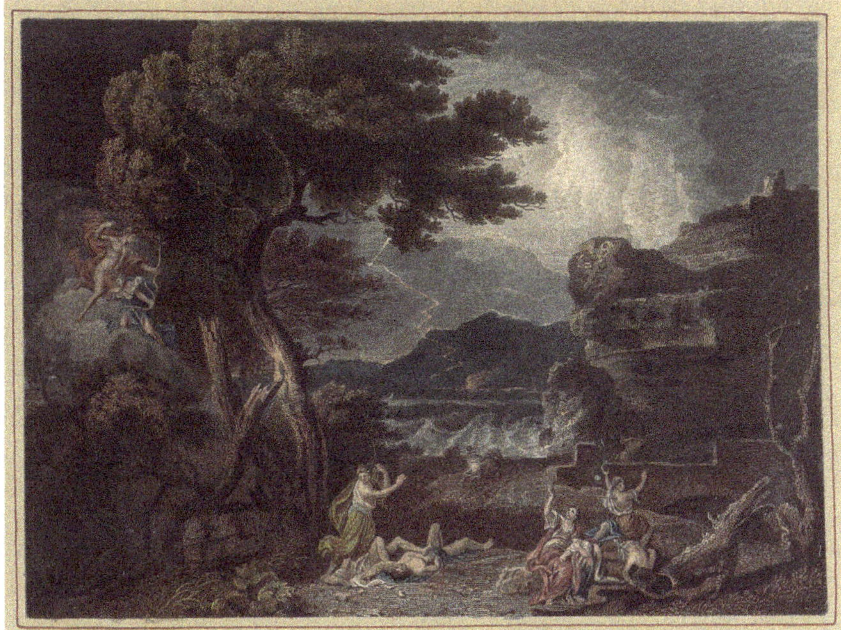

FIGURE 4.2 *After Richard Wilson, 'Niobe' from William Young Ottley,* Engravings of the Most Noble the Marquis of Stafford's Collection of Pictures in London, *London: Longman, Hurst, Rees, Orme, and Brown, 1818, engraving. Yale Center for British Art, Paul Mellon Collection.*

as described in Chapter One. That British pictures were given pride of place at Trentham suggests that the quintessentially 'English' genres of landscape and subject painting were still thought better suited to display in the country house, which powerfully symbolized the interrelationship of land ownership and cultural and political power. European, particularly Italian and French, forms of culture such as painting, music and sculpture, continued their reign amongst the British aristocracy as the most prestigious even as the British elite had begun the process of reforming its taste and manners from within.[11]

Cleveland House was the metropolitan face of a family with landed interests dispersed throughout the British Isles, from the canals and potteries of Staffordshire to the mountains of northern Scotland. Cleveland House was so rich in continental masterpieces that a few writers characterized it as a 'National Museum'.[12] In practice, however, the effort to unite the various parts of Britain under a single cultural umbrella was a fractured process, as 'national' culture was invariably understood to be English and 'Englishness' was itself a contested idea. As historians including Linda Colley and Gerald Newman have demonstrated, a true national identity did not automatically follow upon the union of English, Scottish, Welsh and Irish territories into

Great Britain, but was deployed to draw attention away from the fissures which continued to exist amongst these distinct groups.[13] The geographical and cultural divide separating rural parts of the country from growing urban centres was often difficult to reconcile and the notion that the 'national' culture being forged in the Cleveland House gallery was truly intended for a seamlessly integrated Great British public is self-evidently problematic. Whatever the theoretical framing of Cleveland House as a space for the 'public', in practice it was open to an international, cosmopolitan group of upper-class people. Its audiences did not include the working classes of the British Isles, nor even Lord and Lady Stafford's own tenants, who existed in a parallel universe to the glamorous and urbane life it represented.

The Marquess and Marchioness of Stafford's own family history is emblematic of the tensions inherent in reconciling regional and national identities. Stafford was born eldest son of John Leveson-Gower, the First Earl Gower, a Tory politician and representative of the Leveson-Gower family who were long-time landowners in Staffordshire. Likewise Lady Stafford, as noted above, inherited the massive Sutherland estate and its associated benefits and responsibilities after her parents died in 1766 when she was still a baby.[14] She was raised by her grandmother, Lady Alva, in Edinburgh, 200 miles to the south of the family seat, before bringing the Sutherland estate to her marriage in 1785.[15] Elizabeth's wedding to George cemented her family's place amongst the metropolitan aristocracy. Edinburgh was geographically and culturally removed from the Highlands; Elizabeth's subsequent move to London symbolized her rise from regional landowner to leader of taste on the national stage and her marriage was emblematic of the consolidation of Scottish and English aristocracy during the eighteenth and nineteenth centuries. The English aristocracy was in a state of crisis as fortunes dwindled and male lines died out; as David Cannadine has argued, their intermarriage with Welsh, Irish and Scottish landowners gave these old families a new lease on life and created an aristocracy that was truly 'British'.[16]

Although Lady Stafford exemplified the model of the Scottish aristocrat who had made the social journey from province to capital, the real estate she brought to the marriage was a mixed blessing. At the time of her marriage the Sutherland estates encompassed more than 750,000 acres of northeastern Scotland known as the 'Highlands' because of their mountainous and rocky terrain. In raw acreage, they dwarfed the holdings of any other aristocratic family in Britain, but the land was of meagre quality for farming. Tenants in Sutherland had been overwhelmingly poor for decades and incomes derived from rents had long been insufficient to entice landlords to carry out meaningful improvements. In contrast, her new family's estates in Staffordshire represented Sutherland's near opposite in terms of modernity and prosperity. The value of the Stafford family's holdings had increased rapidly during the latter part of the eighteenth century due to the construction of the Duke of Bridgewater's canal network and from related processes of industrialization. As Eric Richards has written, upon the marriage of Elizabeth and George, 'the most unmodernised remote corner of the British Isles became interlocked with the most dynamic sector of its most advanced region – Lancashire and the West Midlands'.[17] After Bridgewater named Stafford his heir, the family's enormous land holdings received a massive infusion of wealth in the form of income from industry, not to mention Cleveland House and its collection of pictures. George and Elizabeth Leveson-Gower, Marquess and Marchioness of Stafford, were now the richest couple in Britain.

Both clearance/improvement and the construction of the gallery were enabled by the influx of cash that followed Bridgewater's death. As discussed in detail in Chapter One, Lord and Lady Stafford undertook the construction of the gallery in London shortly after receiving news of the Bridgewater inheritance in 1803. Simultaneously, they embarked upon a scheme of improvements to the Sutherland estate. Preparation for improvement proceeded swiftly, with a general outline of the plans in place by August of 1805.[18] Clearances on the Sutherland estate began in 1806 (within months of the gallery's completion and opening) and proceeded sporadically between 1806 and 1815. Because the Sutherland estates were Lady Stafford's birthright, it appears that it was she who initiated the new scheme of land management. The Sutherland estates were *her* ancestral property and it was *she* who bore the dual titles of Marchioness of Stafford and Countess of Sutherland. As Eric Richards argued, Lady Stafford was – at minimum – fully-informed about the possible consequences of the plan and insisted it proceed with all due haste, using 'a proper degree of firmness'.[19]

Lord and Lady Stafford intended to transform Sutherland into an economic engine while moving their Highland tenants to more solid financial ground. A mixture of self-interested and benevolent motives was common in the story of agricultural improvement. From the landlord's point of view, enclosure was intended to transform land that was failing to reach its full potential into something more fruitful. From the tenant's point of view, enclosure and related efforts to improve the agricultural landscape represented the conversion of traditionally public, common assets into private property by landed interests. More to the point, in practical terms, enclosure often involved evicting tenants from land and houses where their families had lived for generations; 'enclosure' was a euphemism smoothing over a process that was always contentious and sometimes violent. Consolidation, enclosure and the landowner's attack on customary rights left many Highlanders unemployed, hungry and uprooted from longstanding communities.[20] First-person accounts of evictions carried out by the Staffords' representatives are vivid, though most were not written down until many years after the fact. For example, Betsy MacKay, who was sixteen at the time her family was evicted in 1814, recalled:

> Our family was very reluctant to leave and stayed for some time, but the burning party came round and set fire to our house at both ends, reducing to ashes whatever remained within the walls. The people had to escape for their lives, some of them losing all their clothes except what they had on their backs. The people were told they could go where they liked, provided they did not encumber the land that was by rights their own.[21]

The result of Clearance on the Sutherland estate was widespread outrage. Anger quickly turned to violent resistance in the form of rick-burning (wagon-burning) and related means of protest.

The brutality of enclosure was enabled by the geographical and cultural distance between the Scottish people and their landlords, many of whom lived in Edinburgh or even further afield in London. Wishing to distance themselves from the 'primitive' peoples amongst whom they dwelt, the Scottish upper classes had increasingly embraced Englishness in an attempt to become cozier with the cosmopolitan society of the south. Scotland was commonly regarded in English circles as an undeveloped backwater, peopled by uncivilized clans of subsistence farmers. Particularly in the wake of the Jacobite Rising of 1745, Scottish culture and politics were widely regarded as subservient to English concerns and it was only much later, after the process of Clearance was well underway, that the romanticization of Scottish culture and history that characterized the nineteenth century began in earnest.[22] At the turn of the nineteenth century, Scots, and Highlanders in particular, were still widely understood as people who, by virtue of outlook, ethnicity and language – most spoke Gaelic – only uneasily fit under the umbrella of British identity.

Examples of Highlanders being derided as ethnic and cultural outsiders are ubiquitous in the literature of the period. In 1775 Samuel Johnson wrote, 'Till the Union made them acquainted with English manners, the culture of their lands was unskillful and their domestick life unformed; their tables were coarse as the feasts of Esquimaux and their houses filthy as the cottages of Hottentots'.[23] Lady Stafford largely embraced the view that her tenants were primitive and backward people whose customs and beliefs reflected a worldview that had long since disappeared from her own circles. Writing to one acquaintance, she described them as 'an infinite multitude roaming at large in the old way, despising all barriers and regulations and firmly believing in witchcraft'.[24] In 1813 William Young, a promoter of improvements on the Sutherland estate, complained about its tenants in frankly racial terms. 'Such a set of savages is not to be found in the wilds of America', Young wrote. 'If Lord and Lady Stafford do not put it in my power to quell this banditti we may bid adieu to all improvement'.[25] As David Solkin has argued, in the late eighteenth century, images of *banditti* conjured the anxiety an imperial power felt toward indigenous people they attempted to bring under their control.[26] Young's self-serving use of words like 'savages' and 'banditti' to describe Sutherland tenants suggests that

English (and Lowland Scottish) landowners did not regard Highlanders as well-fed and free British farmers, but as 'natives' of a foreign land who must be brought to heel.

Even writers who were clearly sympathetic to the plight of Highlanders made frequent recourse to the imagery of colonization. In 1803 the Rev PB Homer wrote, 'the life of the poor is here the most destitute and the most deplorable that an imagination can conceive. In the supply of its necessary wants, it is not raised one degree above that of the savages of Otaheite'.[27] Looking back on this period in 1819, after the Romantic recuperation of the Highlands had begun, an article in the *New Monthly Magazine* observed woefully, '[The Highlanders] were shunned as a race with which no dealings could be made and on whose faith no dependence could be placed; who had no law but the word of a proud chief and no sense of moral obligation but that capricious feeling of honor which frequently obtains even among a community of robbers'.[28] Although years of enclosures in Sutherland had encouraged the metropolitan press to view Highlanders in a more compassionate light, their frequent elision of Highlanders with native peoples of North America and Africa positioned Scots as childlike, savage and subservient to the English in matters of culture and, by extension, political authority.

Changing Subjects: *Etchings from Original Pictures in the Cleveland-House Gallery*

Clearance produced a strong reaction amongst the local population, which one of the Marchioness' representatives euphemistically called a 'Commotion'.[29] One of many such incidents took place in Golspie, the coastal village neighbouring Dunrobin Castle, Lady Stafford's ancestral home. Hearing of the violent outbreak she wrote:

> At present I am uneasy about a sort of mutiny that has broken out in one part of Sutherland, in consequences of our new plans having made it necessary to transplant some of the inhabitants to the sea-coast from the more inland parts. The same plan has succeeded in other parts of the estate, but the people in one parish resist it, which I fear has rendered it necessary for the sheriff who went to quiet them to send for the assistance of the military.[30]

Apparently unable to satisfactorily reconcile her own perspective with that held by the 'refractory' tenants, she continued, 'London is more full and gay, if possible, than usual'.[31]

Elizabeth's words reflect a desire to change the subject, from unpleasant dealings in Sutherland to the ease and pleasure of her life in London. Though the logic of improvement was generally accepted within metropolitan circles, reports of the sheer scale and brutality of Clearance circulated by word of mouth and in the press. Prominent landlords like the Staffords could not escape the scrutiny of reformers who had begun to regard improvement through the lens of ethics rather than as a clear-cut matter of economics. In 1798 the Rev Thomas Garnett observed:

> All the advantages [of enclosure] have, in my opinion, been more than counterbalanced by the effect which this system has produced on the population of the country. By joining together two, three, or more farms and converting them into a sheep walk, twelve or sixteen tenants, with their families, are thrown out of their usual line of employment, the greater number of whom are obliged to emigrate. Where one man occupies the space which would be occupied by these, his private gains will by no means compensate for the public loss.[32]

Garnett argues that at stake was not just agricultural productivity but the loss of community on a scale that was impossible to calculate. In London, Lord and Lady Stafford opened their house and the art objects it contained with the express intention of making their cultural wealth accessible to a wider public and welcomed the admiration these actions garnered amongst their peers and in the periodical press. In Scotland, they moved to restrict access to lands which had long been understood as a public resource by the Highlanders, expecting to do so with relative freedom from scrutiny.

Despite efforts to squelch criticism in the press, by 1808 the estate was issuing 'flat denials' in response to critical reports in Scottish newspapers.[33] By 1810–1811, the first round of Clearance was winding down and another was in the works. In 1812 James Loch, a Scottish attorney, entered the Staffords' employ as their main representative in matters pertaining to their estates and finances, after which time Clearance in Sutherland increased in frequency and intensity. Around this time, rumours began to circulate amongst members of Lady Stafford's own social network, which she took steps to rebut. To one acquaintance, she wrote:

> We have lately been much attacked in the newspapers by a few malicious writers who have long assailed us on every occasion. What is stated is most perfectly unjust and unfounded, as I am convinced from the facts I am acquainted with and I venture to trouble you with the enclosed . . . If you meet with discussions on the subject in Society, I shall be glad if you will show this statement to anyone who may interest him or herself on the subject.[34]

The Marchioness was taking active steps to manage her family's reputation by personal appeal. Certainly, she was not the only woman of this era to do so. In the later decades of the eighteenth century, 'women of quality' found themselves regularly scrutinized for failings of character, both real and imaginary.[35] Elizabeth herself had been the subject of chatter regarding a number of affairs and, most disconcertingly, rumours surrounding the paternity of her youngest son, Francis, born in 1800. Though there is no reliable written evidence of the truth of these allegations, Sylvester Douglas, Lord Glenbervie, claimed in his gossip-filled diaries that 'the intrigue, the *éclat* and the subsequent pacification [of Lord Stafford's fury] were matters of general conversation at the time'.[36]

As the events outlined above were underway, Lord and Lady Stafford made a number of commissions, including a privately-printed catalogue that appeared in 1812, a picture of the Marchioness by society portraitist Thomas Lawrence and a genre painting by acclaimed Scottish artist David Wilkie, which was exhibited at the Royal Academy in 1817 before being put on display at Cleveland House. I have found no letters or other writings that offer any explicit declaration of intent prompting any of these commissions. Even so, their appearance between 1812 and 1817 coincides with a period during which Lord and Lady Stafford – and the Marchioness in particular – were under particular scrutiny with regard to their Highland tenantry.

The first of these commissions is a slim volume consisting of six engravings after pictures from the Old Gallery at Cleveland House, where more than 100 of the collection's Dutch and Netherlandish pictures were on display. I have written at length elsewhere about this portfolio of etchings.[37] Titled *Etchings from Original Pictures in the Cleveland-House Gallery*, the book and engravings are attributed to Cleveland House's porter, William Cantrill. This book is an extraordinarily unusual object, filled with engravings by a member of household staff with no known training in drawing or engraving. As Cantrill's dedication acknowledges, they are clearly the work of an inexperienced artist. He writes, 'May it please your ladyship, the following six etchings, being first attempts by an untutored hand, from the fine originals in the gallery at Cleveland-House, are most humbly dedicated by your Ladyship's obedient, grateful and dutiful servant, William Cantrill, Your Ladyship's Porter.'

These few words are the only stated reason given for the book's creation and the only clue to the underlying relationships and concerns that produced it. As Helen Smith has written, the dedication is an enormously tricky literary form. Dedications can be understood as both 'speaking inwards by illuminating questions of influence and construction and outwards to readers real and imagined, as well as to the social world in which the text has been nourished . . . and brought forth'.[38] As noted in Chapter Two, Cantrill was a long-time employee; account books confirm that by 1812 he had worked at Cleveland House at least since 1805 when construction on the gallery was underway and it is almost certain that he had been employed by the family well before that date.[39] The dedication is, as Smith writes, a format that 'perform[s] intimacy' but, in this case, it makes public an apparent exchange of encouragement (on Lady Stafford's part) and appreciation (on Cantrill's part) between two people of vastly different social standing.[40] Having entered the public realm it functions as a memento honouring Lady Stafford, while silently reminding the reader of her beneficence as an employer, patroness and benefactress of the arts. Cantrill's dedication, which implied an easy and naturally-ordered relationship between the Marchioness and himself (and, by extension, her many other dependents), frames the catalogue as a private, personal homage to a benevolent mistress rather than as a patriotic tribute to a great (read: male) collector. It also implies that the bond between aristocrat and dependent was not as broken as events in the Highlands might suggest.

Etchings from Original Pictures is precisely the type of object that might circulate within the intimate circles of a family. A few crucial hints as to the book's intended audience and possible use may be gleaned from the evidence that survives in the form of the object itself. Its generous size, approximately 29 x 37cm, makes it very unlikely to have been carried in the gallery. It was privately printed, but the title page bears a price, a relatively inexpensive 12s and indicates it was available for purchase at a number of leading booksellers, including Ackermann, Colnaghi and Molteno. However, its present scarcity suggests that it did not circulate widely.[41] The copy illustrated here was inscribed by the Revd Henry John Todd, who donated it shortly after its publication to the library of the Society of Antiquaries, where it remains (see Figure 4.3). Todd had a distant but personal connection to Lord and Lady Stafford, having served as private chaplain to the Seventh Earl of Bridgewater, a cousin of the late Duke.[42] As this connection suggests, the book's audience was probably primarily family and friends and it was most likely intended to be leafed through and contemplated in private.

Subject or genre painting, the category to which all of the pictures included belong, was particularly well-suited to constructing narratives that could be understood across the boundaries of social class separating Cantrill, his patroness and the book's presumed audience.[43] There is no explicit evidence as to who chose the paintings Cantrill copied, but the circumstances of its publication suggest that it was a collaboration between Lady Stafford and her employee. Both dedication and choice of images gloss over the subject of unrest on the Scottish estates. When a viewer 'reads' the book – looks at the series of images in the order they appear – a narrative emerges telling a story of rural poverty redeemed by a benevolent female patron. The sequence begins with etchings after paintings like Jan Fyt's *The Starving Dog*, Antoine LeNain's *The Village Piper* and David Teniers' *Boors Playing Cards* and *Ducks in Water*, all of which were reproduced in William Young Ottley's 1818 *catalogue raisonné* (see Figure 4.4). The selected images present various aspects of poor, rural life to their well-heeled, metropolitan viewers as charmingly picturesque and – to an extent – inevitable.

The final engraving in the book, which Cantrill made after Quirijn van Brekelenkam's *Returning Thanks*, focuses the viewer's attention on a female figure praying over a humble meal (see Figure 4.5). The praying woman is

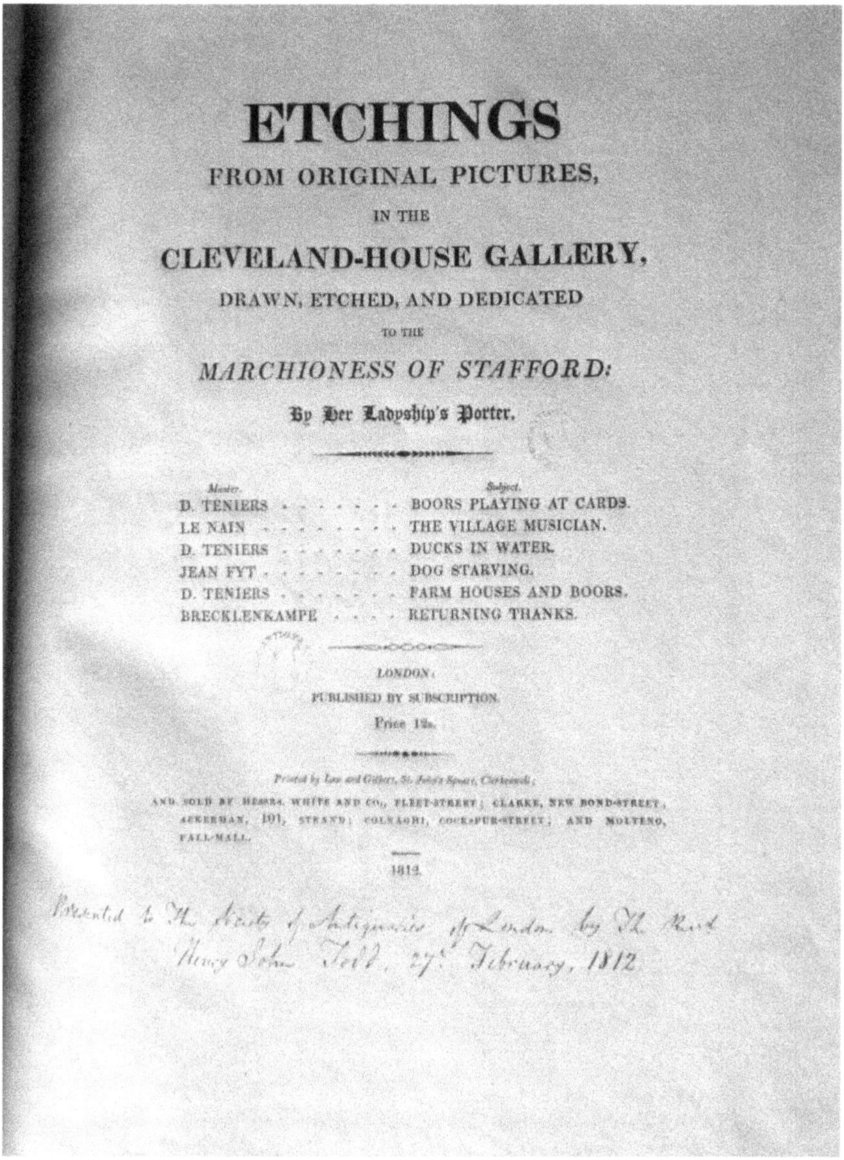

ETCHINGS
FROM ORIGINAL PICTURES,
IN THE
CLEVELAND-HOUSE GALLERY,
DRAWN, ETCHED, AND DEDICATED
TO THE
MARCHIONESS OF STAFFORD:
By Her Ladyship's Porter.

Master.	*Subject.*
D. TENIERS	BOORS PLAYING AT CARDS.
LE NAIN	THE VILLAGE MUSICIAN.
D. TENIERS	DUCKS IN WATER.
JEAN FYT	DOG STARVING.
D. TENIERS	FARM HOUSES AND BOORS.
BRECKLENKAMPE	RETURNING THANKS.

LONDON:
PUBLISHED BY SUBSCRIPTION.
Price 12s.

Printed by Law and Gilbert, St. John's Square, Clerkenwell;

AND SOLD BY MESSRS. WHITE AND CO., FLEET-STREET; CLARKE, NEW BOND-STREET, ACKERMAN, 101, STRAND; COLNAGHI, COCKSPUR-STREET; AND MOLTENO, PALL-MALL.

1812.

Presented to the Society of Antiquaries of London by the Revd Henry John Todd, 27th February, 1812

FIGURE 4.3 *Title page inscribed by the Revd Henry John Todd, 27 February 1812. [William Cantrill]* Etchings from Original Pictures in the Cleveland-House Gallery *(London: Published by subscription, 1812). Reproduced with the permission of the Society of Antiquaries of London.*

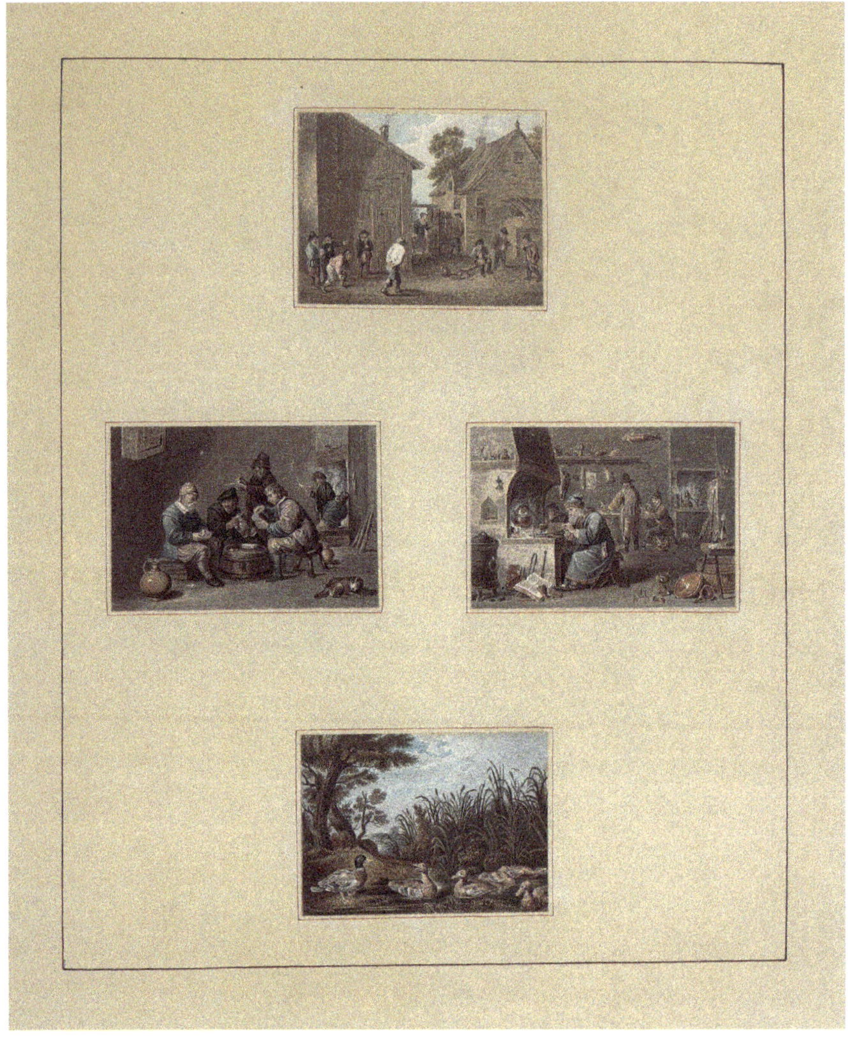

FIGURE 4.4 *After David Teniers, 'Farm Houses and Boors' (top), 'Boors Playing Cards' (centre left) and 'Ducks in Water' (bottom) from William Young Ottley,* Engravings of the Most Noble the Marquis of Stafford's Collection of Pictures in London, *London: Longman, Hurst, Rees, Orme, and Brown, 1818, hand-coloured engraving. Yale Center for British Art, Paul Mellon Collection.*

understood to deserve the viewer's empathy by virtue of the (mostly) orderly domestic interior that surrounds her. A viewer considering Brekelenkam's image within the framework of Cantrill's catalogue could have easily made a connection between this woman and the Marchioness of Stafford's Highland tenants, grateful to a benevolent mistress for access to housing and

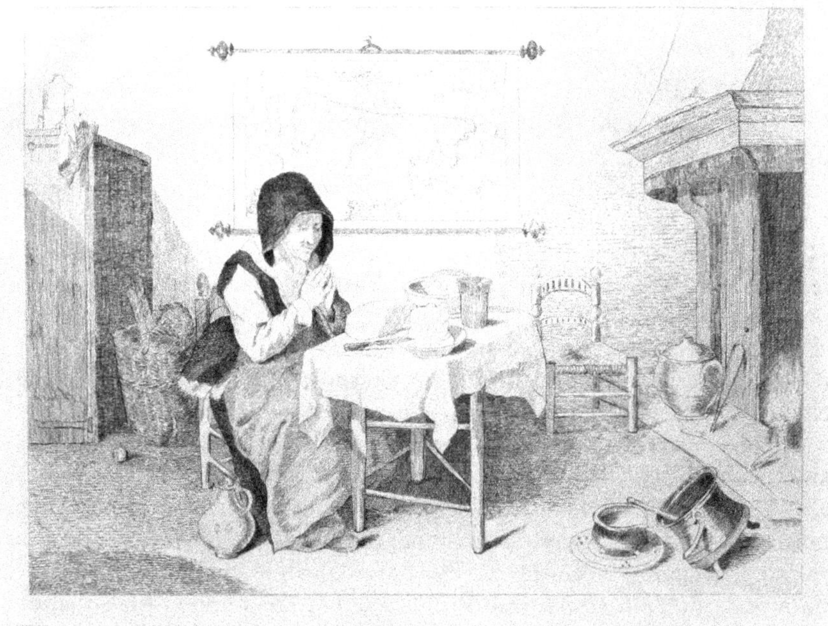

FIGURE 4.5 *William Cantrill after Quirijn van Brekelenkam, Returning Thanks from* Etchings from Original Pictures in the Cleveland-House Gallery *(London: Published by subscription, 1812). Reproduced with the permission of the Society of Antiquaries of London.*

the bread on her table. *Returning Thanks* emphasizes a mutually-beneficial relationship between superior and dependent; images of female piety and domesticity burnish the Marchioness' stylish reputation by associating her name with an image of industriousness, wisdom and gratitude.

Cantrill's book offers a way of thinking about the gallery and its purpose that runs counter to the public virtues that the gallery had elsewhere been used to promote. Other catalogues focused on Lord Stafford's patriotic and noble example, presenting him as a gentleman enacting his duty to the nation in making his collection accessible to the public. Cantrill's is dedicated exclusively to Lady Stafford. Where other catalogues prioritise the prestigious Italian religious and history paintings that were the gallery's main draw, Cantrill's focuses exclusively on genre scenes depicting 'low' life. Certainly, copying these pictures would have been considered more appropriate to the talents of a self-taught artist who had emerged from the working classes. At the same time, the shift in focus from Lord to Lady Stafford made an appeal to the book's audience along traditionally gendered lines, linking the collection to the conventionally feminine (and private) virtues of domesticity and conscientious household management.

'Domestic Realities': David Wilkie's *The Breakfast*

Cantrill's catalogue may have played a role in quelling anxieties about Clearance within Lady Stafford's circles in the early 1810s, but all previous publicity paled in comparison to the firestorm of controversy that erupted in June 1814. Patrick Sellar, a factor, or property manager, on the Sutherland estate was carrying out evictions in the village of Badinloskin when witnesses said Sellar ordered his officers to burn the houses and crops of tenants who refused to move. Burning the rafters of houses was a relatively common practice during Clearance, intended to prevent reoccupation of houses after the clearing party had moved on. In this case, Sellar was accused of burning the cottage of a man named William Chisholm, knowing that Chisholm's elderly, bedridden mother-in-law, Margaret McKay, was inside. Donald Macleod, a memoirist who recorded his impressions of these events decades later, claimed that when Sellar discovered McKay was too infirm to leave the cottage he declared, 'Damn her, the old witch; she has lived too long. Let her burn!'[44] Accounts of what actually happened on the day of the clearance varied. The family was able to move her to another building before the burning began, but court records indicate that the stress of the situation – which caused 'great fright and alarm' – hastened her illness and she died less than a week later.[45] Sellar was put on trial in April 1816 for two deaths, including that of Mrs McKay, and related crimes of endangerment.[46]

A month later, a new portrait of Lady Stafford by society portraitist Thomas Lawrence debuted at the annual Royal Academy exhibition. This commission dated back to 1813, just after Cantrill's catalogue began to circulate; Joseph Farington reported that Lawrence was beginning work on a full-length portrait of the Marchioness.[47] Lady Stafford had been painted previously in half-length by Sir Joshua Reynolds, John Hoppner and George Romney, all of whom were acclaimed portraitists of the period (see Figure 1.4). These earlier portraits circulated widely in the form of engraving, but it is unsurprising that at the height of her social influence and at a moment of reputational stress she should have sought a portrait in the grand style for which Lawrence, by now the portraitist of choice amongst the *beau monde*, was so celebrated.[48] Many upper-class people turned to portraiture to burnish their reputations, especially at a time when attacks on their character – and, by extension, their claim to moral authority – had become endemic within British society.[49] Lawrence never completed this full-length portrait; the half-length appeared instead at the 1816 exhibition. She appears as glamorous as ever, wearing a fur-trimmed turban and displaying a large bejewelled brooch, but she looks out at the viewer with a sober expression in keeping with the seriousness of shocking events that had unfolded in Scotland during the period between when the portrait commission was first discussed and the finished picture's unveiling at a public venue.

The Sellar trial described a horrific scene of Highlanders being burned alive in their own homes – regardless of whether it was precisely accurate – to newspaper readers nationwide. The possibility that either Lord or Lady Stafford had explicitly authorized or permitted the burning of cottages and the endangerment of their tenants was anathema to prevailing ideals of aristocratic conduct. Tenants were dependent upon landlords to exercise restraint, sympathy and good judgment because the consequences of landlords' decisions fell disproportionately on them. Since inheriting Bridgewater's estate more than a decade prior, the Staffords had taken dramatic steps to demonstrate their public spiritedness. The construction of the gallery, the founding of the British Institution, the support of a wide-range of charitable organizations, even the well-meant (if patronizing and destructive) attempt to improve the lives of their Highland tenantry through enclosure and clearance, had been undertaken with that goal in mind. Events in Badinloskin and Sellar's trial cast a shadow over all of these efforts.

As this series of Clearances and their tragic consequences were unfolding, Lord Stafford was in the process of ordering a picture from renowned Scottish genre painter David Wilkie. Wilkie had made a name for himself a decade prior by exhibiting sensational blockbuster pictures like *Village Politicians* and *The Blind Fiddler* at the Royal Academy and became one of the most popular and sought-after painters of the period.[50] The first evidence of the commission is found in a letter from Wilkie to his sister in May 1813, in which the artist describes having been approached by the Prince Regent and Stafford before a dinner at the Royal Academy. Stafford expressed his wish for the artist to fulfill a long-standing promise to paint him a picture, though at least another year and a half passed before Wilkie and his patron agreed on a subject.[51] During this period, Wilkie painted one of his most celebrated pictures, *Distraining for Rent*, which explicitly depicted the tragedy that could result from landlord-tenant disputes and seemed to align the artist's sympathies with the tenants (see Figure 4.6).[52] (Wilkie sold *Distraining for Rent* to the British Institution, which was buying pictures for donation to a national gallery in the event that one would be founded in the future. Stafford was a member of the purchasing committee.[53]) Certainly, Wilkie did not discuss the practice of Clearance nor take a position on its efficacy or morality in his private correspondence. When the artist explicitly referenced Highland people in his work, he did so in the spirit of the revival of interest in Scottish culture found in the novels of Sir Walter Scott (whom Lady Stafford also patronized) and encouraged by the Prince Regent. Wilkie's *The Highland Family*, for example, depicts a loving family in a humble yet neat interior setting (see Figure 4.7). If anything, *The Highland Family*, dating from 1824, would appear to depict the continued viability of the Highland way of life.

In the end, Wilkie came to terms with Stafford by proposing a subject that would appear *Distraining for Rent*'s opposite, at least as far as the possibility of any political connotation being attributed to it. In December

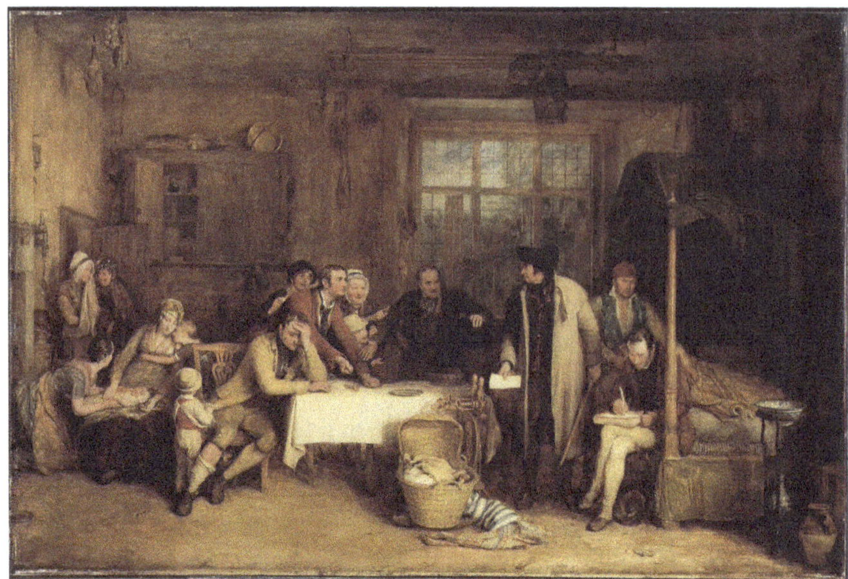

FIGURE 4.6 *Sir David Wilkie,* Distraining for Rent, *oil on panel, 1815. National Galleries Scotland, Purchased 1975.*

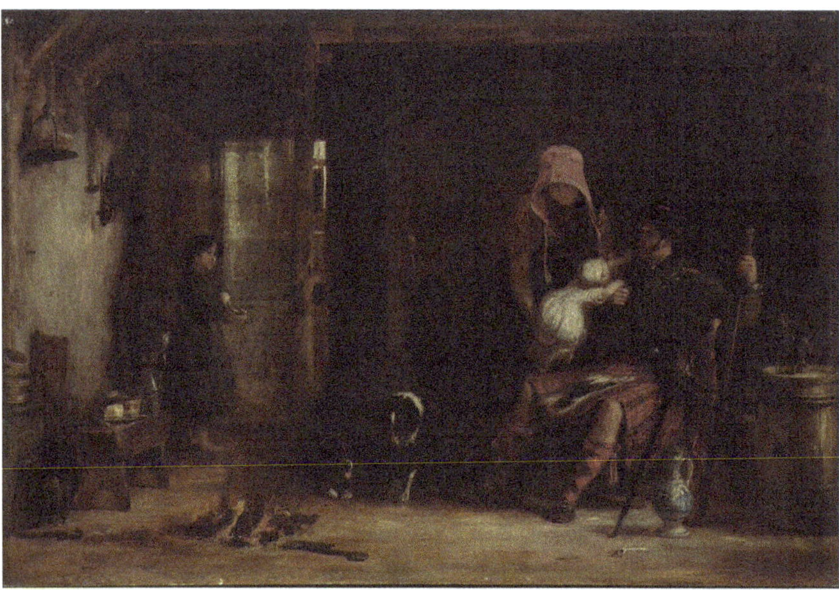

FIGURE 4.7 *Sir David Wilkie,* The Highland Family, *1824. Oil on wood. The Metropolitan Museum of Art, New York, Bequest of Maria DeWitt Jesup, from the collection of her husband, Morris K Jesup, 1914.*

1815 Wilkie wrote, 'I have been very unsettled in my studies, from the difficulty of making an arrangement with the Marquis of Stafford. I have at last however, succeeded in satisfying him with a sketch . . . The subject is a breakfast scene'.[54] *The Breakfast*, which Wilkie exhibited at the Royal Academy in 1817 before it was hung in the gallery at Cleveland House, is a scene of comfortable, middle-class domestic life (see Figure 4.8). An elderly lady and two younger men, one of whom is absorbed in his newspaper, come together for their morning meal. The interior is simply but comfortably furnished with carpets, Chinese porcelain on the mantel, an upholstered armchair and folding screen in the background lending elegance to its

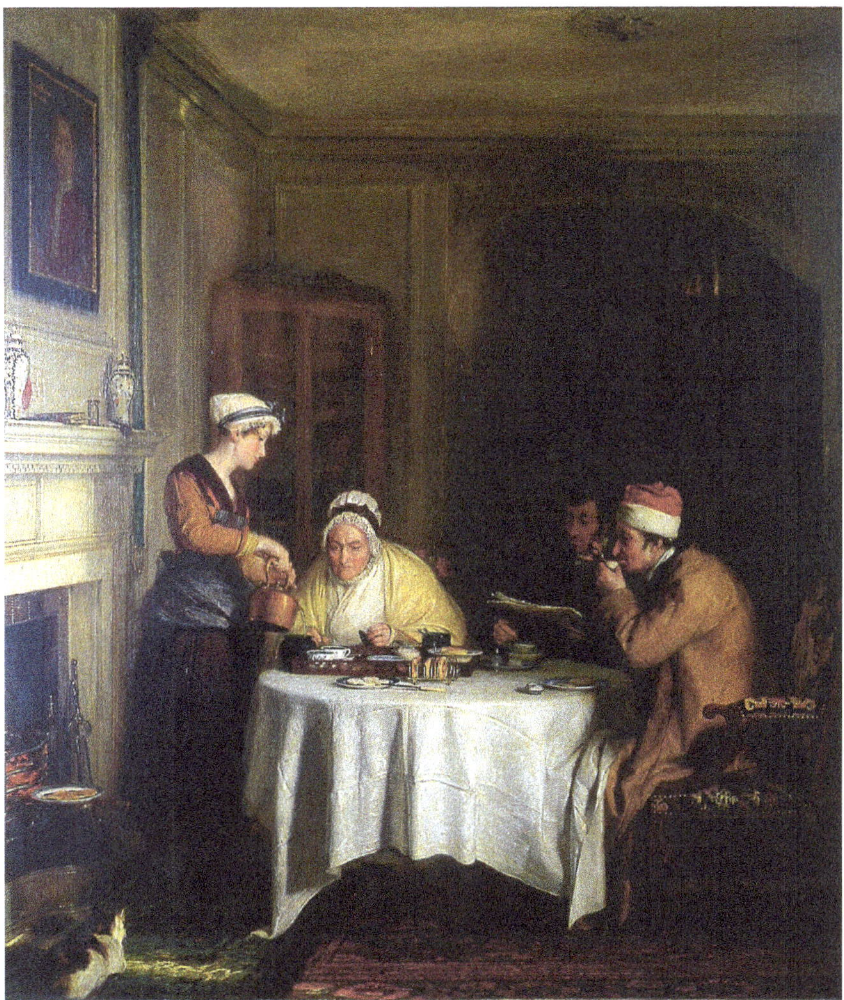

FIGURE 4.8 *Sir David Wilkie,* The Breakfast, *1817. Sutherland Dunrobin Trust, Dunrobin Castle.*

spaces. A young maid, her pale complexion highlighted with glowing pink cheeks, serves her mistress, while a cat snoozes next to the glowing grate in the lower left-hand corner. In a letter to the Earl of Leven Wilkie wrote, 'it has no story in it, but as it contains a great number of objects that look very pleasing upon canvas & as the family are supposed to be in good circumstances it affords the means of conveying an idea in the Picture of the most complete English comfort'.[55] Wilkie's gloss on the picture suggests that the artist himself understood the profusion of objects in the private interior as an index of concepts like Englishness, comfort and domesticity.

In March 1817, Wilkie wrote to fellow painter Benjamin Robert Haydon to mark completion of *The Breakfast.*

> The Marquis and Marchioness of Stafford have been to call and are exceedingly satisfied with my picture. I am to take it to their Gallery and see it beside some of the old pictures before it goes to the exhibition. It is now so far finished that I am at work upon other things.[56]

Wilkie was handsomely paid by the Marquess for his efforts. He wrote to his patron in July, 'My picture of The Breakfast I have had this morning the pleasure of delivering at Cleveland House. The groom of the chambers has paid me, by your lordship's desire, 400l. for it, a sum which, as it exceeds the price, 350 guineas, I engaged to paint the picture for, I have received as a liberal mark of your lordship's approbation of the work'.[57]

The Breakfast was one of only a handful of British pictures by living artists to be displayed at Cleveland House during the 1810s. Although Old Masters were the primary source of the gallery's prestige, during the Napoleonic Wars Stafford had begun to balance his collection somewhat by purchasing or commissioning paintings from contemporary British artists. As discussed earlier in this chapter, these commissions also suggest an increasing openness to understanding contemporary British artists within the context of their historical and European predecessors. Wilkie's work exhibited the anecdotal charm of subject painting as well as the gravitas and ambition of history painting, making him an obvious choice to join Wilson and Turner representing the best of British art on the gallery's walls. However, as Nicholas Tromans has noted, *The Breakfast* demonstrated neither painterly ambition nor the impulse to heroicize the daily lives of ordinary people that originally made his work such a sensation.[58] Critics were unenthusiastic and *The Breakfast* has never been considered amongst Wilkie's most significant or memorable work.[59] Even so, thanks to Wilkie's reputation and, perhaps, the status of his patron, *The Breakfast* garnered several long notices in the papers at the time of its exhibition at the Royal Academy. Robert Hunt, reviewing in *The Examiner*, began with faint praise: 'This is a much less interesting subject than most which Mr. Wilkie chooses, for it is a portraiture of body and bodily action with but a glimmering of mind'.[60] Yet Hunt simultaneously drew attention to Wilkie's gift for bringing a scene of 'domestic realities' so convincingly to life:

> Though the *Breakfast* might have been additionally enlivened by an audience listening to a reader of the newspaper, or debating on its contents, more than by the gentleman so relishingly sipping an egg, by the old lady carefully watching the filling of the tea-pot and by the quiet paper reader, – yet these are such counterparts of vitality, such domestic realities, that they relieve the feelings, after looking at so many sophisticated canvasses as crowd an Exhibition room; and the Breakfast is a refreshment still more welcome, from the pretty, modest maid who brings it in and who holds the kettle. She is a portrait of moral and personal graces, of innocence and beauty.[61]

Hunt locates the picture's charm in its modesty and, by implication, its lack of sophistication in comparison to many of the other canvasses filling the exhibition room that year. He also draws attention to the way in which ordinary household objects – tea-pot, kettle, egg in its cup – communicate much of its meaning.

Despite any reservations critics felt when the picture was at the Royal Academy, it was praised after being moved to Cleveland House. James Elmes' *Annals of the Fine Arts*, a publication that fervently encouraged British patrons to support British artists, called Wilkie's 'Breakfast scene, now at Cleveland-house, one of the best, of his best style'.[62] A few months later, the *Annals* more pointedly praised the appearance of a contemporary British picture amongst Cleveland House's distinguished collection of Old Masters:

> We congratulate Lord Stafford on the appearance of Wilkie's picture of the Breakfast Scene, in his noble Gallery, which is just opened to his friends; and we congratulate Wilkie himself on the appearance of this picture at Cleveland-house. It keeps its place in the presence of the finest pictures of the Dutch school; and it was a most gratifying sight to us, to see a picture of the British school of art honouring, not disgracing the walls, of a noble mansion.[63]

To those disposed to see it as such, *The Breakfast* was an example of contemporary British painting that could hold its own in a collection that emphasized continental Old Masters. More importantly, it was a proof of concept for the gallery itself. Once artists had access to studying the works of the masters, the British School would prove itself worthy of inclusion in a collection of national and international significance.

Yet in the wake of the scandalous murder trial in Inverness, the 'domestic realities' that Robert Hunt detected in Wilkie's picture must have been understood in the context of the metaphorical language of Clearance. Landlords' legal right to move or destroy the dwellings of their tenants was at the heart of the controversy of Clearance; the house as an emblem of domesticity was embedded in the very principle of clearance itself. The *Oxford English Dictionary's* definition of 'clearance', which refers specifically to the removal of 'old houses' and 'inhabitants', attributes the first use of this term to Henry Mayhew's *London Labour and the London Poor*, an illustrated book of essays concerned with the situation of the London working and impoverished classes published in 1851.[64] The term 'clearance' itself was not yet in common usage in the late Georgian period. Instead 'eviction' and 'removal' were commonly used during the period of the most aggressive improvements on the Sutherland estate. Both 'eviction' and 'removal' evoke dismantling domestic arrangements and uprooting people from traditional homesteads. In the early nineteenth century the term 'eviction' had an explicit legal connotation of 'the action of evicting or dispossessing a person of property', a meaning which is still felt in its modern day usage to refer to the eviction of tenants from land or housing.[65] Similarly, 'removal' suggests the 'act of transferring the furniture and other movable property of a household to a new residence', as well as the act of moving a person or thing from one place to another.[66] These terms suggest that the crux of conflict on the Sutherland estate was the moving of people from their houses without their consent and the destruction of dwellings which were, to their Highland occupants, homes. Tying together the hundreds of disparate accounts of events in the Highlands, the imagery of 'houses', 'homes' and the comfort of the 'cottage' are a near-constant refrain.

The apparently rude state of Highland dwellings in the period immediately predating the Sutherland clearances had often been given as one of the most pressing reasons for clearance to proceed. Advocates of improvement claimed that the tenants' housing was dirty and unsafe and the language and imagery they employed to describe it reflects that view. James Loch was the foremost agent of improvement on the Sutherland estate; he characterized the houses, which typically took the form of turf huts, as lodgings of 'miserable description'.[67] He wrote:

> It was impossible that it should ever be swept; and when the accumulation of filth rendered the place uninhabitable, another hut was erected in the vicinity of the old one. The old rafters were used in the construction of the new cottage and that which was abandoned, formed a valuable collection of manure for the next crop.[68]

Loch's view was that these homes are literally disposable, to be composted into manure to fertilize crops once they are no longer fit for human habitation. Robert Southey, who was no fan of Highland landlords, described such cottages succinctly as 'men-sties'.[69] Writers who took a sympathetic view of Highland dwellings deployed the language of home and domesticity to highlight the pathos inherent in the destruction of Highlanders' houses. One witness later recalled:

> There was . . . much personal suffering from their having to pull down their houses and carry away the timber of them to erect houses on their new possession, which houses they had to inhabit immediately on being

> covered in and in the meantime to live and sleep in the open air, except for a few who might be fortunate enough to get an unoccupied barn or a shed from some of their charitable newcome neighbors.[70]

Such descriptions did not conjure the image of impoverished tenants desperate for assistance, but instead of self-sufficient people whose homes were being destroyed for no discernable reason.

The imagery of the home as a marker of the stability and morality of the working classes had become a staple of genre painting by the late eighteenth century. The juxtaposition between images of poverty and self-reliance quoted above recalls paired genre pictures like George Morland's *The Pleasures of Industry* and *The Miseries of Idleness* (see Figures. 4.9 and 4.10). Morland uses the family and the domestic interior as shorthand for the relative merits of the hardworking vs the idle poor, a discourse which was a powerful subtext to the Clearances. The landlord's role was paternalistic; part of the stated goal of clearance was to root out the 'ignorant and savage' among the tenantry and improve the lives of the 'industrious and diligent', who 'deserved careful nurture'.[71] The Staffords' representative James Loch became infamous for

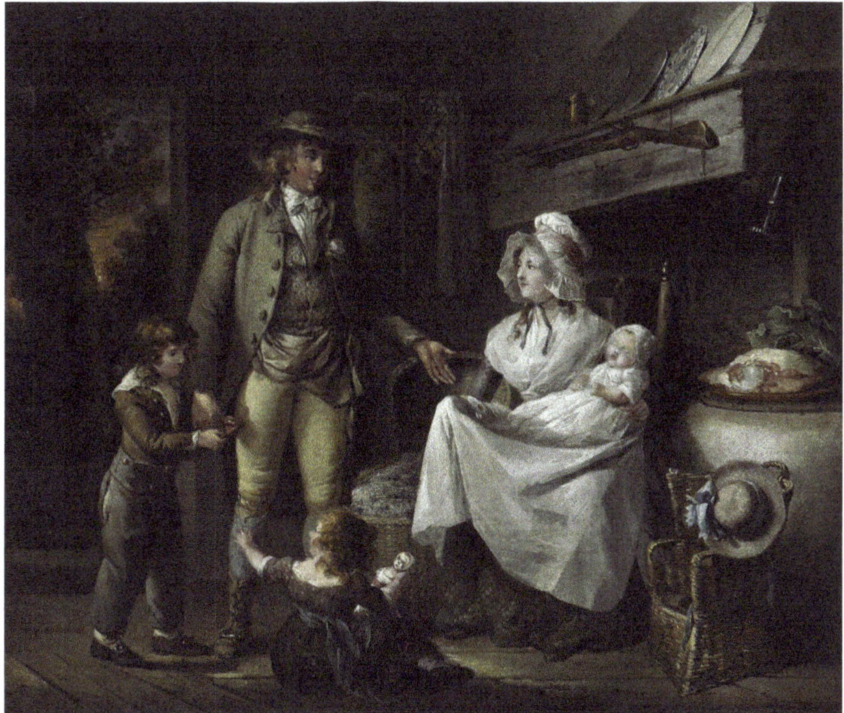

FIGURE 4.9 *George Morland,* The Comforts of Industry, *oil on canvas, before 1790. National Galleries Scotland, Hon Alexander and Lady Margaret Shaw Gift 1935.*

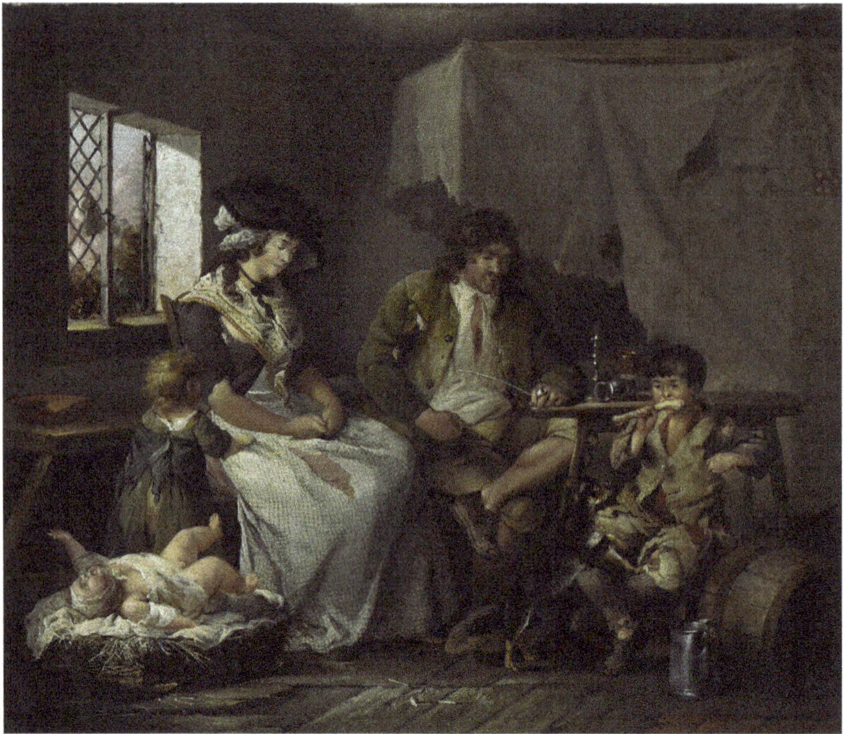

FIGURE 4.10 *George Morland,* The Miseries of Idleness, *oil on canvas, before 1790. National Galleries Scotland, Hon Alexander and Lady Margaret Shaw Gift 1935.*

apologist accounts of the clearances in Sutherland, making frequent recourse to the spectre of 'idleness' to explain why improvements had been necessary. He wrote that the Highlanders had led 'a life of irregular exertion, with intervals of sloth', continuing, 'they deemed no comfort worth the possessing, which was to be acquired at the price of regular industry; no improvement worthy of adoption, if it was to be obtained at the expense of sacrificing the customs or leaving the homes of their ancestors'.[72] As for those who preferred emigration to being relocated to coastal fishing villages, Loch wrote that 'the idle and lazy alone', would contemplate this possibility.[73] It was by then widely acknowledged that many Highlanders, disinclined to accept forced movement to the coasts, were instead departing for foreign shores.

The Highlands, which had been so frequently regarded as a dirty and primitive backwater, had begun to attract more attention in the London press, much of which was now sympathetic to the Highlanders themselves. After touring Scotland in 1819, Robert Southey succinctly recorded both the popular view of what had occurred and his summation of its ethical implications:

> Here you have a quiet, thoughtful, contented, religious people, susceptible of improvement and willing to be improved. To transplant these people from their native mountain gleans to the sea coast and require them to become some cultivators, others fishermen, occupations to which they have never been accustomed – to expect a sudden and total change of habits in the existing generation, instead of gradually producing it in their children; to expel them by process of law from their black-houses and if they demur in obeying the ejectment, to oust them by setting fire to these combustible tenements – this surely is as little defensible on the score of policy as of morals.[74]

By the end of the decade, the incongruity between the deplorable living conditions in some parts of the Highlands and the London lifestyles of their landlords had become too distinct to avoid comment in the metropolitan press. One commentator questioned how Stafford, whom he described as 'a highly esteemed nobleman' and 'the general arbiter of taste' could be implicated in gravely unethical acts.[75] More pointedly, 'B.G.', writing in the *New Monthly Magazine* in 1819, delivered this crushing assessment: 'When all is amassed that law and threats of displacement can procure, the parties enriched leave the parties impoverished, to squander their earnings and to forget their woes amid the luxuries of the metropolis.'[76]

That 'improvement' might come at the expense of long-established communities and family homes formed a striking contrast with the Staffords' attempts to claim moral authority based in the domestic sphere. Even as the imagery of destroyed and abandoned houses underwrote the logic of clearance, it also conjured its double: the secure, untroubled domesticity betokened by *The Breakfast*. Wilkie's painting drew attention to the virtues the gallery promoted, aristocratic respectability and commitment to public duty, by distilling them into a straightforward image of comfortable middle-class life. *The Breakfast* bears no resemblance to daily activities as experienced by Lord or Lady Stafford, but nevertheless depicts themes of home that were emblematic of Clearance itself in a visual language that was easily interpreted by an urban audience. By commissioning this picture from Wilkie at this moment, Lord and Lady Stafford nodded to their duty to patronize living British artists, while bringing Scotland into the 'nation' that the gallery represented.

Conclusion

The language and rhetoric surrounding the Clearances had centered on the imagery of the home and its destruction. Sometimes the squalid conditions of Highland homes were evoked to provide a moral framework as a rationale for Clearance. But equally, the imagery of domesticity was mobilized as a proof of the immorality of eviction. The *Morning Chronicle* described the

Sutherland tenants as 'Driven from their native homes . . . scattered over the neighboring counties . . . and . . . extremely poor'.[77] Emigration, of course, represented the *ne plus ultra* of removal – the home was not just moved, but destroyed and abandoned, only to be rebuilt in some far-flung part of North America or Australia. It should also be noted, though it is beyond the scope of this chapter, that many Scots who emigrated found work on plantations in the American South, where the cycle of displacement and violence continued.[78]

The abandoned or demolished family home as the central metaphor of Clearance has persisted to the present. In 1963, John Prebble drew liberally on the imagery of domestic life to tie the destruction of Scottish cottages to the motives of the landlords. As he memorably put it, '[The tenants] held to the spirit of the clan when the chief was bartering it for a house in Belgravia.'[79] (Prebble likewise used a rhetorical appeal to domesticity in condemning Lady Stafford herself, writing acerbically that 'she was as English in mood and taste as the furniture of a London drawing-room', a comment which he clearly did not intend as a compliment.[80]) The image of a house in Belgravia, one of London's most expensive enclaves though it did not develop this reputation until the mid- to late-nineteenth century, pointedly draws distinctions between the daily lives of Highlanders and their landlords that Lord and Lady Stafford preferred to elide. In 2014, historian James Hunter tweeted a photograph of a ruined foundation accompanied by the text, 'Badinloskin. 200 yrs ago today Margaret MacKay died here aftr her home was burned by Sutherland factor Patrick Sellar.'[81] That a photograph of rubble in an empty field could conjure such memories two centuries later indicates how powerful the imagery of home remains in the contested history of the Highlands.

The series of commissions described in this chapter are material artifacts that memorialized the incongruity between the glamour and prestige of the gallery and the lives of working people throughout Great Britain. These objects reveal a subtle but unmistakable desire to change the subject away from Lord and Lady Stafford's actions as landlords back to their accomplishments as collectors and cultural leaders. British paintings were understood to be objects of absorbing interest for the aristocratic English collector, but at the same time, they were largely absent from metropolitan collections which were, thanks to men like Stafford, coming to represent a core element of national artistic heritage. The division of the two aspects of the collection – continental Old Masters painted by artists understood to be of international importance in the urban townhouse, 'English' pictures in the country estate – is emblematic of the division between the metropolitan aristocracy that carried out land management policy in a vacuum from the direct consequences of their actions and the tenants living in the landscape that English painting often took as its subject.

In his guidebook, John Britton implies that the country house is in many ways a more logical place for these paintings to be situated, in keeping with the widely pervasive association of the very concept of 'Englishness' with the countryside. By way of contrast, the townhouse gallery, by definition located in an urban setting, called for the installation of a broad, art historical survey to appeal to a national (and international) audience. In Chapter Five, I will explore the network of gentlemen's galleries that proliferated in London after Cleveland House opened. In the years immediately following Britain's victory in the Napoleonic Wars, an influential group of gentleman collectors sought to create a national culture of fine art focused on the space of the private house. Some found a way to highlight British artists in the context of the urban dwelling, while others continued to collect and display Old Masters. What they had in common was the drive to find a 'home' for the fine arts in the context of the private, domestic sphere, which shaped thinking about how and where paintings should be seen for generations to come.

5

'To private collections alone': The Apotheosis of the Private Gallery

In 1818, William Young Ottley's *Engravings of the Most Noble the Marquis of Stafford's Collection of Pictures in London* was published. Ottley's book represented a remarkable feat of the engraver's art. It included the set of 13 laid-out interior plans discussed in Chapter Three, as well as more than 290 individual reproductions of paintings then hanging in the gallery at Cleveland House. Engraver Peltro William Tomkins took a leading role in the project, but the efforts of nearly 30 additional artists were required to bring it to fruition over the course of ten years.[1] The sheer extent of human endeavour and capital investment in the production of such a luxurious object, not to mention its imposing physical presence, signal that the book was meant to be a public statement of Cleveland House's significance on the national – and imperial – stage. As its Dedication to King George III put it, the book's purpose was to cultivate 'the arts of elegance, the delight they afford the human mind, the importance they maintain in the empire of commerce and splendour they diffuse'.[2]

It is not surprising that Ottley was keen to establish Cleveland House's rightful position as an art gallery for the nation. Historians have conceptualized the eighteenth and early nineteenth centuries as the period of the 'birth of the museum'.[3] As discussed in Chapter One, in Britain, the drive to compete with public venues on the continent led to numerous experiments focused on making fine art accessible to the public, especially in London. These ranged from the British Institution to the Dulwich Picture Gallery to the long-hoped-for National Gallery, which opened in April 1824. After the National Gallery's founding, many national and municipal cultural institutions began to appear across the country, implementing the vision of cultural reformers who regarded them as vital to the creation of a well-educated and well-disciplined general public.[4] By the end of the century, museums and public galleries were widespread, offering education and entertainment to visitors from a wide range of occupations and social classes.

Yet even as the concept of the public art museum was developing in fits and starts toward the end of the Georgian era, private art galleries were becoming integral to London's art world. Led by Stafford's example and motivated by the general sense of patriotism and optimism that attended Britain's victory in the Napoleonic Wars, gentlemen from a range of social ranks and tastes began opening their houses and collections to the public. Supporters of private townhouse galleries promoted them as accessible urban spaces for looking at art, a cultural gap that other venues had inadequately filled.[5] By 1819 the number and quality of private galleries had increased dramatically. The *Literary Gazette* noted:

> It is gratifying to find that with peace we find the arts of peace cultivated in the manner which is most likely to ensure them general patronage and success. The Marquis of Stafford's Collection, Mr. Hope's and Mr. Angerstein's, had considerable effect in calling the attention of the fashionable world to the splendor which the Arts were calculated to shed upon their Patrons and the noble decorations they furnished to the mansions of the great.[6]

The ranks of collectors whose houses were open to the public now included professional men like John Soane, who opened his dwelling in Lincoln's Inn Fields full of paintings, casts, genuine antiquities and architectural models to students in the early 1810s. A few enjoyed regular publicity in the press, especially Sir John Leicester and Walter Ramsden Fawkes, collectors of contemporary British art who opened their houses in 1818 and 1819 respectively. The phrase 'noble decorations' to refer to these men's collections points to the elision between 'Fine Art' and interior décor that often characterized descriptions of private galleries in this period.

Chapter Five will explore the cultural terrain upon which both 'private gallery' and 'public museum' sought to establish themselves as the best possible system for collecting and exhibiting fine art to eager and rapidly expanding audiences. In her work on strategies for display in public museums in the later nineteenth and twentieth centuries, Charlotte Klonk has observed that, in general, histories of art institutions have leapt from what she calls the 'market stall' model to the 'spiritual/non-material' model without dealing with the messy territory in between.[7] This chapter aims to wade deeply into this messy territory, describing how, as support for the idea of a state-owned National Gallery grew, a vocal (and powerful) contingent maintained that the burgeoning network of private townhouse galleries outlined above was the best system for exhibiting important artworks to the public.

Ultimately, the public museum as an institutional type was buoyed by political and cultural trends that aristocrats and private collectors were unable to hold at bay. Yet collectors, with the support of their boosters, artists and journalists, successfully established the notion that private interiors were ideal spaces for looking at art and that private spaces promoted true connoisseurship in ways that bustling public institutions never would. This assumption, which fuels a powerful counter-narrative to the dominance enjoyed by state- and municipal museums in the cultural landscape, continues to operate as an influential undercurrent in discussions of national patrimony and cultural heritage. The idea has informed a range of developments from the late nineteenth century to the present, from the founding of the National Trust in 1895 to the resurgence of interest in stately homes as sites of 'national identity' in the mid to late twentieth century, to the proliferation of 'private museums' in the twenty-first.

1806–1819: Private Galleries Proliferate

Before embarking on his project to catalogue all of the paintings on display at Cleveland House, William Young Ottley was a prominent collector in his own right and an amateur writer on art. The son of a West Indian plantation owner, Ottley spent much of the 1790s in Rome where he was able to collect important works of Italian art and assisted others in his circle in forming their own collections. He returned to London in 1799 and how exactly he became involved in the project to catalogue the collection at Cleveland House is unclear. However, in March 1807, Joseph Farington reported that 'Longman & Rees in Paternoster Row, have issued proposals for a publication of Prints from celebrated Pictures . . . the whole to be under the management of Ottley & Tresham [R.A.]; & it is sd. The former is to have 1000 guineas for His trouble, & the latter 500'.[8] Ottley's junior partner in the project was Irish history painter Henry Tresham and, in 1808, they published a prospectus for *The British Gallery of Pictures.*

As outlined in Ottley and Tresham's prospectus, *The British Gallery of Pictures* was an enormously ambitious enterprise. Hand-coloured engravings based on the 'all the best and most interesting Paintings' in British collections were to be issued in monthly instalments. The list of men whose pictures were to be engraved for the project included such illustrious collectors as Stafford, Carlisle and Grosvenor, the Marquis of Lansdowne, Lord Northwick and Lord Radstock. Subscribers would receive two engraved plates and descriptive letter-press on a monthly basis, at a range of price points depending on the size of the paper and the option to have the engravings 'highly finished in Colours, in imitation of the original pictures'.[9] PW Tomkins was listed as the head engraver on the project and engravings that had already been completed were available for review at Tomkins' shop at 49 New Bond Street.

In time the scope of Ottley's project expanded well beyond the initial prospectus. (Tresham, who was in poor health and died in 1814, left the project early on.)[10] Instead of presenting engravings after only the most important pictures from each collection, Ottley now proposed to catalogue and illustrate each collection in full. The *catalogue raisonné* of the Stafford collection was to be the first in a series of such *catalogues raisonnés* that would document every significant private collection in Britain – what Ottley called 'all the Paintings in every collection of magnitude in the United Kingdom' – for the benefit of the public. Undertaken on such a scale, Ottley proclaimed, the plan 'may truly be termed NATIONAL', sure to stir 'patriotic feelings' in all who encounter it.[11]

Ottley was developing his project at a moment when several prominent figures had begun to argue that publicly funded support for the arts and more particularly, a state-funded art museum, was a necessary step for the nation. The founding of the *Musée du Louvre* in 1793, which came into focus for British travellers during a brief period of peace in 1803, had posed a cultural challenge that many were keen to emulate.[12] In 1805, Royal Academician Martin Archer Shee gave eloquent voice to this view, writing: 'A few fine examples of the different schools, collected with judgment and placed within the reach of the student . . . is a desideratum of the highest consequence to the advancement of British art and an object certainly not unworthy the interference of the government to effect'.[13] Shee's *Rhymes on Art* found an eager audience amongst influential people and contributed to the general mood that somehow prominent collectors needed to find way to answer the Louvre. The British Institution, in which Stafford took a leading role, represented one possible response to this challenge, the gallery at Cleveland House itself, another.[14] But these were both private enterprises, organized and managed at the convenience of rich and connected collectors like Stafford. Shee argued that British artists sorely needed a venue where they could study great works of art without the necessity of foreign travel – or visits to private collections which depended on the largesse of the collector. As he wrote, the 'gazing groups of periodical visitors' who gained entry to 'our celebrated collections' gained little more than a 'tantalizing glimpse' of the treasures they held. In his view, seeing paintings 'in the eagerness of hurried examination' would neither 'satisfy curiosity nor improve taste'.[15]

Schemes to establish a National Gallery had been floating around for many years, even before the founding of the Louvre introduced a sense of urgency to the discussion. Decades earlier radical MP John Wilkes had proposed that Parliament purchase the Houghton Collection, a group of paintings assembled by the former Prime Minister, Robert Walpole, as the kernel of a state-sponsored National Gallery. Instead the pictures were purchased by Catherine II of Russia (Catherine the Great) and bundled away to the Hermitage in 1779.[16] During the 1790s, private ventures like Boydell's Shakespeare Gallery attempted to create spaces that were freely open to the public and celebrated 'English' culture, as represented by contemporary paintings after Shakespearean subjects.[17] There were also a number of idiosyncratic efforts to create a state-owned public art gallery. In 1804, Joseph, Count Truchsess de Zeyl-Wurzach opened a picture gallery in the New Road, London and advertised a subscription scheme (suggested donation: £5) to turn the gallery into a 'Grand and Permanent National Exhibition'.[18] Truchsess claimed to be an aristocrat attempting to recoup some of his losses from the French Revolution; the guidebook accompanying the exhibition urged potential donors to consider 'the everlasting honour that must accrue to individuals, from having concurred in the creation of so useful an establishment, that every public-spirited Briton is invited to become a subscriber or donator'.[19] Truchsess' plan did not gain traction.

For proponents of a state-owned gallery, most frustrating of all had to be the numerous, probably cavalier, promises made by the Prince Regent, later King George IV, to open his collection to the public. As Prince of Wales, George was a founding patron of the British Institution and in subsequent years he made periodic promises that he would make sizable donations of both pictures and exhibition space to the Royal Academy. Joseph Farington wrote in 1812, for example, that 'the Prince Regent intended to give Carlton House to the Royal Academy'.[20] Around 1820, when George became King, a flurry of rumours circulated that he intended to commission architect John Nash to design a new building to display pictures from the royal collection, presumably for public access. Then, in 1822, came 'a categorical assurance that he would present much of his own collection as the nucleus of a new national gallery'.[21] Again, nothing came of this promise. Finally, after 1824, he raised hopes that he would donate a group of 164 pictures from Carlton House, which was by that time slated for demolition, to the new National Gallery. Instead, these pictures were hung in the private picture gallery Nash designed for Buckingham Palace, to which the public did not have access.

In the face of these challenges, the public was increasingly aware of a growing network of private galleries in London – and throughout the country – that were open to visitors at least some of the time. The opening of Cleveland House in 1806 had acted as a catalyst encouraging collectors to open their art-filled residences to the public and, in the subsequent 15 years, their numbers increased steadily. It is difficult to trace which houses were open and exactly when, but guidebooks offer some general insight into the state of affairs over the course of this period. The first edition of John Feltham's popular guidebook, *The Picture of London*, appeared in 1802 and named 18 'private collections of our nobility and gentry', beginning with the Queen's Palace in St James's Park and concluding with Charles Townley, whose collection of sculpture and antiquities was well known to connoisseurs (see Figure 1.18). According to the *Picture of London*, a subset of these, including Townley's house, Thomas Hope's house and the Duke of Bridgewater's original gallery at Cleveland House, were accessible 'by application'.[22] Feltham died in 1803, but his guidebook continued though many editions. The 1809 edition of *The Picture of London* listed an additional 16 collections, including those kept at the largest freestanding townhouses including Northumberland House, Devonshire House and Marlborough House. John Julius Angerstein's collection, displayed in his relatively small terraced house and described as being 'formed at the greatest expence, in proportion to its numbers', also joined their ranks.[23] Angerstein emigrated from Russia in the mid-eighteenth century and made a fortune, in part as a key player in the development of insurer Lloyd's of London. Angerstein began assembling his collection, which was located in his townhouse at 100 Pall Mall and included masterpieces including Sebastiano del Piombo's *The Raising of Lazarus* (1517–1519) and Raphael's *Portrait of Pope Julius II* (1511), available to visitors under a scheme of admission following the model set by Stafford sometime in the early 1810s; it was his collection that later formed the nucleus of the National Gallery.[24] The 1809 edition contained a list of slightly less grand houses and collections, including those owned by prominent art-world figures like Sir George Beaumont, Mr Richard Payne Knight and Mr Prince Hoare; it also appended a list of collections found 'around the metropolis' – that is to say, in suburban or rural areas near the urban centre – such as Chiswick House, Strawberry Hill and Hampton Court. Of this group, eleven were explicitly described as accessible to the public in some fashion.[25] When the enlarged and improved edition of the *Picture of London* appeared in the mid-1820s, with John Britton as editor, an exhaustive list was no longer included; instead the 28 most noteworthy galleries were individually written up.[26] In all cases, the gallery at Cleveland House was described as 'perhaps, the finest in England' and was always listed first after the royal palaces. In later editions, the 'perhaps' was edited out.[27]

The escalating numbers suggest that collectors were beginning to regard the opening of houses to the public to be an essential aspect of the performance of public duty or, at a minimum, a beneficial public relations exercise. Implicit in the size and ambition of Ottley's project to collect all of the great pictures of Britain in print form was the notion that collections like the ones described above were effectively usurping the role of any theoretical future national gallery. Ottley appears to take for granted that none of the attempts to create a state-owned gallery were likely to succeed, particularly in a country where the ownership of private property – understood as not only land but also houses, pictures, furniture, jewels and other possessions of value – was the bedrock upon which the very notion of English liberty was founded, seen as a natural right and mark of Britain's civilization, in contrast to other countries and parts of the world.[28] As late as 1818, six years before the National Gallery opened to the public, Ottley foresaw no possibility – or hoped to forestall the possibility – that the collection of an extravagantly wealthy English peer would make its way into public ownership:

> It may be confidently asserted, that at this period no country in Europe contains so many valuable Cabinet Pictures of the Great Masters as Great Britain; nor is there any in which their beauties are more intensely felt or

> more judiciously appreciated. To unite the most select of these in a grand NATIONAL GALLERY, however desirable to the lovers of art, is a task beyond the limits of possibility, as long as private opulence and security continue to be the happy results of the public tranquility.[29]

Ottley's appeal to enduring British values of 'private opulence' and 'security' are an implicit reference to France and the fate of the Louvre. After Napoleon's defeat, many artworks from the Louvre's collection were repatriated to their sites of origin; in retrospect, the Louvre could appear more cautionary tale than cultural achievement. John Scott, editor of the *Champion* newspaper, described the Louvre under Napoleon as 'rich . . . in the sole survivors of general wrecks and ruins' and wrote that 'magnificent galleries of foreign productions do little or no credit to the mind of a country and perhaps it would not be too much to say, that they are positively injurious to its mind', because they would encourage 'acquirement as opposed to genius . . . imitation as opposed to invention'.[30] These are similar to arguments that critics like William Hazlitt, as we shall see later in this chapter, used to argue against art academies and other institutions in favour of the sublime, near-spiritual experience to be found in private galleries.

Ottley presents 'private opulence' and 'security' as mutually-reinforcing ideals, the prevalence of which render obsolete any necessity for a state-owned collection of art. Under such circumstances, a series of *catalogues raisonnés*, available to all, could create a virtual National Gallery, at least for anyone who could afford to buy them or otherwise access them. Ottley's project sought to bring the collections of Britain together in one place as an alternative to the tour of town and country houses that would otherwise be required to see these pictures, 'bring[ing] into one point of view the riches dispersed through such a number of magnificent collections as are possessed by the Nobility and Gentry of these kingdoms'.[31] Allowing a network of private galleries to accumulate and display important collections of art to the public permitted Britain to amass cultural treasures without the trauma of state intervention and to embrace an ideology of 'Englishness' that prioritized the actions of private individuals as the best route to progress in the public sphere.

'Englishness' and the Private Art Gallery

Sometime in the 1810s, Thomas Rowlandson made a sketch of a gentleman's top-lit art gallery (see Figure 5.1).[32] Rowlandson depicts a room that is tidily domestic and welcoming of polite sociability. A lady in a fashionable white muslin gown reads in an armchair next to a crackling fire. Other visitors discuss the paintings, while in the centre of the image, a group assembles around a library table to examine books that could well be the very *catalogues raisonnés* that made collections like the one depicted accessible

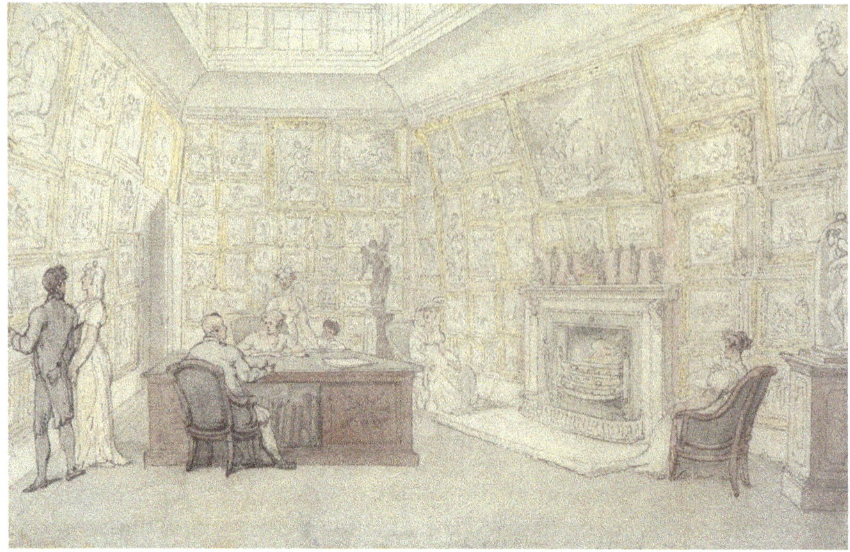

FIGURE 5.1 *Thomas Rowlandson, 1756–1827,* A Gentleman's Art Gallery, *undated. Watercolour and graphite with pen and grey ink and pen and brown ink on medium, slightly textured, cream wove paper. Yale Center for British Art, Paul Mellon Collection, B1981.25.2682.*

to the public. The social encounters depicted are easy yet refined, implying that the gallery nurtures familial relationships while simultaneously exhibiting important examples of painting, sculpture and print to visitors.

Although representations of private art galleries are relatively scarce, those that do exist, like Rowlandson's, embrace the notion that these were first and foremost social spaces. Stafford's earliest supporters, like John Britton, had insisted on the notion that Cleveland House was a private space even while promoting it as a public one of national interest, as discussed in Chapter One. Ottley's catalogue attempted to walk a similar line, depicting Cleveland House simultaneously as private treasure and national resource. As discussed in detail in Chapter Three, Tomkins' laid-out plans prioritized the decoration of the interior as a signifier of the gallery's identity as private space. His view of the Anti-Room to the Old Gallery, for example, depicts a relatively small room supplied with a suite of sofas and chairs facilitating conversation and rest (see Figure 5.2). The image features a black lacquer cabinet supporting an object that may represent Chinese blue-and-white porcelain which, in turn, partially obscures a mirror encased in an exuberant gilded rococo frame. Though many objects in the gallery at Cleveland House had been designed and made by Tatham to reflect the inspiration of classical antiquity, the aristocratic interior of the period usually included objects that referred to the wider world beyond as a mark of its owner's taste and sophistication. In the context of Ottley's ambitious project, images of the interior became ballast anchoring the gallery to the private realm, even as the catalogue's prospectus and size implied that it functioned as a resource making art available for readers across a range of social classes and, in theory, to all parts of the empire. Certainly, many saw the growing empire and its inhabitants as equally important constituencies for the gallery as those living 'at home' in the British Isles. In 1812 one observer wrote, 'The Stafford, Carlisle and Grosvenor collections of pictures; the Spencer, Marlborough, Devonshire, Bridgwater and Pembroke libraries are national treasures, becoming a people who are contending for the empire of the world.'[33]

Writers and artists who promoted gentlemen's galleries enthusiastically adopted the viewpoint that luxurious domestic interiors could operate as signs of masculine virtue and public spiritedness. The representation of two houses in particular offer a case study of the visual and verbal language of

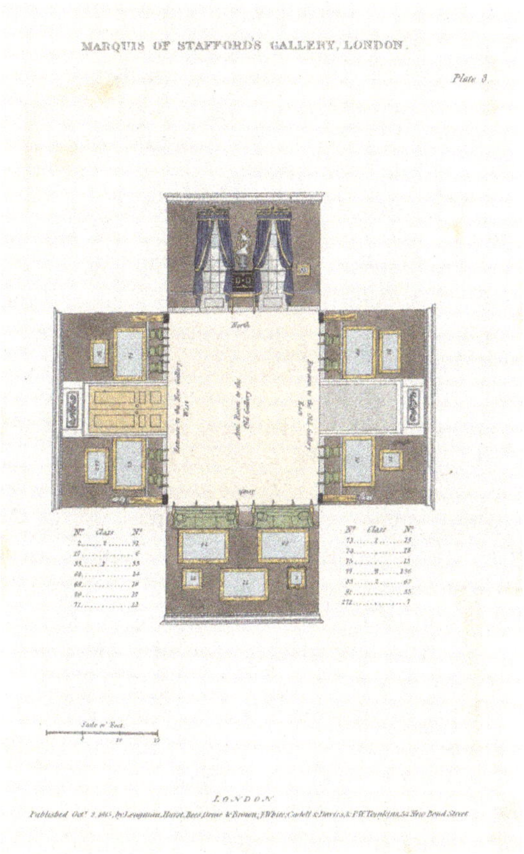

FIGURE 5.2 *[PW Tomkins, engr.] 'Anti-Room to the Old Gallery' from William Young Ottley,* Engravings of the Most Noble the Marquis of Stafford's collection of pictures in London, *London: Longman, Hurst, Rees, Orme, and Brown, 1818, engraving. Yale Center for British Art, Paul Mellon Collection.*

domesticity that their boosters were keen to promote. Since the opening of Cleveland House, few galleries had received sustained attention from journalists until Sir John Leicester, later created Baron de Tabley and Walter Fawkes, a Yorkshire landowner, opened their houses to visitors in 1818 and 1819, respectively. What set them apart and attracted the particular notice of periodical writers was that both men were ardent patrons of native-born artists whose galleries focused almost exclusively on British painting. Leicester and Fawkes both belonged to the social class just below the peerage. Leicester was the first-born son of a Baronet, the lowest-ranking hereditary title which did not bestow the right to sit in the House of Lords. Even so, Leicester sat for some time as an elected Member of Parliament as did Fawkes, who was born to Yorkshire gentry. Focusing on British art may have been an entry point into the world of London collectors which, at the beginning of the century, was still dominated by extraordinarily wealthy and high-ranking people.[34] Certainly, both were taking part in a more general trend toward patriotic or national-minded collecting that gained traction after the 1790s.[35] The patronage of British art had garnered increasing acceptance as a tool to improve the 'taste' of the British public; to improve public taste would in turn improve British design and manufactures and encourage international commerce.

The culture of collecting at the turn of the nineteenth century, then, characterized Leicester and Fawkes as patriotic, public-minded men. Fawkes specialized in collecting landscape painting, widely embraced as a genre in which British artists particularly excelled.[36] An early and regular patron of JMW Turner, Fawkes displayed Turner's work at his house in Hill Street and at his country seat, Farnley Hall. Leicester's collection was more varied and included works by artists like Turner and Benjamin West in a range of genres from landscape and portraits to historical and mythological subjects and genre painting.[37] This last category included one of Leicester's most-prized pictures, Thomas Gainsborough's *The Cottage Door* (1780), which was famously displayed in a 'tent room' in his gallery.[38] These men's focus on collecting the productions of native-born British painters attracted significant attention from fellow collectors and connoisseurs, artists and the periodical press. The galleries and their owners alike were warmly embraced by the contemporary press, who lauded them for their devotion to the English school and to patriotic values.[39]

In order to display their growing collections Leicester and Fawkes created galleries in townhouses situated within a short distance of Cleveland House. Their focus on British art notwithstanding, the principle underpinning their galleries had much in common with the aristocratic examples to which they were occasionally compared. Fawkes's gallery occupied a suite of rooms on the first floor of his house at 45 Grosvenor Place. Similarly, Leicester hired architect Thomas Cundy Sr to convert the library at 24 Hill Street, Mayfair, into a gallery featuring a circular lantern after acquiring the house in 1805, as Dongho Chun has demonstrated.[40] Leicester opened his gallery to the public in 1818 on many of the same terms set by Stafford at Cleveland House.[41] Prospective visitors were required to apply for tickets, though in practice, as at Cleveland House, most successful applicants were already part of his extended circle.[42] Leicester's gallery was open from one to four o'clock on Monday afternoons from March to May and, according to some reports, could be visited by 500 people in a single afternoon. On 20 May 1819 *The Morning Post* reported that more than 700 people had visited on its final opening date of the season.[43]

Following the pattern set by other galleries, Leicester and Fawkes commissioned catalogues that served both the practical functions inherent to guidebooks and the less tangible functions of social gatekeeping. Like Britton's, guidebooks to Leicester and Fawkes's galleries included images of their interiors. Sir John Leicester commissioned artist John Buckler, known for architectural views, to record both the gallery at his country estate Tabley House and the newly built town gallery at Hill Street (see Figure 5.3). Buckler depicts a room defined by architectural and decorative references to classical antiquity and outfitted with skylighting, picture rails, chandeliers and an array of furnishings. Buckler's view, made around 1806, depicts Leicester's gallery soon after completion and furnished with an array of seats and tables scattered around the room as if a larger party has only recently left. A trio of ladies in fashionable Grecian-style day dresses look at

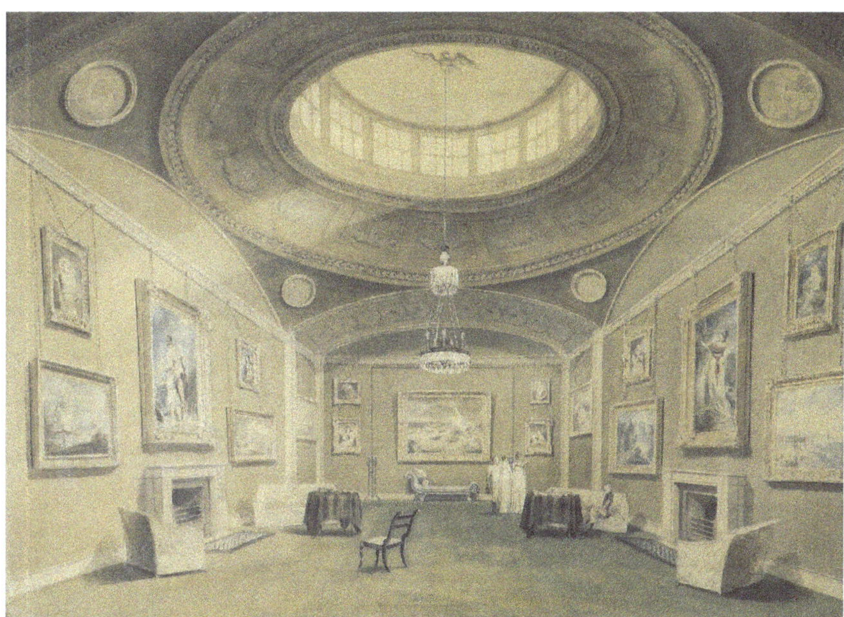

FIGURE 5.3 *John Buckler,* Sketch of Sir John Leicester's Gallery of Pictures by British Artists, Hill Street, Berkeley Square, *1806. Pencil & wash on paper. Tabley House Collection, University of Manchester, UK. Bridgeman Images.*

the paintings while a gentleman seated nearby looks on. Made prior to the publication of Smith's view of the New Gallery at Cleveland House in 1808, Buckler's image understands the gallery as a social space in which viewing of pictures is but one amongst a range of possible activities.

Likewise, an image of Fawkes' gallery was made for one of the two catalogues of his collection that appeared in 1819.[44] Fawkes commissioned JMW Turner to make a view of the Large Drawing Room in his house at 45 Grosvenor Place, which was subsequently engraved by Henry Moses for inclusion in the guidebook printed by Benjamin Bensley.[45] Turner depicts the room as almost strangely full of furniture and seating in a range of types, left at odd angles as if a large party has just departed the room. Particularly unusual is the large square settee – an object which may almost certainly be described as an 'ottoman' – at the centre of the image. Turner's original watercolour indicates that the ottoman was upholstered in blue-and-white striped fabric matching the other armchairs, stools and sofas in the room (see Figure 5.4). As I have written elsewhere, ottomans became popular in the early nineteenth century thanks to their exotic associations and may have been considered particularly appropriate for private but social spaces. In 1808, furniture designer George Smith wrote, 'Ottomans are particularly

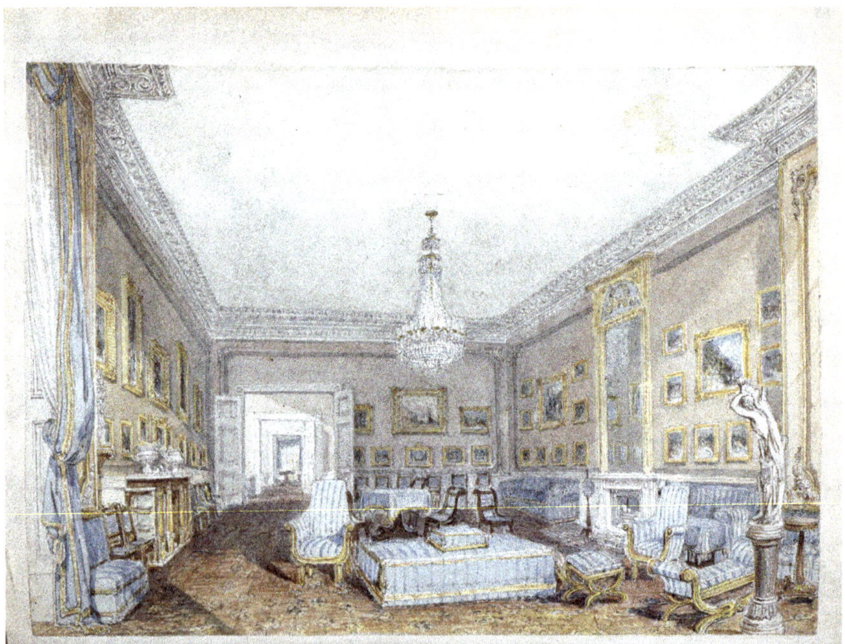

FIGURE 5.4 *Joseph Mallord William Turner*, Drawing Room of 45 Grosvenor Place, *1819. Watercolour and pen and ink on paper, 152 × 216mm. Private collection. Photo: Tate.*

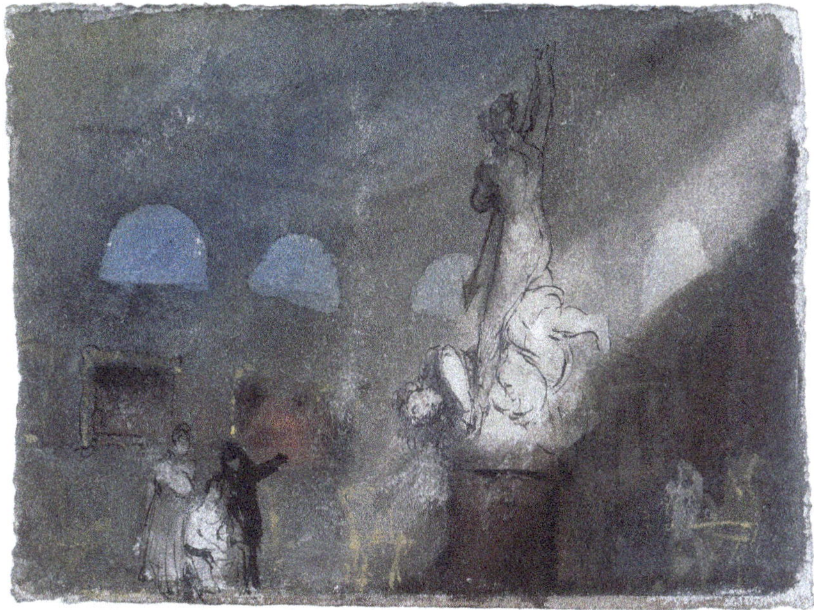

FIGURE 5.5 *Joseph Mallord William Turner,* The North Gallery at Night: Figures Contemplating Flaxman's Statue, 'St. Michael Overcoming Satan', *1827. Ink, watercolour and bodycolour on paper, 141 × 192mm. Tate, accepted by the nation as part of the Turner Bequest, 1856. Photo: Tate.*

useful in Picture Galleries, their projection from the wall preventing the pictures being fingered, which is too often practiced'.[46] Its presence in Fawkes' gallery nods to the room's quasi-public status. Turner's view is an outlier when considered in the context of other gallery interior views made in the early nineteenth century. Turner had a close relationship with his patron, who had purchased well over 200 of his works by the time this image was made and the view of the gallery's interior, which also documents Turner's own pictures displayed on its walls, must also to an extent reflect the intimacy of this particular relationship. It is perhaps more reminiscent of the views Turner made of interiors at Petworth House nearly a decade later, which captured the chaotic idiosyncrasy of that household's domestic arrangements through loosely painted impressionistic sketches (see Figure 5.5).[47]

Buckler and Turner's views share a sense of the active connoisseurship and lively conversation that flowed from the domestic setting that gentlemen's galleries were thought to enable. The galleries are depicted as lived spaces where furniture is moved around with use and people circulate. About a decade after Buckler's view was made, Leicester's gallery was engraved again for inclusion in a guidebook written by William Paulet Carey. Comparing

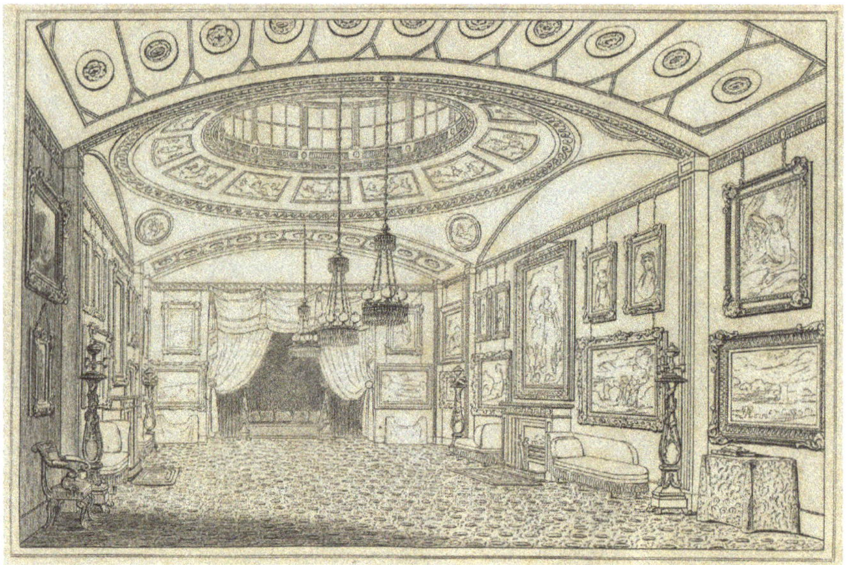

FIGURE 5.6 *Anon, Frontispiece from* A Descriptive Catalogue of a Collection of Paintings by British Artists, in the Possession of Sir John Fleming Leicester, Bart. *(London: J Nichols, 1819). National Gallery of Art, Washington, DC.*

this view with Buckler's earlier one gives the impression that as the process of readying the gallery for the 'public' took place, there was also an attendant sense that some of the inherent untidiness of social intercourse had to be organized and arranged. This unsigned view of the gallery's interior depicts the room empty, ready for ticketed visitors, furniture arranged neatly along the walls of the room and a bound picture list placed on a table at the composition's right (see Figure 5.6).[48] Even so, when Turner's view of Fawkes' Large Drawing Room was translated into engraving for the same purpose, all of its peculiarity remained intact.[49] All the images of Fawkes' and Leicester's galleries mentioned above envision them as holistic environments in which lighting, furniture and textiles attract the visitor's interest. Pictures are not prioritized in the visual field, but are instead embedded within the decorated interior, an approach that would be mirrored in written descriptions of galleries, in both guidebooks and periodicals.

Promoting Commerce: The 'solid and pure taste of England'

Fashionable periodicals used Englishness as a defining characteristic of the private collectors and galleries featured in their pages. This was especially true of men who specialized in collecting British art like Leicester and Fawkes but, as the variety of examples discussed in this book have demonstrated, all private galleries were lauded as patriotic when they made a gesture towards admitting the general public. The *Repository of Arts*, which as discussed in Chapter Three appealed to middle-class readers who looked to the magazine for news about fashionable metropolitan culture, seems to have been particularly invested in promoting private galleries. It also promoted consumerism as a route to national prosperity. One review of Walter Fawkes' gallery asserted that 'the influence of the arts is now sensibly felt by the public; their power of . . . aiding and enhancing the various manufactures of our country, is now universally admitted'.[50] The stated goal of many collectors – to 'improve' public taste – dovetailed conveniently with the *Repository's* assumption that commercial consumption was the best route to prosperity. If collections of Old Masters promoted manufacturing and commerce, then art collectors were key actors in the development of the national economy and international commerce, which were in turn dependent on the maintenance and growth of empire.

Irish art dealer and critic William Paulet Carey become one of the most zealous advocates in favour of private collections being opened to the public, an idea for which he advocated in language that was frankly embedded in discourses about masculinity and empire. Carey consistently described Sir John Leicester in terms of his 'manliness and public spirit' and was likewise explicit that Leicester's efforts should be understood on an imperial stage.[51] Discourses on empire in the late eighteenth- and nineteenth-centuries frequently focused on the implications of imperial activities on the health and manliness of the body politic and Carey aimed this strain of argument at those who would collect Old Masters at the expense of living British artists:

> . . . there was but one gentleman of rank and fortune in the empire, who had manliness to stem the tide of public prejudice and patriotism to give an exclusive preference to the works of his countrymen . . . that gentleman, although he admired the beauties of the old masters, admitted only the works of British artists, when embellishing the principal apartments of his splendid mansions in town and country.[52]

Describing the Leicester Gallery as the 'rallying ground of British genius', Carey deployed a martial metaphor to argue that British art was central to the formation of a national culture that could represent Britain's importance (not to mention dominance) on a world stage.[53] Carey took special notice of the number of 'foreign' visitors to be seen regularly in private galleries, describing the crowd at Leicester's as 'multitudes of foreigners of eminence, Americans and Asiatics, as well as Europeans of every country'.[54] It is implied that the presence of people from around the globe in the gallery was proof of its efficacy in promoting the cause of British art.

This attitude ran counter to the Royal Academy's longstanding prescription that art and commerce be kept strictly separate – or at a minimum, that the interconnections between the two be cleverly camouflaged. An important achievement of private galleries was to remove the display of art from sites associated with commerce, like dealer's rooms, auction rooms and artists' studios and to re-site it in the tasteful domestic spaces of those who achieved status through birth, not business. Writing about Walter Fawkes' house, for example, the *London Chronicle*'s correspondent asserted:

> We must first mention the house, as a very stately and noble mansion, furnished with great elegance, not with French elegance, but something we like much better, the solid and pure taste of England. Without having previously known the owner's habits, we should have pronounced it to be the house of an opulent and manly-minded English landholder.[55]

This writer declares that the manliness of the house is communicated by its décor, which evokes the 'solid and pure taste of England', obscuring the distinction between public and private virtue. The notion that Fawkes' house was clearly that of a 'landholder' marks its owner as a member of the privileged classes, whose 'pure taste' surely flowed from their status as men whose fortunes did not depend on trade. So accepted was this view that the *Repository of Arts* proclaimed that it was 'needless to dwell on the obviously patriotic motive of Sir John Leicester in forming this fine collection and throwing open, at no small expense and very considerable domestic inconvenience, his gallery to the lovers of art'.[56] In early nineteenth-century political discourse linking the concepts of patriotism and domesticity was not unusual, as aristocrats and other elites increasingly sought to mobilize the vocabulary of patriotism to reaffirm their own fitness to rule.[57] Of course, the notion that the financial fortunes of landed gentleman were rigorously disconnected from industry and commerce was ludicrous. The Bridgewater and Stafford fortunes that paid for Cleveland House and the collection it contained had been built by investment in a network of canals that enabled the rise of Britain's industrial midlands in the late eighteenth and early nineteenth centuries.

In light of the desire to downplay any connection between commerce and collecting, many proprietors of galleries eschewed or forbade any kind of financial transaction to take place. This again marked a shift from the context of the country house tour, where visitors were usually granted admission by housekeepers or other servants who doubled as tour guides and earned tips in exchange. In the London townhouse gallery, the purported absence of any such financial transaction was a point of pride. At Leicester's 'a paper on the staircase desires most explicitly that "no money shall be given to his servents (sic)"'.[58] Naturally, of course, such remonstrations did not necessarily eliminate this practice; Louis Simond complained in 1810 that a visit to Grosvenor House was 'dear' because a visitor felt obliged to 'give gold at the door'.[59] Even so, descriptions of galleries preferred to maintain the impression that such transactions never took place. A fictionalized account of a visit to Cleveland House referred to freedom from tipping as a source of easy interaction between visitor and household staff:

> Sir Felix much pleased with the polite attention of the domestic who conducted them through the different apartments, to whom Miss Macgilligan offered a gratuity, but the acceptance of which was, with courteous acknowledgements, declined.[60]

The Marquess of Stafford, Sir John Leicester and others who followed this model were actively seeking to distance their galleries from public exhibitions charging entry fees. A side effect was that they elided the distinction between invited guest and ticketed tourist.

The sense that one was freely invited to explore the house without tipping symbolized the politeness of both the gallery space and of the visitors who entered. If and when visitors did not exhibit the manners expected of guests in private houses – especially if they exhibited the sense of entitlement to enter that a ticket in hand might reasonably bestow – condemnation or ridicule were sure to follow. In 1817 Thomas Rowlandson gently caricatured the unsuitable characters who might present themselves at a gentleman's gallery, depicting four visitors to Matthew Michell's gallery in his house in Enfield, north of London (see Figure 5.7). A country clergyman, clad in black, stands with two men, one of whom appears to wish to be thought a connoisseur, leaning back with an air of detachment and raising a glass to his eye. Behind him, a woman dressed in what appears to be a common day dress and mob-cap, stands with her hands deep in her pockets, a sign that she has not yet mastered the codes of polite gentility. *The Examiner* for March 1819 derided both 'shabby-looking fellows' and 'persons above the middle class of society' who 'attempted to obtrude themselves into' private galleries:

> A member of the 'privileged orders', who has so exorbitant a wish to extend those privileges, by forcibly entering a private residence, forgets that the courtesy of its proprietor . . . ought to have been a new motive for holding it sacred from assault, beside the universally acknowledged one, that 'every man's house is his castle'. A friend, in speaking of this absurd attempt to walk into a private abode as he would into a coffee-house, says, 'he had better call for tea and toast while he is about it'.[61]

This writer consciously deploys the language of idealized domesticity, using both a religious metaphor and a phrase comparing houses to castles that was already well-worn by the end of the 1810s. The invocation of the 'coffee-house' conjures a space that had first developed to accommodate public debate in the seventeenth century as a foil to the privately owned

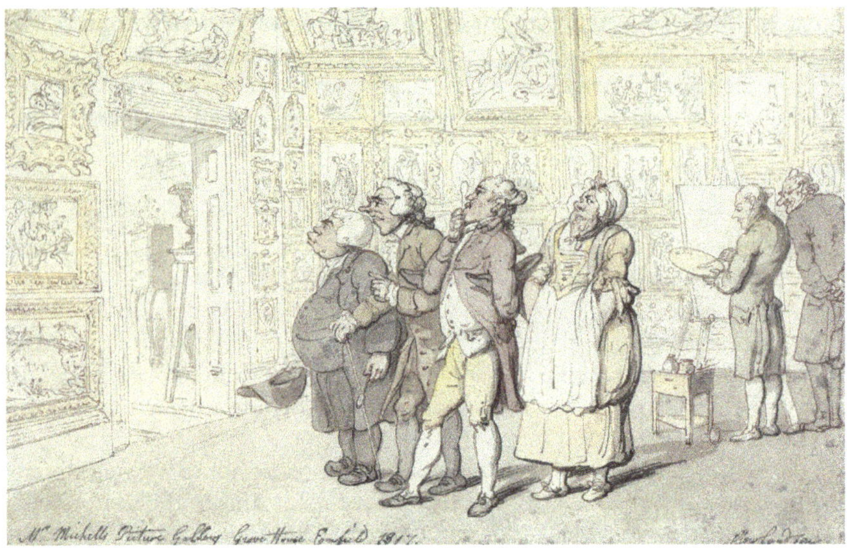

FIGURE 5.7 *Thomas Rowlandson, 1756–1827, British,* Mr Michell's Picture Gallery, Grove House, Enfield 1817, *1817, Watercolour and graphite with pen and grey ink and pen and brown ink on medium, moderately textured, cream wove paper, Yale Center for British Art, Paul Mellon Collection, B1975.4.911.*

gallery, for which any claim to publicity is far more limited.[62] The writer makes clear that whatever processes private collectors used to manage the public, their galleries should not be comparable to 'coffee-house[s]' but should be approached as domestic spaces where any visitor must abide by all the social conventions that would usually apply.

Supporters of the private gallery system unwaveringly hailed a gentleman's tolerance of disruption to his domestic arrangements as a symbol of patriotic fervour and unstinting embrace of public duty. At the same time, these supporters tended to gloss over restrictions on admissions which became standard practice, including those described above such as very limited admission hours, advanced ticketing, closures in 'wet and dirty' weather and the requirement that visitors arrive in carriages. On occasion, more radically-minded critics dared to suggest that such restrictions should be seen for what they were and that attempts to restrict audiences were not in keeping with the 'national' mission that such collectors had embraced. The *Literary Gazette* ran a series of articles in 1818 and 1819 suggesting that the English private gallery system was still sorely lacking, as 'they manage these matters better in France'.[63] Of restrictions in place at Walter Fawkes' gallery the *Literary Gazette* acerbically commented:

> Taking it for granted that . . . no persons in habits of filth or mud would present themselves, we cannot help being sorry that such an English-

> looking drawback as this notice is, should have been tacked. It is indeed almost whimsical and may induce foreigners to think there is some truth in the oft-repeated assertion, that our variable atmosphere and frequent bad weather have in fact considerable effect upon British Taste and National Genius.[64]

In both cases, an appeal to a brand of patriotism that favoured cosmopolitan values over parochial ones ('English-looking') was intended to spur the owners of collections to think more broadly about both the national and international audiences their collections might attract. Fashionable magazines, which tended to take the perspective of the gentleman collector over that of the insouciant member of the public, responded to criticisms like these with derision. To one complaining letter-writer the *Repository of Arts* sarcastically retorted, 'What a pity, that when a public-spirited gentleman throws open a splendidly furnished mansion on stated days to promote the popularity of the fine arts, he is not also to give shelter on a rainy day to every lounger, with the additional privilege of wiping his boots on superb Persian carpets!'[65] The *Repository* consistently reinforced the notion that a private gallery was first and foremost a domestic haven and that temporary invasion by visitors should not endanger its status as such.

In the eyes of periodical literature aimed at a middle-class audience, particularly in publications such as the *Literary Gazette* or the *Repository of Arts*, it was the luxurious, domestic and masculine interior cultivated in the private galleries of men like Fawkes and Leicester that provided the best setting for a truly thorough appreciation of the fine arts. Art and social life were not opposed or incompatible activities; they went hand-in-hand, each enhancing the other. Ideally, the private gallery created an environment that bolstered the appreciation of art by cocooning it within a social space where visitors could feel themselves guests rather than interlopers. As one of Leicester's boosters, identified as 'W', wrote in the *Literary Journal*:

> The pleasure which this Gallery affords, must be enjoyed to be felt and this is most liberally permitted on proper application to its general possessor, without being taxed by the servants, or being made to feel, while you are there, that you have driven away the owner from his mansion during your stay and that he indulges his vanity at the expense of his comforts. Here, on the contrary, the noble owners participate in the pleasure they create; they are usually in the Gallery and they add to the delight of the scene.[66]

'W' sets up a direct contrast between visiting a gallery in a town house and visiting a country house. The 'comforts' of its owner may be accommodated alongside the 'liberal' admission of the public. Visitors are admitted to Leicester's gallery without the burden of a financial transaction and welcomed by the owner himself. These acts transformed the experience of the gallery visit into a social rather than a solitary one.

Such writers argue that the situation of the gallery in an occupied dwelling positively benefitted both collector and visitors. The benefit could extend even further, transmitting the qualities of the selfless and morally-upstanding gentleman to his visitors by a process of social osmosis:

> If all the opulent and honourable persons who have fine specimens of the Arts were to open their doors once a week during the summer, . . . Bazaars and Bond-street might lose their loungers, but the saloon and the study would be filled and the domestic virtues might find a powerful reinforcement in the pursuits which made home a place at once of diligence, taste and imagination.[67]

The *Chronicle* pitted 'bazaars and Bond-street', the twin spectres of commercial enterprise and fashionable life, against the pleasures of 'domestic virtue'. The 'home' referred to was understood as a site of moral authority, where gentlemen and ladies were educated about matters of public importance within a domestic environment that was made possible through the munificence of the private gentleman. In this formulation, the 'lounger', a perennial target of contemptuous writers, is transformed from a foppish character concerned with Bond Street's delights into a figure of 'taste and imagination'. The gallery's transformative power was manifested when the 'saloon and study are filled' with former loungers turned educated connoisseurs.

Yet there were, of course, many who were not so keen to embrace the private gallery as the answer to the British art world's problems. They worried that relying on the whims of individual private collectors could never permit the British School to reach its potential. William Paulet Carey, despite being an ardent and vocal supporter of Sir John Leicester, wondered if the British reliance on private patronage and display could ever produce an artist to rival the great masters:

> Could Michael Angelo, or Raffaelle, have worked all the wonders of the Vatican in a private apartment? We need not any further argument to show that the country, which would excel in this style of poetry, painting and sculpture, must employ the Fine Arts to decorate her churches with the noblest subjects of sacred history and her other principal public buildings with representations of great national events. She must do all this, besides laudably calling forth genius to furnish the splendid apartments of private persons with elegant embellishments.[68]

Carey powerfully contrasts the feminine, decorative 'embellishment' achieved through private patronage with the masculine, 'noblest subjects' that will result from thoughtful church and state patronage. While Carey leaves room for artists to be employed in the decoration of 'splendid apartments' he is clear that, in order to awaken dormant British genius, some system of public patronage would have to be established. In Carey's view, it was inevitable that public collections in the form of state-owned galleries of art would need to be developed so that London could establish itself as a truly cosmopolitan centre.

'The Mind's True Home': William Hazlitt and Ideal Gallery

Connoisseurs and artists alike had long struggled to find a venue in London that could properly educate and train the eye of the public to appreciate Old Master paintings. Writers celebrated the dynamic, rambunctious world of modern London while training a critical eye on it. The annual exhibitions of the Royal Academy, where practicing artists and Academicians displayed their work to the public, attracted large crowds of people from all walks of life as well as foreign tourists. As the Academy exhibitions became 'the rage', everything related to the art world was drawn into its vortex, from standards of display, to the behaviour of the crowds in attendance, to the development of modern painting itself.[69] Certainly, an oft-repeated criticism was that the exhibitions were so visually stimulating and the crowds there so full of fashionable people and celebrities that looking at the art became at best challenging and at worst an afterthought. As the *Repository of Arts* put it in 1819, 'the eye is dazzled at one moment by the blaze of colour on the canvas and then diverted from the pictures to the company, so that it is absolutely impossible to get a calm and steady view, so as to appreciate the real merit of the works'.[70] These attitudes toward the annual exhibitions extended to other metropolitan venues and were cheekily illustrated by Thomas Rowlandson's view of the exhibition, which was included in Rudolph Ackermann's three-volume subscription series *The Microcosm of London* in 1808 (see Figure 5.8). As Ann Bermingham has argued, the *Microcosm* sought to encapsulate the best that modern, commercial London had to offer by illustrating the city's diverse range of spaces devoted to business and sociability, featuring art exhibitions alongside board rooms, schools, courthouses, places of worship, theatres and markets.[71] Rowlandson's view took the sociable, rambunctious atmosphere of the Great Room as its focus, taking a documentary approach to the architecture of the room and the paintings that hung on its walls while training a playful eye on the social types that typically populated it.[72] Ladies and gentlemen, old and young, clergymen and military officers talk, whisper and stroll; they examine the pictures and, not infrequently, each other.[73]

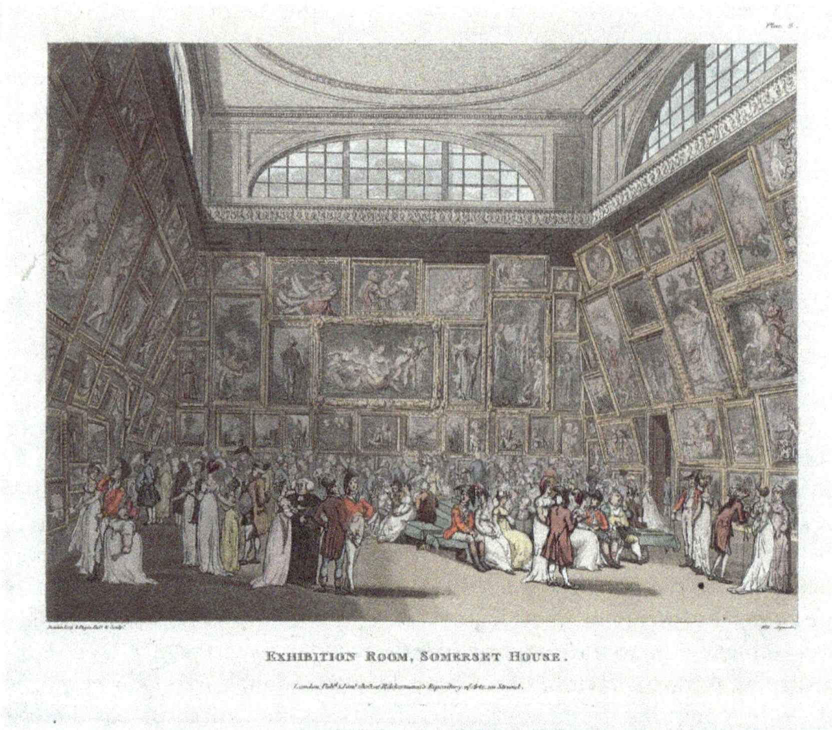

FIGURE 5.8 *Thomas Rowlandson, 'Exhibition Room, Somerset House' from* Microcosm of London, *pl 2 (London: Ackermann, 1808). Hand-coloured etching and aquatint. The Metropolitan Museum of Art, New York, Harris Brisbane Dick Fund, 1917.*

Critics regularly lamented that the crowded visual field and social scene found in spaces like the Royal Academy exhibitions usurped the serious appreciation of art.[74] Perhaps the most eloquent voice taking up this argument was that of critic and essayist William Hazlitt. Hazlitt claimed that the riotous environment focused on fashion and consumerism fostered by the Royal Academy was in fundamental conflict with the type of serious reflection necessary for understanding works of art. In general, Hazlitt was sceptical of the widely accepted view that all the British school needed to thrive was more attention and patronage from the upper classes and the crown. Instead, he argues that academies and public education do not produce great art, which was actually the product of individual artistic genius perceived by the discerning eye of the gifted connoisseur.[75] Fundamentally, Hazlitt did not subscribe to the notion that art needed to appeal to the masses and argued instead for a 'republic of taste' ruled by 'aristocrats of intellect and sensibility rather than of blood' as John Barrell has written.[76] Hazlitt saw the popularization of connoisseurship as a serious problem for the arts; it became a 'fashion' rather than a calling; the new 'connoisseurs' were 'pretenders to taste, through vanity, affectation and idleness'.[77] While elsewhere Hazlitt was a vigorous champion of the labouring classes, he wished to protect the fine arts from 'ignorance and vulgarity', which were equally or more likely to be found amongst the fashion- and celebrity-obsessed middle or upper classes.[78]

> We really do not see how the man of genius should be improved by being transplanted from his closet to the anti-chambers of the great, or to a fashionable rout. He has no business there – but to bow, to flatter, to smile, to submit to the caprice of taste, to adjust his dress, to think of nothing but his own person and his own interest, to talk of the antique and furnish designs for the lids of snuff-boxes and ladies' fans![79]

Hazlitt extends the distinction between true connoisseurs and mere pretenders to objects themselves, viewing works of art as superior in a hierarchy of value to luxury items like clothing or furniture, which were subject to the mercenary values governing the consumption of other expensive goods. Characterizing 'taste' as changeable and implicitly feminine, he links it to fashion, a frivolous form of consumption. When artists become distracted by the production of lucrative objects that circulate in an elite milieu, like 'snuff-boxes and ladies' fans', they neglect the imaginative works Hazlitt unequivocally linked to artistic genius and connoisseurship, both coded masculine.

Yet paradoxically Hazlitt was drawn to the notion that private – even aristocratic and royal – collections might provide the ideal space for knowledgeable connoisseurs to encounter art. These ideas are most fully elucidated in a series of essays published in *The London Magazine* in 1822–1823 before being collected in *Sketches of the Principal Picture-Galleries in England* in 1824. The series describes visits to a number of important collections, including Cleveland House, the Angerstein Gallery, Grosvenor House, Windsor Castle and Hampton Court. (The Dulwich Picture Gallery is the only public collection included in the series.) Read as a whole, the essays offer implicit and explicit critiques of the most well-known fashionable West End arts venues (the Royal Academy, for example) while concentrating on the positive experiences to be found in a range of alternatives. The most frequently-cited of these essays is Hazlitt's account of a visit to Angerstein's gallery, first published in December 1822 before the house at 100 Pall Mall had been transformed by Act of Parliament into the National Gallery. The animating spirit of the essay is Hazlitt's declaration that 'a visit to a genuine Collection is like going a pilgrimage – it is an act of devotion performed at the shrine of Art!' which expresses the writer's desire to re-invest the act of looking at paintings with a seriousness bordering on the sacred. He continues, 'This is not a bazaar, a raree-show of art, a Noah's ark of all the Schools, marching out in endless procession; but a sanctuary, a holy of holies, collected by taste, sacred to fame, enriched by the rarest products of genius'.[80] Hazlitt was certainly not the only writer of the period to invest the act of looking with the notion of the sacred; the French critic Quatremère de Quincy, for example, was writing in a similar idiom to transform the practice of looking at art into a religious, or transcendental experience.[81]

Hazlitt begins the essay by contrasting the bustle of the city, evident as he walked along Pall Mall before arriving at Angerstein's door, with the quiet space found within. It is a distinction that becomes key to his framing of the art viewing experience:

> We know of no greater treat to be admitted freely to a Collection of this sort . . . it is a cure (for the time at least) for low-thoughted cares and uneasy passions . . . The business of the world at large and even its pleasures, appear like a vanity and an impertinence. What signify the hubbub, the shifting scenery, the fantoccini figures, the folly, the idle fashions without, when compared with the solitude, the silence, the speaking looks, the unfading forms within? – Here is the mind's true home.[82]

Invoking a metaphor of domesticity, Hazlitt locates the 'mind's true home' in a private art gallery. It is clear that this experience is possible because he has been admitted at a time when the crowds are at bay; able to completely ignore the other objects that surround him, he devotes two-and-a-half pages to a detailed and poetic account of the *Raising of Lazarus* by Sebastiano del Piombo. At the same time, Hazlitt's writing, which fuses an embodied mode of looking with a descriptive house tour, necessarily depends upon the discourses of privacy, domesticity and publicity that were being worked out around Cleveland House and other private galleries. He contrasts the 'unfading', tacitly unchanging, highly privileged and private spaces of high art with the public world characterized by the folly and capriciousness of fashion. Championing private houses as the best spaces in which to appreciate works of art, he seeks to elevate paintings and fine art above the furnishings and interior décor that surround them. The act of looking was to be understood as a private, or solitary, experience, but also one that was embodied by a person travelling through the spaces of the house and its grounds – making a 'pilgrimage', Hazlitt would have said – to arrive on the threshold of experience.

Even so, Hazlitt had reservations about private collections. The quiet and focused study that could take place there was too often disrupted by an inevitable intrusion of the demands of sociability. Questioning whether artists truly benefitted from access to such spaces he wrote, 'The assumed familiarity and condescending goodness of patrons and vice-patrons will serve to intoxicate rather than to sober the mind and a card to dinner in Cleveland-row or Portland-place will have a tendency to divert the student's thoughts from his morning's work, rather than to rivet them upon it'.[83]

Hazlitt's mention of dinners at 'Cleveland-row' and 'Portland-place' – references to Cleveland House and to Thomas Hope's antiquities-filled house respectively – reflects his ambivalence about the social environment fostered by such spaces, where the experience of looking at art may be subsumed by the social pressures of fashionable society.

My intention in focusing on Hazlitt is not to claim him as an exception, but rather to use his evocative (and, admittedly, idiosyncratic) body of work to trace developments in attitudes regarding the display of fine art in the early nineteenth century. Most periodical publications wholeheartedly embraced the notion that the public taste could be improved by the wider accessibility of fine collections of art. What these writers shared with Hazlitt, though few could summon his mastery of language, was the assumption that the practices of looking at art were fundamentally interwoven with the social practices that governed those spaces, whether they be public exhibitions, auction venues, or private houses.

The economic and political security of post-Napoleonic Britain was used as an argument in favour of keeping collections in private hands and the trope of the beneficent private collector was one to which defenders of the status quo made frequent recourse. Hazlitt was not the only one writing about private galleries and collections in this period. Liberal journalist PG Patmore wrote his own series on private galleries and collections for the *New Monthly Magazine* that was later collected under the title *British Galleries of Art* in 1824. (A third writer, Charles Molloy Westmacott, a more conservative figure who adopted a deferential attitude toward the perspective of the aristocracy, also published a collection of essays, *British Galleries of Painting and Sculpture,* in the same year.[84]) Each in his own way, Hazlitt and Patmore wrestled with the implications of the imminent founding of the National Gallery and what it could mean not only for collectors, but also for artists and for art lovers who wished to have access to superb collections of painting.[85] Following the model established by William Young Ottley, Patmore suggests looking at the network of private collections across the country as akin to a collective 'National Gallery', a public resource nevertheless best kept in private hands. The allusion to 'Britishness' in his book's title attributed a national significance and common mission to what was, in reality, a diverse assemblage of houses and other spaces. Patmore celebrates moderately sized, gentlemanly collections in private houses as 'natural', ideal sites to hold the nation's treasures. Their settings, interiors and connections to family history make them ideal for both displaying and looking at art.[86]

The essay in *British Galleries of Art* that perhaps best encapsulates these ideas concerns itself with Knole Park, a Jacobean country house in Kent. Knole had been owned by the Sackville family since the early seventeenth century, during which time an important collection of family portraits, augmented with works by Old Masters like Peter Paul Rubens and Jacob Jordaens, had accumulated on its walls. Further it had been open to tourists since early in the Sackville family's residence and was recognized as an important repository of furniture and art.[87] Patmore takes his reader along on an imaginative tour of the house, beginning with the approach through its extensive grounds adorned by a 'beautiful company of beeches'. As an aside it is worth noting that by the early 1820s, when these essays were published, the possible benefits of the countryside setting for looking at art had re-emerged as a topic of discussion amongst parties interested in creating venues for display of art to the public. At the time of Dulwich Picture Gallery's founding during the previous decade, Sir Francis Bourgeois had hoped that it might eventually serve as a National Gallery, since the suburban or rural location could be thought to provide fresh, clean air which was beneficial both for the preservation of artworks and to transform the gallery visit into a healthful excursion into the English landscape. Discussion regarding the question of whether the urban, suburban, or rural setting best supported the mission of the public art museum continued for decades.[88]

After several pages describing the grounds and the exterior of the house ('a finely preserved monument of grey antiquity') Patmore crosses its threshold to present an overview of the collection. He leads his reader through the house, using textual clues to describe how paintings are organized in the interior and in relation to one another and occasionally commenting on particularly notable decorative objects such as the 'noble ebony wardrobe' found in the 'Spangled Bed-room'.[89] Paintings, Patmore argues, originally commissioned in many cases for grand domestic spaces such as those Knole offers, must remain in these spaces to be fully appreciated and understood. Praising the collection of family portraits at Knole, which he is careful to note are kept in the family's own apartments, he writes: 'They are only remarkable generally for the delightful air of comfort which breathes through them, arising from the total absence of all pretensions at modern ornamental splendor'.[90] Grounds, house and collection together present a 'pure and unfaded ... picture of the olden time, as it respects architecture, internal arrangement, furniture and the habits and customs which these illustrate and recall'.[91] Patmore's celebration of Knole and his reference to the 'olden time', prefigures an early Victorian fixation on ideas about national identity rooted in the Tudor and Stuart periods.[92]

In the 1840s, James Holland painted the Lady Betty Germain bedroom at Knole, depicting it as a feminine space (see Figure 5.9). Knole featured a series of such 'Show Rooms' – the Spangle Bedroom mentioned above is another – which are still in place in the house today under the auspices of the National Trust and can be toured by visitors as they would have been in the eighteenth or early nineteenth centuries. The figures in Holland's painting, however, do not appear to be tourists. One lady in contemporary dress reads near the low-burning fire, flowers strewn at her feet, while another stands at a mirror framed by candles that appears as much as anything as a shrine to the room's namesake, Lady Betty, who had died in 1769 at the age of almost 90. Furnished with draperies, carpets, fire screens

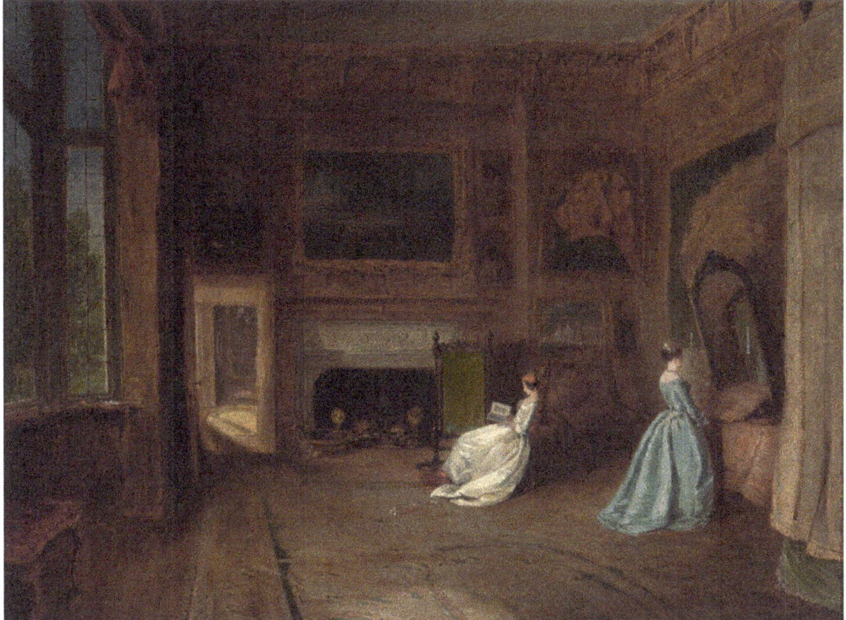

FIGURE 5.9 *James Holland, 1799–1870, British,* The Lady Betty Germain Bedroom at Knole, Kent, *1845, Oil on canvas, Yale Center for British Art, Paul Mellon Collection, B1976.7.43.*

and other objects, the bedroom's moody atmosphere seems to evoke a private, interior world with but a hint of a view to the landscape outside. At Knole, artworks form an essential part of the domesticity the image conjures; Patmore and Holland render completely unthinkable the possibility that they could be removed to a gallery elsewhere and exhibited as works floating free from the palimpsest of family history Knole epitomized.

Patmore deployed the imagery of domesticity, which had been used so successfully to solidify the privacy of galleries like Cleveland House even as they were opened to the public, to justify his belief that the best paintings in Britain belonged in private collections. In fact, his essay on Knole begins unexpectedly, with a long discussion on the evils of nationalization, one of the processes by which the Louvre had amassed its renowned collection. Lamenting that the Louvre had perhaps too many 'perfect beauties', he notes that 'it is not in human nature . . . to appreciate that which it obtains with ease, or can have by asking for'.[93] A bit of difficulty in gaining access to works of art – a journey into the countryside, an application for a ticket – may render the visitor all the more alive to what the collection has to offer. Palaces filled with the spoils of war, like the Louvre, he writes, may grow too large and dilute the power of their own collections.[94] Turning from this critique to his description of Knole, it is clear that Patmore sees private collections, not national or state-owned ones, as a remedy to these concerns:

> It is to private collections alone that the lover of art should perhaps look for the true encouragement which art needs and without which it cannot support its due claims to the attention and admiration of mankind: and these can never, like the late collection at the Louvre, counteract their natural and proper effect, by growing to an inordinate and unnatural size and (like Aaron's rod), swallowing up all the rest.[95]

In all of the essays in this series, Patmore draws on assumptions about aristocratic domesticity to make a case that, as he writes above, 'it is to private collections alone' that connoisseurs may look to provide the proper setting for important works of art.

Conclusion

The foundational principle behind William Young Ottley's project, of which his enormous catalogue of the Marquess of Stafford's collection at Cleveland House had been intended as only the first instalment, was the notion that a network of private galleries could – and should – stand in for a single state-owned institution. Just as Ottley's idea was being elaborated and disseminated through the writings of men like Hazlitt and Patmore, the National Gallery was founded in 1824 by an Act of Parliament. Ottley's grand project – to unite the private galleries of Britain into a virtual national collection – had been rendered obsolete almost before it began. He was unable to sell sufficient copies of his catalogue of Cleveland House to turn a profit and, within a year, the engraved plates had been put up for auction.

When art writer and gossip columnist CM Westmacott published his own book describing the private galleries of the metropolis, which in many ways amounted to an abridged version of Ottley's original vision, he justified its publication by stating that:

> In the present advanced state of the arts, it is singular that no general catalogue of a critical and descriptive nature, directing the promoter and admirer to the choicest collections in the metropolis, noticing every work of art separately and pointing out what is best worthy of his attention, should have preceded this attempt.[96]

Westmacott notes that while some 'splendid and elaborate works of some few of the Collections' had been published, their circulation had been limited by 'their extravagant price', which 'has confined the knowledge of these treasures of art to the more wealthy patrons'.[97] Though Westmacott is needling Ottley for his failure to complete his vision, his underlying observation is correct. Ottley sought to make the contents of Britain's private galleries available to the public, but doing so proved prohibitively expensive for his project to carry out its intended mission in any meaningful way.

The demise of Ottley's project and the founding of the National Gallery point to a shift in momentum away from private galleries as viable alternatives to public collections of art. Purchased for the nation, Angerstein's house and collection were transformed into a metaphorical and literal 'home' for the nation's art, an uneasy hybrid of public and private space.[98] The new National Gallery emerged in a climate in which the private gallery had been the archetypal format for looking at Old Master paintings for more than 20 years. During its first decade, the new National Gallery did little to overturn the expectations associated with display in private houses, but a drive for greater professionalism in its management and keeping of pictures did push the next generation, emblematized by men like Charles Lock Eastlake, to develop new strategies for display in public museums that distinguished them from aristocratic interiors.[99]

The very fact that the pictures in the new National Gallery came from a single private collection – which had been offered by its owner as a ready-made gallery complete with house to contain it – assuaged any concerns that the state had coerced private individuals to part with their personal property. Even those arguing in favour of the Bill in Parliament explicitly refrained from suggesting that pictures belonging to the English aristocracy, private institutions or, most crucially, the crown, had any place in a National Gallery of Art. In his budget speech of 23 February 1824, Frederick Robinson, the Chancellor of the Exchequer, called the new gallery a 'splendid' establishment full of 'ornaments', declaring that 'every Englishman who paces it may gaze with the proud satisfaction of reflecting, that they are not the rifled treasures of plundered palaces, or the unhallowed spoils of violated altars'. Robinson explicitly rejects the idea that the purchase of Angerstein's collection bore any resemblance to the nationalization of private possessions or pillaging of foreign treasures that characterized the founding of the Louvre. Some historians have argued that Robinson 'erected' this 'rhetorical pillar' of the ideology supporting the National Gallery.[100] By this point, however, it should be clear that the way for Robinson's line of argument had been paved by a range of voices arguing in print and in image that the private house was a protected space where fine art could – and should – be kept in trust for the nation.[101] The notion that the gallery might be both 'splendid' and for 'every Englishman' draws an elision between the space of the public art gallery and the private space of the home. The idea of 'home' as a space that nurtures private property ownership and an appreciation of fine art objects was part and parcel of this national project rather than a break from it.

Conclusion: The 'Home' of Art

This book began by picturing how an imaginary visitor to London in 1805 might have used John Feltham's guidebook, *The Picture of London*, to find out where to go to look at art. Over a period of more than 20 years, a number of new guidebooks appeared, all of which sought to help visitors to the metropolis make sense of its vibrant network of spaces and places for entertainment, culture and art. In 1824, the same visitor might have consulted *Leigh's New Picture of London* which included a map of 'Remarkable Objects in London', featuring myriad places it deemed of interest to any resident or visitor (see Figure 6.1). Municipal sites including the Gas Works, Guy's Hospital and the King's Bench Prison jostle for space with commercial venues like the Corn Exchange and the South Sea House. The map includes churches, schools and popular entertainment venues such as theatres and art exhibitions. Benjamin West's Gallery appears, as does the nearby gallery of Joseph Backler, a maker of painted and stained glass and the gallery of Miss Linwood, known for her reproductions of fine art in embroidered wool.[1] So too the map alerts our visitor to the ongoing importance of private art galleries and important townhouses as 'remarkable objects' within the urban landscape. Cleveland House (indicated as 'Marqs of Stafford's') appears at centre left, just south of Piccadilly. Nearby points mark the locations of Apsley House, Spencer House ('Earl Spencer's), Lansdowne House and Buckingham House shortly before its transformation into Buckingham Palace. What this map did not depict was the National Gallery, still months away from opening to the public at the time the guidebook appeared.

Soon after the National Gallery's founding in 1824, however, the sense of promise that surrounded private art galleries in the early nineteenth century began to decline. Whether that is directly related to a shift in public values represented by its founding may be impossible to say. Leicester and Fawkes's galleries faded from view after enjoying just a few years of focused attention from critics and audiences. Collectors, like Sir George Beaumont, began to donate pictures to the fledgling National Gallery, prompting others to follow their example. The gallery at Cleveland House, which had done more than any other to promote the idea that private collecting and public benefit were mutually reinforcing, continued on, but Stafford suffered a stroke while visiting

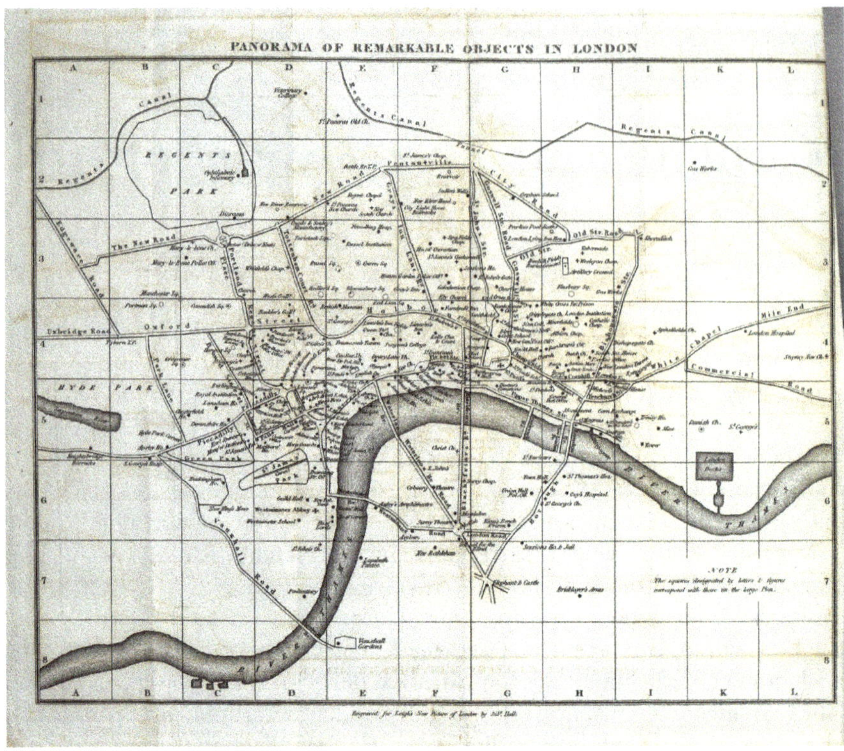

FIGURE 6.1 *Sidney Hall, engr., 'Panorama of Remarkable Objects in London' from* Leigh's New Picture of London *(London: Samuel Leigh and Baldwin, Cradock and Joy, 1824–1825). RB 68903, The Huntington Library, San Marino, California.*

Paris in 1822, after which his health and energy for his prized art gallery never entirely recovered. When Stafford died in 1833 at age 75, having been elevated in rank to Duke of Sutherland, his youngest son, Francis Leveson-Gower, inherited Cleveland House, the gallery and the collection of pictures it contained. He changed his name to Francis Egerton, Earl of Ellesmere ('Ellesmere') in compliance with the terms of the Duke of Bridgewater's initial bequest (the Duke's name was also Francis Egerton). Ellesmere continued the family tradition of making the pictures available to the general public.

The expectation on the part of the public that Cleveland House should remain open to the public had become entrenched after 30 years of continuous practice, but the question of whether they should feel entitled to admission remained fraught. Historian Peter Mandler has argued that widespread tourism to stately homes began in the 1830s and 1840s as new forms of transportation opened up access to the countryside. As private houses became tourist destinations on a scale that had been impossible given the exigencies of eighteenth-century travel, the burdens of accommodating them became more onerous and owners increasingly resisted participating in the ritual.[2] As early as 1824 the intransigence toward the public displayed by many owners of important collections angered William Hazlitt:

> Do these Noble Persons wish to set bounds to and disappoint public curiosity? Do they think that the admiration bestowed on fine pictures or rare sculpture lessens their value, or divides the property as well as the pleasure with the possessor? Or do they think that setting aside the formality of these new regulations, three persons in the course of a whole year would intrude out of an impertinent curiosity to see *their* houses and furniture, without having a just value for them as objects of art? Or is the expence of keeping servants to shew the apartments made the plea of this churlish, narrow system? The public are ready enough to pay servants for their attendance and those persons are quite as forward to do this who make a pilgrimage to such places on foot as those who approach them in a post-chaise or on horseback with a livery servant, which, it seems, is the prescribed and fashionable etiquette![3]

Hazlitt perceives, with his usual acuity, that for some collectors freely showing objects to tourists might feel uncomfortably close to the act of literally 'dividing' property with them.

While it is often argued that nationalization of property was never a genuine threat in Great Britain, the undercurrent of possessiveness Hazlitt detected upon visiting such houses suggests the concern had not completely disappeared from the propertied mind. The Duke of Wellington, who had become a beloved public figure following the Napoleonic Wars, found that members of the public were increasingly assertive in their attempts to see his house. He installed a plaque at Stratfield Saye, his estate in Hampshire, which stated: 'Those desirous of seeing the Interior of the House, are requested to ring at the door of entrance and to express their desire. It is wished that the practice of stopping on the paved walk to look in at the windows should be discontinued'.[4] The plaque demonstrates the difficulty of wishing to appear welcoming to the public while setting limits on invasions of privacy. To be sure, the phenomenon of country house visiting was distinct from the way in which galleries in town were managed; while country houses still required a journey by coach or train, houses in town were as accessible as they ever had been.

Cleveland House (and later Bridgewater House) was no exception to these more general trends. Ellesmere continued the family tradition of keeping both open to the public so that the family's renowned collection of art could be seen, but within a few years had become fed up with what he called the public's 'intolerable conduct'. In 1841 he wrote to his picture dealer, John Mountjoy Smith:

> The fact is that I have been unable to make up my mind as to what way or under what limits I can possibly shew my pictures. I have been cured of liberality in doing so by the intolerable conduct of those who come to see them and I have been not unwilling to cure the public at large of the notion they had received from my father's practice and my own, that they had the right to see them. The thing is now the more difficult because I live in the rooms. I should always be glad to have them seen by anybody who is fit to look at them, & if while I am absent from town you can arrange with my housekeeper so as to shew them yourself to persons of this description, by which I mean foreigners & visitors to London who want to see the pictures & not to clean their shoes on my carpets, read my books and open the bedroom doors, say two days a week, I have no objection and you may shew her this letter. I believe Mr. Ramsbotham is not in town or you might arrange it with him. I will thank you to keep a list of these who come.

By the time this letter was written, Cleveland House had been demolished and Ellesmere's new house, Bridgewater House, was underway. He concluded, 'I wish it to be well understood that the mass of man & womankind who come to London to see homes & paw furniture must wait till Mr. Barry has built my new house, which may be a long time, as I shall not hurry it on their account'.[5] Forty years prior, John Britton had called his father's actions a mark of 'exemplary liberality'. Now, Ellesmere himself feels 'cured' of that same liberality by the troublesome nature of a public who feel entitled to read his books and open his bedroom doors. This letter, while intended for the eyes of Ellesmere's dealer, is redolent with the language of domesticity that earlier publications about Cleveland House had been at pains to establish.

The notion of the home as an ideal gallery space and the metaphor of 'pilgrimage' as a mode of viewing were widely influential. After the publication of Hazlitt's *Sketches of the Principal Picture-Galleries in England* in 1824 the religious metaphor for looking at art gained currency and became intrinsic to later nineteenth- and twentieth-century viewing and exhibition practices. The Grosvenor Gallery, which opened in 1877, was called 'The Temple of Art' and incorporated both the institutional markers of the museum and the exhibition style of the private house, as Colleen Denney has argued.[6] These trends were in no way limited to Britain. In a groundbreaking article Martha Ward demonstrated that the impulse to display art in spaces resembling private interiors was adopted by Impressionist painters and, as Morna O'Neill has written, the intertwining aesthetics of the private home, dealer's shop and museum were a driving force behind the establishment of the Hugh Lane Gallery in Dublin in 1908.[7]

In the decades following the publication of Hazlitt's book, the pilgrimage metaphor was fully absorbed and attenuated by some of the most widely read art critics, including German art historian and museum curator Gustav

Waagen and feminist literary critic and philosopher Anna Brownell Jameson.[8] Waagen visited London in 1835 in the course of compiling his enormous and influential tome *Art and Artists in England*. Following Hazlitt's template, Waagen emphasized physical and emotional experience when describing the spaces in which artworks were hung. For example, in a townhouse in Curzon Street he wrote, 'My gratification was enhanced by the circumstance that, in the drawing-room, I saw myself surrounded by excellent Italian pictures, of the time of Raphael and was therefore in the sanctuary of the arts, the study of which was the sole object of my journey'.[9] At one stroke, any suggestion of base materialism is cast away and the collector is bestowed with an aura of protector and guardian of sacred relics.

Visiting Stafford House (now called Lancaster House, Stafford House was adjacent to Cleveland House and became the London stronghold of Stafford's eldest son and heir, the Second Duke of Sutherland, see Figure 0.5) Waagen indicates that its interior had a magnetic draw, despite remarkable views to the landscape beyond:

> From the windows you enjoy a free, beautiful view; for on one side you overlook the whole of the Green Park and on the other side St. James's Park, with lofty trees of the most luxuriant growth, between which the towers of Westminster Abbey rise in the background. Yet the eye always returns to the interior of the apartments, where it is attracted by a variety of objects; for, besides the riches and the splendour which the hangings, curtains and furniture everywhere display, the more noble and refined enjoyment which works of art alone can afford, is nowhere wanting.[10]

While the view from the house offers the opportunity for a totalizing and empowering gaze, Waagen's literal and metaphorical eye is trained on the 'refined enjoyment' to be experienced within. Stafford House, like the other large townhouses Waagen visited, is filled with much more than a superb collection of pictures; he deems 'hangings, curtains and furniture' worthy of attention as well. Significantly, though, the pictures are viewed as 'noble' objects, far superior in intellectual and, by implication, aesthetic, value to the more mundane trappings of wealth found nearby. Waagen makes clear that for him, artworks and especially those by Italian Old Masters, are part and parcel of the house's interior world. It is possible that, from Waagen's viewpoint, no public space could ever provide a truly elevated experience if it were not somehow intertwined with the aesthetics of the private interior. Paradoxically, Waagen was an early outspoken proponent of the need to educate the masses in the appreciation of high art; his language reveals a deep-seated ambiguity between the private home as a 'sanctuary' for art and the need to provide accessible spaces that were freely available to the general public.

Similarly, Anna Jameson used the metaphorical language of domesticity to defend the right of collectors to protect their privacy despite her advocacy of public art galleries for the masses. Jameson forcefully articulated her disgust at the desire of the 'public' to invade the private spaces in aristocratic houses:

> We can all remember the public days at the Grosvenor Gallery and Bridgewater House. We can all remember the loiterers and loungers, the vulgar starers, the gaping idlers, we used to meet there – people who, instead of moving amid these wonders and beauties, 'all silent and divine,' with reverence and gratitude, strutted about as if they had the right to be there; talking, flirting, peeping and prying; lifting up the covers of chairs, to examine the furniture; touching the ornaments – and even the pictures! Now English residences are not like the great, empty, unfurnished, uncarpeted palazzi of the Italian nobles. Can we wonder that men of taste – Englishmen, who attach a feeling of sanctity to their home – should hate the idea of being subjected to such vulgar intrusion, merely because they have a Raphael or Rubens of celebrity?[11]

The idea of religious sanctity in Jameson encompasses two important, mutually reinforcing spheres of influence. One of these is the 'home', a word she applies to the 'English residences' of 'men of taste' in contrast to the 'unfurnished, uncarpeted palazzi' of the Italian nobility. While Jameson does not support removing these works to a public gallery, neither does she condone disrupting a private dwelling.

For Jameson, the other sanctified domain is the realm of art itself. She uses the language of pilgrimage and the divine to set the world of pictures apart from other decorative accoutrements in the grand house. Her writing directly evokes domestic ideology – firmly associated with the middle classes by the early Victorian period – to affirm the system of private ownership of pictures by the aristocracy and rich collectors. She adopted this attitude to argue against the nationalization of private works of art:

> In referring to the vast number of first-rate pictures now in England, scattered through many houses and galleries – in distant counties – in remote country seats – in town houses, shut up half the year – I have heard the wish expressed, that these treasures were assembled in one place – in one national gallery, easily and constantly accessible to all. I cannot say I sympathize with the wish; no: not if the object could be effected without wrong to individuals and with advantage to the pictures themselves, would I wish this.[12]

The idea that pictures are best viewed within the context of the private house flows from the notion promulgated by Hazlitt that the private gallery provides a privileged space for the study and appreciation of art. Jameson continues: 'One hears a great deal of nonsense talked upon this subject, as if a picture were buried, because we have to make a pilgrimage to it.'[13] Jameson took Hazlitt's approach to its logical extreme. The art object itself is sanctified, as are the social practices that enable its viewing and appreciation.

A belief in 'worship' as the proper metaphor for deep aesthetic engagement, which emerged in historically specific conditions, nevertheless has persisted to the present. There are many examples of art galleries being built to resemble places of worship and to recreate the sense of ritual performed within, as Carol Duncan argued in her pioneering work of museum criticism *Civilizing Rituals* (1995).[14] Another astute observer of these trends was conceptual artist and art critic Brian O'Doherty, whose essay series *Inside the White Cube*, written in 1976, explored the ideological underpinning of the twentieth century, modernist exhibition space:

> The ideal gallery subtracts from the artwork all clues that interfere with the fact that it is 'art.' The work is isolated from everything that would detract from its own evaluation of itself. This gives the space a presence possessed by other spaces where conventions are preserved through the repetition of a closed system of values. Some of the sanctity of the church, the formality of the courtroom, the mystique of the experimental laboratory joins with chic design to produce a unique chamber of esthetics. So powerful are the perceptual fields of force within this chamber that, once outside it, art can lapse into secular status.[15]

O'Doherty understood that the connection between art appreciation and sacred experience, which originated at the beginning of the nineteenth century, had become completely embedded within the logics of viewing and display by the late twentieth. The ideology of art as sacred combined with what O'Doherty calls 'chic design' – as filtered through earlier practitioners like Alfred Stieglitz or Alfred Barr, to name two American examples – ensured a space in which art need not compete with any other signifiers such as furniture, windows or wall colour.[16] Neither does the modern gallery space accommodate the body of the viewer:

> Indeed the presence of that odd piece of furniture, your own body, seems superfluous, an intrusion. The space offers the thought that while eyes and minds are welcome, space-occupying bodies are not – or tolerated only as kinesthetic mannikins for further study.[17]

Hazlitt had pushed for a space in which the 'mind' could be at home, but not in denial of the physical presence of the body. Hazlitt recognized that the gallery was a social space, allowing him to assess the negative impact it had and search for meaningful alternatives. Hazlitt's London offered a range of possibilities, including the Royal Academy, British Institution, Christie's and other auction houses, the Water-colour Society and artists' studios. Hazlitt chose to hold up the private, gentlemanly collection and the remote Dulwich Picture Gallery as the best London had to offer.

At the heart of Hazlitt's writing on display lay a profound tension. While continuing to champion private spaces and to code the viewing experience itself as private, he also sought to elevate fine art above the furnishings and interior décor that framed it. The notion that art should be viewed in a pristine environment, free from distractions, rather than in the domestic settings in which it was traditionally kept, was a principle that underpinned the gradual move toward the 'white cube' of contemporary art museums that O'Doherty described. Moreover, Hazlitt's view that private galleries provided important venues for the arts contradicted many of his own radical political principles, which were anti-aristocratic and anti-private property.

Ultimately, the National Gallery drew attention and energy away from great private collections of continental art and its founding represented a major turning point in the era of the private gallery. Domesticity is a durable metaphor, as the title of Jonathan Conlin's 2006 history of the National Gallery, *The Nation's Mantelpiece*, makes clear. Drawn from John Summerson's description of the building's architecture as an overly ornamented mantelpiece, the phrase conjures the notion that the National Gallery is not just a temple of art, but its spiritual 'home', with all the word implies.[18] The notion that art could be seen and, perhaps, better-appreciated within the private houses of Britain's elite had been established by two decades of concerted effort by boosters.

The lure of the private gallery remains potent and has even seen a resurgence in the twenty-first century as public commitment to funding the arts has languished and the list of high net-worth collectors who have the means to open private museums has increased dramatically.[19] London's tourist scene is still dominated by major public and internationally renowned institutions such as the National Gallery and the British Museum. However, across the country, a substantial network of private houses remain open to the public under the auspices of the National Trust, which promotes the narrative that private, domestic dwellings represent a specific form of British culture that speaks to and for all. The nineteenth-century housing reformer Octavia Hill helped found the National Trust in 1895 on the premise that both the preservation of ancient buildings and landscapes and access to beautiful art and interior spaces was of essential importance to all Britons, regardless of social class.[20] While in the early nineteenth century country houses, such as those that now form the National Trust, were still operated on an individual and idiosyncratic basis, a common sense of purpose united the owners of their urban counterparts, giving rise to a strand of art criticism that held up the private gallery as the ideal setting for both the display and wider appreciation of art. This rhetoric has retained its power to the present day, lending British historic houses and collections an enduring appeal.

NOTES

Introduction: 'The Finest in England'

1 John Feltham, *The Picture of London for 1805: Being a Correct Guide to All the Curiosities, Amusements, Exhibitions, Public Establishments, and Remarkable Objects in and Near London* (London: Richard Phillips, 1805), 265.

2 *Ibid.*, 264.

3 *Ibid.*, 265.

4 FHW Sheppard, ed. *Survey of London*: *Volumes 29 and 30, St James Westminster, Part I* (London: London County Council, 1960), 30: 491–495; Feltham, *Picture of London for 1802*, 212.

5 A note on naming: Just before his death in 1833, Stafford was elevated to the title Duke of Sutherland and so many authors refer to him as Sutherland and to the collection as the Sutherland Collection, since this is how it is still known. However, given that he was known as Stafford throughout the time period covered by this book, I will refer to him as Stafford throughout for clarity.

6 There is a substantial literature on these sites and institutions, but works that give a general overview of the development of public spaces for the display of art in London in this period include Richard Altick, *The Shows of London* (Cambridge MA: Belknap Press, 1978), David Solkin, *Painting for Money: The Visual Arts and the Public Sphere in Eighteenth-century England* (London: Yale University Press, 1992), Celina Fox, ed. *London – World City 1800–1840* (London: Yale University Press and the Museum of London, 1992), Brandon Taylor, *Art for the Nation: Exhibitions and the London Public 1747–2001* (New Brunswick, NJ: Rutgers University Press, 1999) and Giles Waterfield, *The People's Galleries* (London: Yale University Press, 2015).

7 Waterfield, *Palaces of Art: Art Galleries in Britain, 1790–1990* (London: Dulwich Picture Gallery, 1991), 75. See also Waterfield, 'The Town House as Gallery of Art', *London Journal* 20/1 (May 1995): 47–66 and Waterfield, *People's Galleries*. Other notable work on Cleveland House to date includes Peter Humfrey, *The Stafford Gallery: The Greatest Art Collection of Regency London* (Norwich: Unicorn Press, 2019) and Susannah Brooke, 'Private art collections and London town houses, 1780–1830' (PhD thesis, Queen's College, University of Cambridge, February 2013). See also Anne Nellis Richter, 'Glitter and Fashion in the "Louvre of London"' in *The Georgian London Town House: Building, Collecting and Display* ed. Susanna Avery-Quash and Kate Retford (London: Bloomsbury, 2019), 233–46 and Brooke,

'The Display and Reception of Private Picture Collections in London Town Houses, 1780–1830', *The Georgian London Town House*, 149–58.

8 Of these, only Spencer House still stands and retains its character as an eighteenth-century townhouse. Joseph Friedman, *Spencer House: Chronicle of a Great London Mansion* (London: Zwemmer, 1993).

9 Artist Benjamin Robert Haydon recorded in September 1839 that the house was to be demolished, see *The Diary of Benjamin Robert Haydon* ed. Willard Bissell Pope (Cambridge MA: Harvard University Press, 1960–1963) IV: 581, but the *Survey of London* dates demolition to 1840 or 1841. 'Cleveland Row', in *Survey of London: Volumes 29 and 30, St James Westminster, Part 1*, ed. FHW Sheppard (London: London County Council, 1960), 487–509. *British History Online*, accessed 18 September 2023. Available at: www.british-history.ac.uk/survey-london/vols29-30/pt1/ pp 487–509.

10 For the history of Stafford House/Lancaster House see James Yorke, *Lancaster House: London's Greatest Town House* (London: Merrell Publishers, 2001).

11 PJ Atkins, 'The spatial configuration of class solidarity in London's West End 1792–1939', *Urban History Yearbook* 17 (1990), 36–65, 56.

12 Even John Summerson's foundational work on the built environment of Georgian London mentions neither Cleveland House nor its architect, Charles Heathcote Tatham. See Summerson, *Georgian London* (London: Yale University Press, 2003).

13 Spencer House, about which Friedman has written extensively, is an important exception to these losses. Friedman, 'Town and Country: The Spencers of Althorp', in Avery-Quash and Retford, *The Georgian London Town House*, 112.

14 Retford, 'Introduction', in Avery-Quash and Retford, *The Georgian London Town House*, 2–6.

15 Important scholarship on the London townhouse includes Yorke, *Lancaster House*, Friedman, *Spencer House*, Christopher Simon Sykes, *Private Palaces: Life in the Great London Houses* (New York: Viking, 1986), MH Port, 'West End Palaces: The Aristocratic Town House in London, 1730–1830', *The London Journal* 20:1 (1995): 17–46, Rachel Stewart, *The Town House in Georgian London* (London: Yale University Press, 2009), Susanna Avery-Quash and Kate Retford, eds *The Georgian London Town House: Building, Collecting and Display* (London: Bloomsbury, 2019), Adriano Aymonino, *Enlightened Eclecticism: The Grand Design of the 1st Duke and Duchess of Northumberland* (London: Yale University Press, 2021) and Manolo Guerci, *London's Golden Mile: The Great Houses of the Strand, 1550–1650* (London: Yale University Press, 2021).

16 Richard Rush, *Memoranda of a Residence at the Court of London* (Philadelphia: Key & Biddle, 1833), 4.

17 On the collection, see especially Peter Humfrey, *The Stafford Gallery* and Nicholas Penny, *The Sixteenth Century Italian Paintings, v. 2, Venice, 1540–1600* (London: National Gallery, 2008), 461–470.

18 Jürgen Habermas, *The Structural Transformation of the Public Sphere*, trans Thomas Burger (Cambridge: Polity Press, 1989) and David Solkin, *Painting for Money*.

19 Important works dealing with exhibitions and galleries in this period include Andrew Hemingway, 'Art Exhibitions as Leisure-Class Rituals in Early Nineteenth-Century London', in *Towards a Modern Art World* ed. Brian Allen (London: Yale University Press, 1995), David Solkin, *Art on the Line: The Royal Academy Exhibitions at Somerset House, 1780–1836* (London: Yale University Press, 2001), Solkin, *Painting for Money*, Ann Bermingham, ed, *Sensation & Sensibility* (New Haven CT: Yale University Press, 2005), K Dian Kriz, *The Idea of the English Landscape Painter* (London: Yale University Press, 1997), Francis Haskell, *The Ephemeral Museum: Old Master Paintings and the Rise of the Art Exhibition* (London: Yale University Press, 2000), Rosie Dias, *Exhibiting Englishness: John Boydell's Shakespeare Gallery and the Formation of a National Aesthetic* (London: Yale, 2013) and Waterfield, *The People's Galleries* (London: Yale University Press, 2015).

20 For a wide-ranging study of the history of public art museums in the nineteenth century, see Giles Waterfield, *The People's Galleries.*

21 Important re-engagements with Habermas' theory include Nancy Fraser, 'Rethinking the Public Sphere' in *Habermas and the Public Sphere* ed. Craig Calhoun (Cambridge MA: MIT Press, 1992), Dena Goodman, 'Public Sphere and Private Life: Toward a Synthesis of Current Historiographical Approaches to the Old Regime', *History and Theory* 31 (1992), Amanda Vickery, 'Golden Age to Separate Spheres: A Review of the Categories and Chronology of Women's History', *Historical Journal* 36 (1993), 383–414, Lawrence E Klein, 'Gender and the Public/Private Distinction in the Eighteenth Century: Some Questions about Evidence and Analytic Procedure', *Eighteenth-Century Studies* 29:1 (1995), 97–109 and JA Downie, 'The Myth of the Bourgeois Public Sphere' in *A Concise Companion to the Restoration and Eighteenth Century* ed. Cynthia Wall (London: Blackwell, 2005).

22 Colley, *Britons: Forging the Nation 1707–1830* (London and New Haven CT: Yale University Press, 1992), 177.

23 Flowing from the example set by Nobert Elias' early work on the history of manners and Philippe Ariès and Georges Duby's series *A History of Private Life* published in 1985, a range of scholars working within different methodological traditions have been fleshing out the picture of how the notion of 'privacy' and the related notion of 'intimacy' developed over the course of the sixteenth through nineteenth centuries. Notable works in this field, particularly in literature and history, that relate to the history of Britain include Michael McKeon's *The Secret History of Domesticity* (Baltimore: Johns Hopkins University Press, 2005) and Patricia Spacks, *Privacy: Concealing the Eighteenth-Century Self* (Chicago: University of Chicago Press, 2003).

24 Catherine Hall and Leonore Davidoff, *Family Fortunes: Men and Women of the English Middle Class 1780–1850* (London: Hutchison, 1987), Stella Tillyard, *Aristocrats: Caroline, Emily, Louisa and Sarah Lennox 1740–1832* (London: Chatto & Windus, 1994) and Amanda Vickery, *The Gentleman's Daughter: Women's Lives in Georgian England* (New Haven CT & London: Yale University Press, 1998).

25 See for example Freya Gowrley, *Domestic Space in Britain, 1750–1840: Materiality, Sociability and Emotion* (London: Bloomsbury, 2022).

26 See for example Rosie Dias and Kate Smith, eds *British Women and Cultural Practices of Empire, 1770–1940* (London: Bloomsbury, 2018) and Margot Finn and Kate Smith, eds *The East India Company at Home, 1757–1857* (London: UCL Press, 2018).

27 Kate Retford, *The Art of Domestic Life: Family Portraiture in Eighteenth-century England* (London: Yale University Press, 2006) and Retford, *The Conversation Piece: Making Modern Art in Eighteenth-Century Britain* (London: Yale University Press, 2017).

28 Amanda Vickery, *Behind Closed Doors: At Home in Georgian England* (London: Yale University Press, 2009), Jon Stobart, *Comfort in the Eighteenth-century Country House* (New York and Abingdon: Routledge, 2022), Stobart ed. *The Comforts of Home in Western Europe, 1700–1900* (London: Bloomsbury Academic, 2020) and Jon Stobart and Mark Rothery, *Consumption and the Country House* (Oxford: Oxford University Press, 2016).

29 See, for example, Mario Praz, *An Illustrated History of Furnishing from the Renaissance to the Twentieth Century* trans. William Weaver (New York: George Braziller, 1964), Peter Thornton, *Authentic Décor: The Domestic Interior 1620–1920* (London: Weidenfeld & Nicholson, 1989), Annik Pardailhé-Galabrun, 'Home Decoration' in *The Birth of Intimacy: Privacy and Domestic Life in Early Modern Paris* trans. Jocelyn Phelps (Philadelphia: University of Pennsylvania Press, 1991), Mary Sheriff, 'The Dynamics of Decoration' in *Fragonard: Art and Eroticism* (Chicago: University of Chicago Press, 1990), Katie Scott, *The Rococo Interior: Decoration and Social Spaces in Early Eighteenth-century Paris* (London: Yale University Press, 1995), Mariet Westermann, ed. *Art & Home: Dutch Interiors in the Age of Rembrandt* (Zwolle: Waanders, 2003), Patricia Fortini Brown, *Private Lives in Renaissance Venice: Art, Architecture, and the Family* (New Haven CT: Yale University Press, 2004) and Jeremy Aynsley and Charlotte Grant, eds. *Imagined Interiors: Representing the Domestic Interior since the Renaissance* (London: V&A Publications, 2006). For the display of art in British houses see Mark Girouard, *Life in the English Country House: A Social and Architectural History* (New Haven CT: Yale University Press, 1978), John Cornforth, *English Interiors 1790–1848: The Quest for Comfort* (London: Barrie & Jenkins, 1978), Charles Saumarez-Smith, *Eighteenth-century Decoration: Design and the Domestic Interior in England* (Weidenfeld & Nicolson, 1993), Charlotte Gere, *Nineteenth-Century Decoration: The Art of the Interior* (New York: Harry N Abrams, 1989), Clive Wainwright, *The Romantic Interior: The British Collector at Home 1750–1850* (London: Yale University Press, 1989) and Ruth Guilding, *Owning the Past: Why the English Collected Antique Sculpture, 1640–1840* (London: Yale University Press, 2014).

30 Nicholas Tromans, *The Private Lives of Pictures: Art at Home in Britain, 1800–1940* (London: Reaktion Books, 2022).

31 Dror Wahrman, *Imagining the Middle Class: The Political Representation of Class in Britain c. 1780–1840* (Cambridge: Cambridge University Press, 1995).

32 On grand London townhouses' decoration and social purpose see the essays in Avery-Quash and Retford, *The Georgian London Town House*, Sykes, *Private Palaces*, Port, 'West End Palaces' and Stewart, *The Town House in Georgian London*.

33 *Catalogue of Pictures at Cleveland House* (London: J Hays, 1806).

34 'Mr Lilley's payments', Staffordshire Record Office D593/R/1/13/1.

35 We do not have a clear statement of intention from the Marquess of Stafford on the subject of the ticketing system or other regulations governing entry, but the guidebook and catalogue written by John Britton, which was published with his permission, implicitly claims to speak for him. While I have found no written correspondence between the Marquess and John Britton confirming this, the inclusion of a floor plan and interior view in the catalogue imply that it could not have been produced without the Marquess' explicit cooperation. For more on access to the gallery at Cleveland House see Richter, 'Opening the Townhouse: Access in the Urban Environment in the Early Nineteenth Century', in *Collecting and Access*, eds Andrea Gáldy, Susan Bracken and Adriana Turpin (Newcastle-upon-Tyne: Cambridge Scholars Publishing, forthcoming).

36 Advertisement found in *Press-cuttings, from English newspapers . . .* National Art Library, Victoria & Albert Museum, London (Shelfmark P.P.17.G), 814. Probably because there were few who could afford such an expensive production, Ottley failed to achieve a return on his investment and declared bankruptcy.

37 John Britton, *Catalogue Raisonné of the Pictures Belonging to the Most Honourable the Marquis of Stafford, in the Gallery of Cleveland House* (London: Longman, Hurst, Rees and Orme, 1808) and William Young Ottley, *Engravings of the Most Noble the Marquis of Stafford's Collection of Pictures in London, arranged according to Schools, and in Chronological Order, with Remarks on Each Picture* (London: Longman, Hurst, Rees, Orme, and Brown, 1818).

38 Advertisement found in *Press-cuttings*, 814.

39 The book described here is the first example I ever encountered. I am very grateful to British book collector Charles Sebag-Montefiore, FSA and Mirjam Foot, Professor of Library and Archive Studies at University College, London, for information on this binding. See also Howard Nixon, *The Broxbourne Library: Styles and Designs of Bookbinding from the Twelfth to the Twentieth Century* (London: Maggs Brothers, 1956), 202.

40 'The Marquis of Stafford's New Residence', [May 1806?] *Press-cuttings*, 1282; Priscilla Wakefield, *Perambulations in London, and its Environs* (London: Darton, Harvey and Darton, 1814), 266.

41 For more on the methodology of using images and interior views as evidence for studying lost interiors and the social practices that took place within, see Anne Nellis Richter, '"The whole is now passed, the House down": Visualising Lost Interiors' in *Reassembling the Social Interior: Historical Spaces from Contemporary Viewpoints* eds Helen McCormack, Jennifer Gray and Anne Nellis Richter (Manchester: Manchester University Press, forthcoming).

42 Michael Yonan, 'Towards a Fusion of Art History and Material Culture Studies', *West 86th* 18:2 (2011), 232–248, 235.

43 Arjun Appadurai, *The Social Life of Things: Commodities in Cultural Perspective* (Cambridge: Cambridge University Press, 1986). Also important for the development of the anthropological approach to consumption are Pierre Bourdieu, *Distinction: A Social Critique of the Judgment of Taste* trans. Richard Nice (Cambridge MA: Harvard University Press, 1984) and Daniel Miller, *Material Cultural and Mass Consumption* (Oxford: Basil Blackwell, 1987).

44 Neil McKendrick, John Brewer and JH Plumb's *The Birth of a Consumer Society: The Commercialization of Eighteenth-Century England* (Bloomington IND: Indiana University Press, 1982). The essays in *Consumption and the World of Goods*, ed. John Brewer and Roy Porter (London: Routledge, 1993) and *The Consumption of Culture: Image, Object, Text*, ed. Ann Bermingham and John Brewer (London: Routledge, 1995) have also been of vital importance in framing the issues addressed by researchers working on consumption. See also Maxine Berg, *Luxury and Pleasure in Eighteenth-century Britain* (Oxford: Oxford University Press, 2005), Woodruff D Smith, *Consumption and the Making of Respectability 1600–1800* (New York: Routledge, 2002) and Frank Trentmann, *Empire of Things: How we became a world of consumers, from the fifteenth century to the twenty-first* (New York: HarperCollins, 2016).

45 Beginning in the 1960s, John Cornforth's body of work for *Country Life* magazine, in addition to numerous other books and publications, revitalised interest in seventeenth and eighteenth-century houses, inspiring a range of important documentary and interpretive works addressing their decoration. See, for example, works cited in fn 29 by scholars and curators including Peter Thornton, Charles Saumarez-Smith, Gervase Jackson-Stops and Charlotte Gere. These classic works have more have recently been built upon by a generation seeking to tie decoration more explicitly to issues of ideology. See, for example, Stacey Sloboda, *Chinoiserie: Commerce and critical ornament in eighteenth-century Britain* (Manchester: Manchester University Press, 2014) and Guilding, *Owning the Past*.

46 Giorgio Riello, 'Things that shape history: Material culture and historical narratives', in *History and Material Culture* ed. Karen Harvey (London: Routledge, 2009). Mimi Hellman's work on the interplay between decoration and social practice in the French context is also essential. See, for example, Hellman, 'Object lessons: French decorative art as a model for interdisciplinarity', in *The Interdisciplinary Century: Tensions and Convergences in 18th-century Art, Literature and History. Studies on Voltaire and the Eighteenth Century* ed. Julia Douthwaite and Mary Vidal (Oxford: Voltaire Foundation, 2005), Hellman, 'Furniture, Sociability and the Work of Leisure in 18th-Century France', *Eighteenth-Century Studies* 32 (Summer 1999), 415–445 and Hellman, 'Enchanted Night: Decoration, Sociability, and Visuality after Dark', in *Paris: Life & Luxury in the Eighteenth Century*, ed. Charissa Bremer-David (Los Angeles: J Paul Getty Museum, 2011).

47 Stacey Sloboda, 'Fashioning Bluestocking Conversation: Elizabeth Montagu's Chinese Room', in *Architectural Space in Eighteenth-century Europe:*

Constructing Identities and Interiors, ed. Denise Amy Baxter and Meredith Martin (Burlington, VT: Ashgate, 2010), Kathryn Norberg, 'Salon as Stage: Actress/Courtesans and their Homes in Late Eighteenth-Century Paris', in *Architectural Space in Eighteenth-century Europe,* Sylvia Harcstark Myers, *The Bluestocking Circle: Women, Friendship, and the Life of the Mind in the Eighteenth-century England* (Oxford: Clarendon Press, 1990), Elizabeth Eger and Lucy Peltz, ed. *Brilliant Women: Eighteenth-century Bluestockings* (London: National Portrait Gallery, 2008) and Daniel Harkett, 'Mediating Private and Public: Juliette Récamier's Salon at L'Abbaye-aux-Bois' in *Women, Femininity, and Public Space in European Visual Culture, 1789–1914,* ed. Temma Balducci and Heather Belnap Jensen (Farnham: Ashgate, 2014), 47–64.

48 Mary Douglas and Baron Isherwood, *The World of Goods: Towards an Anthropology of Consumption* (New York: Routledge, 1996).

49 Hillier and Hanson, *The Social Logic of Space* (Cambridge: Cambridge University Press, 1984), ix.

50 Hannah Greig, *The Beau Monde* (Oxford: Oxford University Press, 2013).

51 E Beresford Chancellor, *The Private Palaces of London Past and Present* (London: Kegan Paul, Trench, Trubner & Co, 1908), 206.

52 For a discussion of the impact of this bombing on the house and art collection, see Christopher Riopelle, 'Lost and Found' in Stephen Bann and Linda Whiteley, *Painting History: Delaroche and Lady Jane Grey* (London: National Gallery, 2010), 22.

53 The pictures were purchased using a combination of public funds and donations from private sources. Mark Brown, 'Second part of £95m Titian pair bought for Britain', *The Guardian*, 1 March 2012. DOI: www.theguardian.com/artanddesign/2012/mar/01/titian-95m-pair-national-gallery.

1 'A very complete business': Designing and Building the Gallery

1 Susan Pearce, 'Material as Style or Material as History? Charles Tatham and the Transformation of the Object', in *Researching Material Culture* ed. Pearce (Leicester Archaeology Monographs 8, Material Culture Research Group, Occasional Papers No 1, 2000), 55.

2 Hannah Greig and Giorgio Riello, 'Eighteenth-Century Interiors – Redesigning the Georgian: Introduction', *Journal of Design History* 20:4 (2007), 286.

3 For a complete overview of the history of the Orléans Collection, see the essays in *The Orléans Collection*, ed. Vanessa I Schmid with Julia Armstrong-Totten (New Orleans: New Orleans Museum of Art, 2018). On the pictures from the Orléans Collection that were purchased by the Duke of Bridgewater and made their way to Cleveland House, see Nicholas Penny, *The Sixteenth Century Italian Paintings, v. 2, Venice, 1540–1600* (London: National Gallery, 2008), 461–70,

Julia Armstrong-Totten, 'Expand the Audience, Increase the Profits: Motivations Behind the Private Contract Sale' in *The Circulation of Works of Art in the Revolutionary Era, 1789–1848*, ed. Roberta Panzanelli and Monica Preti-Hamard (Presses Universitaires de Rennes and Getty Research Institute, 2007). General works on collecting that also focus on the Orléans pictures include William Buchanan, *Memoirs of Painting, with a Chronological History of the Importation of Pictures of the Great Masters into England since the French Revolution* (London: R Ackermann, 1824), Francis Henry Taylor, *The Taste of Angels* (Boston: Little, Brown and Company, 1948), 535–547, Gerald Reitlinger, *The Economics of Taste: The Rise and Fall of the Picture Market, 1760–1960* (New York: Holt, Rinehart and Winston, 1961), 26–38 and Arthur MacGregor, *Curiosity and Enlightenment: Collectors and Collections from the Sixteenth to the Nineteenth Century* (New Haven: Yale University Press, 2008).

4 On the 'Orleans sales' of the 1790s, see Jordana Pomeroy, 'The Orléans Collection: Its impact on the British art world' *Apollo* 145 (Feb. 1997), 26–31 and Pomeroy, 'Conversing with History: The Orléans Collection Arrives in Britain' in *British Models of Art Collecting and the American Response* ed. Inge Reist (Burlington, VT: Ashgate, 2014). On the reception of Old Master painting in the early nineteenth century generally see *The Reception of Titian in Britain from Reynolds to Ruskin* ed. Peter Humfrey (Turnhout: Brepols, 2013) and Maureen McCue, *British Romanticism and the Reception of Old Master Art, 1793–1840* (Burlington, VT: Ashgate, 2014).

5 Peter Humfrey, *The Stafford Gallery: The Greatest Art Collection of Regency London* (Norwich: Unicorn Press, 2019), Peter Humfrey, 'The 3rd Duke of Bridgewater as a Collector of Old Master Paintings', *Journal of the History of Collections* 27:2 (2015): 211–25 and Humfrey, 'The Stafford Gallery at Cleveland House and the 2nd Marquess of Stafford as a Collector', *Journal of the History of Collections* 28:1 (2016): 43–55.

6 Undated note [1803] from Correspondence of the Duchess-Countess and Frances, Lady Douglas, 1790–1811, National Library of Scotland Dep. 313 [744].

7 Letter dated 10 March 1803 in Lady Theresa Lewis, ed. *Extracts of the Journals and Correspondence of Miss Berry* (London: Longmans, Green, and Co, 1865), II: 241. See also Lewis Melville, *The Berry Papers* (New York: John Lane, 1914), 198–99.

8 Eric Richards, *The Leviathan of Wealth: The Sutherland Fortune in the Industrial Revolution* (London: Routledge and Kegan Paul, 1973), 43.

9 Henry Reeve, ed. *The Greville Memoirs* (London: Longmans, Green, and Co. 1905), 3: 20.

10 Anne Nellis Richter, 'Cleveland House as Art Museum? The Short Life of the "Louvre of London"' in Margaret Iacono Wertz and Esmée Quodbach, eds *The Evolving House Museum: Art Collectors and their Residences* (Leiden: Brill, forthcoming).

11 *Will of the Duke of Bridgewater* (London: Stewart and Co. 1839), 6.

12 Stafford's contemporaries were aware that the collection had been marked as an 'heirloom' with all the benefits and challenges that implied. See James Greig, ed. *The Farington Diary* (New York: George H. Doran, 1923–1928), 3: 173.

13 See *The First Modern Museums of Art*, ed. Carole Paul (Los Angeles: J Paul Getty Museum, 2012) for detailed accounts of the continental museums of art that were appearing during the eighteenth century.

14 Michael Yonan, 'The Kunsthistoriches Museum/Belvedere, Vienna: Dynasticism and the Function of Art', in Paul, ed. *The First Modern Museums of Art*, 193–95.

15 As Nicholas Penny put it, the *Palais-Royal* was 'easily visited by amateurs and artists alike'. Penny, *Sixteenth Century Italian Paintings*, 464.

16 Jonathan Richardson, *A Discourse on the Dignity, Certainty, Pleasure, and Advantage of the Science of a Connoisseur* (London: W Churchill, 1719).

17 Sir Joshua Reynolds, *Discourses on Art* ed. Robert Wark (London: Yale University Press, 1997). The literature on artist training is extensive. See Holger Hoock, *The King's Artists: The Royal Academy of Arts and the Politics of British Culture 1760–1840* (Oxford: Clarendon Press, 2005), Matthew Hargreaves, *Candidates for Fame: The Society of Artists of Great Britain, 1760–1791* (London: Yale University Press, 2006) and Martin Myrone, *Making the Modern Artist: Culture, Class and Art-Educational Opportunity in Romantic Britain* (London: Yale University Press, 2020).

18 Adrian Tinniswood, *A History of Country House Visiting* (Oxford: Basil Blackwell, 1989) and Carole Fabricant, 'The Literature of Domestic Tourism and the Public Consumption of Private Property' in *The New Eighteenth Century*, ed. Felicity Nussbaum and Laura Brown (New York: Methuen, 1987). On the expansion of the practice of country house tourism in the nineteenth century, see Peter Mandler, *The Fall and Rise of the Stately Home* (New Haven: Yale University Press, 1997).

19 Jocelyn Anderson, 'Remaking the Space: The Plan and the Route in Country-House Guidebooks from 1770 to 1815', *Architectural History* 54 (2011): 195–212 and *Touring and Publicizing England's Country Houses in the Long Eighteenth Century* (London: Bloomsbury, 2018).

20 *Letters of Sir Joshua Reynolds*, ed. Frederick Whiley Hilles (Cambridge: University Press, 1929), 173.

21 Arthur MacGregor, *Curiosity and Enlightenment: Collectors and Collections from the Sixteenth to the Nineteenth Century* (New Haven: Yale University Press, 2008).

22 Susannah Brooke, 'The Display and Reception of Private Picture Collections in London Town Houses, 1780–1830' in *The Georgian London Town House: Building, Collecting and Display* ed. Susanna Avery-Quash and Kate Retford (London: Bloomsbury, 2019), 149–67. On distinctions between country house and town house visiting see Richter, 'Cleveland House as Art Museum?'

23 Iain Pears, *The Discovery of Painting* (New Haven: Yale University Press, 1988), 176–77.

24 On the founding of the Louvre and its influence on English collectors, see Anne Nellis Richter, '"A Museum within His Own Apartments": Maria Cosway's 'Gallery of the Louvre and the Domestic Interior' in *Visualizing the Nineteenth-Century Home: Modern Art and the Decorative Impulse*, ed. Anca Lasc (Aldershot: Ashgate, 2016). On the influence of the French Revolution on

British culture more generally see David Bindman, *The Shadow of the Guillotine: Britain and the French Revolution* (London: British Museum, 1989).

25 Holger Hoock has argued that the arrival of the Orléans pictures in England prompted renewed calls by members of the Royal Academy for a state-funded national gallery. Holger Hoock, 'Old Masters and the English School: The Royal Academy of the Arts and the Notion of a National Gallery at the Turn of the Century', *Journal of the History of Collections* (2004), 1–18, 16.

26 David Watkin, *Thomas Hope and the Neo-Classical Idea* (London: John Murray, 1968), 10.

27 John Britton, *Catalogue Raisonné of the Pictures Belonging to the Most Honourable the Marquis of Stafford, in the gallery of Cleveland House* (London: Longman, Hurst, Rees, and Orme, 1808), vii.

28 The first exhibition of the BI opened on 17 February 1806, as recorded in Thomas Smith, *Recollections of the British Institution for Promoting the Fine Arts in the United Kingdom* (London: Simpkin & Marshall, 1860), 15. On the British Institution see Peter Fullerton, 'Patronage and Pedagogy: The British Institution in the Early Nineteenth Century', *Art History* 5:1 (1982): 59–72, Morris Eaves, *The Counter-Arts Conspiracy: Art and Industry in the Age of Blake* (Ithaca, NY: Cornell University Press, 1993): 74–78, Francis Haskell, *The Ephemeral Museum* (London: Yale University Press, 2000), and Catherine Roach, *Pictures-within-Pictures in Nineteenth-Century Britain* (New York: Routledge, 2016).

29 Ann Pullan, 'Public Goods or Private Interests: The British Institution in the Early Nineteenth Century' in *Art in Bourgeois Society, 1790–1850* ed. Andrew Hemingway and William Vaughan (Cambridge: Cambridge University Press, 1998), 27–44.

30 Letter from Mrs Howe dated 10 April 1803 in Lewis, *Extracts*, II: 241.

31 For Tatham's full biography, see Howard Colvin, *A Biographical Dictionary of British Architects 1600–1840* (London: John Murray, 1978), 808–10 and Christopher Proudfoot and David Watkin, 'A Pioneer of English Neo-Classicism', *Country Life* (April 13/20, 1972), 918–21.

32 Colvin, *Biographical Dictionary*, 423–26.

33 Proudfoot and Watkin, 'A Pioneer', 918–21.

34 Tatham's activities in Rome are discussed in detail in Frank Salmon, 'Charles Heathcote Tatham and the Accademia di S. Luca, Rome', *The Burlington Magazine* 140 (Feb. 1998), 85–92. His surviving letters and partial autobiography are transcribed in 'Charles Heathcote Tatham in Italy, 1794–96: Letters, Drawings and Fragments, and Part of an Autobiography', ed. Susan Pearce and Frank Salmon, *The Volume of the Walpole Society* 76 (2005), 1–91.

35 On Hope's travel and early collecting see David Watkin, *Thomas Hope*, 7–10 and Philip Mansel, 'European Wealth, Ottoman Travel, and London Fame' in David Watkin and Philip Hewat-Jaboor, ed. *Thomas Hope: Regency Designer* (London and New Haven: Yale University Press, 2008), 2–21.

36 David Watkin, 'Thomas Hope's house in Duchess Street', *Apollo* (March 2004), 31--39.

37 Martin Postle, 'Frederick Howard, 5th Earl of Carlisle as a Collector of Contemporary British Art', *Art & the Country House*. Available at: https://doi.org/10.17658/ACH/CHE526.

38 Christopher Ridgway, 'Castle Howard Introduction', *Art and the Country House*. Available at: https://doi.org/10.17658/ACH/CHE522 and Ruth Guilding, *Owning the Past: Why the English Collected Antique Sculpture, 1640–1840* (London: Yale University Press, 2014), 125–28.

39 David Watkin, 'Thomas Hope's house', 31–39.

40 On colour in galleries, see Ian C Bristow, *Architectural Colour in British Interiors 1615–1840* (London: Yale University Press, 1996), 203–04.

41 John Cornforth, *English Interiors 1790–1848:The Quest for Comfort* (London: Barrie & Jenkins, 1978), 40. In 2012, Jane Davies Conservation carried out paint analysis on the Long Gallery at Castle Howard and concluded that, by 1811 when the gallery was considered complete, the walls were painted an off-white or pale stone shade, while the skirting boards were painted with a marbling effect; overall, the paint choice would have given the room the appearance of stone. Jane Davies' reports, in addition to further documentation of the gallery, were published electronically in December 2021 in a report of a research project conducted by Ben Elliott and Heath Ballowe under the auspices of Castle Howard, The Furniture History Society, British & Irish Furniture Makers Online, and the Foyle Foundation. The digital record of their work is available at: https://castlehowardthelonggallery.commons.bgc.bard.edu/.

42 Anderson, *Touring and Publicizing*, 106.

43 Mansel, 'European Wealth', 16.

44 Staffordshire Record Office D6579/21/1-133 and D6579/24/1-119.

45 Colvin, *Biographical Dictionary*, 809.

46 *London Courier and Evening Gazette* (6 May 1806).

47 Ibid.

48 Rosalys Coope, 'The Gallery in England: Names and Meanings', *Architectural History* 27 (1984), 446–55 and Rosalys Coope, 'The Long Gallery': Its Origins, Development, Use and Decoration', *Architectural History* 29 (1986), 43–72, 74–84.

49 The literature on cabinets and cabinets of curiosity is vast. For an introduction, see Arthur MacGregor, *Curiosity and Enlightenment: Collectors and Collections from the Sixteenth to the Nineteenth Century* (New Haven and London: Yale University Press, 2007).

50 On sculpture galleries in the eighteenth century, see Ruth Guilding, *Owning the Past: Why the English Collected Antique Sculpture, 1640–1840* (London: Yale University Press, 2014) and Malcolm Baker, *The Marble Index: Roubiliac and Sculptural Portraiture in Eighteenth-century Britain* (London: Yale University Press, 2014).

51 Coope, 'The Long Gallery', 64. Additional important sources on the decoration of houses and galleries in the seventeenth and eighteenth centuries include Charles Saumarez-Smith, *Eighteenth-century Decoration* (London: George

Weidenfeld and Nicolson, 1993), Peter Thornton, *Authentic Décor: The Domestic Interior 1620–1920* (London: George Weidenfeld and Nicolson, 1984), and Gervase Jackson-Stops, ed. *The Treasure Houses of Britain* Exh. Cat. (Washington, DC 1985).

52 'The Marquis of Stafford's New Residence', [May 1806] *Press-cuttings, from English newspapers . . .* National Art Library, Victoria & Albert Museum, London (Shelfmark P.P.17.G), 1282; *London Courier and Evening Gazette* (6 May 1806).

53 David Watkin identified the source of the coffering, in Watkin, 'Thomas Hope's house', 37–38.

54 These stoves are not depicted in any visual representations of the gallery. Priscilla Wakefield, *Perambulations in London, and its Environs* (London: Darton, Harvey and Darton, 1814), 268.

55 Giles Waterfield, 'The Town House as Gallery of Art', *London Journal* 20:1 (1995), 47–66.

56 Mark Ledbury, 'Art Versus Life: A Dissenting Voice in the Grande Galerie', *Journal18* 2 (Fall 2016). Available at: www.journal18.org/866. DOI: 10.30610/2.2016.4.

57 'Two hundred and sixty-three vase lamps' quoted in William Thomas Whitley, *Art in England, 1800–1820* (New York: The Macmillan Company, 1928), I: 108. On lighting practices in the early nineteenth century see Alice Barnaby, 'Lighting Practices in Art Galleries and Exhibition Spaces, 1750–1850', in *The International Handbooks of Museum Studies* 1 (2013) and Barnaby, *Light Touches: Cultural Practices of Illumination, 1800–1900* (London: Routledge, 2017).

58 Giles Waterfield, 'The Town House as Gallery of Art', 47–66; Wakefield, *Perambulations in London,* 267–69.

59 Wakefield, *Perambulations in London,* 266.

60 There is an extensive literature on eighteenth-century classicism, but a few important works dealing with its impact in collecting, architecture and the visual arts include Ian Jenkins and Kim Sloan, *Vases & Volcanoes: Sir William Hamilton and His Collection* (London: The British Museum, 1996), Francis Haskell and Nicholas Penny, *Taste and the Antique: The Lure of Classical Sculpture, 1500–1900* (London: Yale University Press, 1981), John Barrell, *The Political Theory of Painting from Reynolds to Hazlitt: 'The Body of the Public'* (London: Yale University Press, 1986), Iain Pears, *The Discovery of Painting* (New Haven: Yale University Press, 1988), Eileen Harris, *The Genius of Robert Adam: His Interiors* (London: Yale University Press, 2001) and Viccy Coltman, *Fabricating the Antique: Neoclassicism in Britain, 1760–1800* (Chicago: University of Chicago Press, 2006).

61 David Udy, 'The Neo-Classicism of Charles Heathcote Tatham', *The Connoisseur* (1977), 269–76.

62 Colvin, *Biographical Dictionary,* 423–26; Summerson described Holland's façade for Carlton House as 'strictly classical and perfectly free from Adam influence'. Summerson, *Georgian London* (New Haven: Yale University Press, 2003), 157.

63 David Watkin, 'Thomas Hope's house: 31–39. See also Watkin and Hewat-Jaboor, *Thomas Hope,* 23–43.

64 Tania Buckrell Pos, 'Tatham and Italy: Influences on English Neo-Classical Design', *Furniture History* 38 (2002), 58–82 and Udy, 'The Neo-Classicism of Charles Heathcote Tatham', 269–76.

65 Susan Pearce, 'Material as Style or Material as History?', 63.

66 Tatham designed one further art gallery, for Brocklesby Park, Lincolnshire, in 1807. Colvin, *Biographical Dictionary*, 808–10.

67 Tatham's surviving letters are transcribed in Pearce and Salmon, ed., 'Charles Heathcote Tatham in Italy.'

68 Viccy Coltman, *Fabricating the Antique: Neoclassicism in Britain, 1760–1800* (Chicago: University of Chicago Press, 2006).

69 CH Tatham, *Etchings, Representing the Best Examples of Ancient Ornamental Architecture* (London: T Gardiner, 1799), 4.

70 Quoted in David Udy, 'The Neo-Classicism of Charles Heathcote Tatham', *The Connoisseur* (1977): 269.

71 Charlotte Gere, *Nineteenth-Century Decoration* (London: Weidenfeld and Nicolson, 1989): 47 and Watkin and Hewat-Jaboor, *Thomas Hope, 66–69.* See Pierre-François Léonard Fontaine and Charles Percier, *Recueil de Decorations Interieurs* (Paris, Pierre Didot l'ainé, 1812).

72 Publications written or sponsored by Hope which included illustrations by Moses include *Household Furniture and Interior Decoration* (London: Longman, Hurst, Rees, and Orme, 1807), *Costume of the Ancients* (London: William Miller, 1809) and *Designs of Modern Costume* (London: Privately printed, 1812).

73 Watkin, 'Thomas Hope's house', 38.

74 Hannah Greig, *The Beau Monde: Fashionable Society in Georgian London* (Oxford: Oxford University Press, 2013), 24–25.

75 On Fonthill Abbey, see Derek E Ostergard, ed., *William Beckford, 1760–1844: An Eye for the Magnificent* (New Haven: Yale University Press, 2001). On the 1822 auction of Fonthill Abbey and the cultural significance thereof, see Anne Nellis Richter, 'Spectacle and Display in the English Country House: The Fonthill Auction of 1822', *Eighteenth-Century Studies* 41:4 (Summer 2008), 543–63. On Strawberry Hill and revived historicism in British design see Richter 'Beauty', in *Interiors in the Age of Enlightenment* ed. Stacey Sloboda (London: Bloomsbury, 2024), 202.

76 Letter dated 9 October 1805, Brighton, Lady B. to G.L.G. in *Lord Granville Leveson Gower: Private Correspondence 1781–1821* ed. Castalia Countess Granville (London: John Murray, 1917), II: 120

77 Thomas Hope, *Household Furniture and Interior Decoration* (London, 1807), 7. Hope's biographers emphasize that because Hope was not British by birth, he was keen to establish himself in English high society. His emphasis on patriotic motives for selecting furnishings for the interior should be viewed in light of his personal ambition. See David Watkin, *Thomas Hope and the Neo-Classical Idea* (London: John Murray, 1968) and Watkin and Hewat-Jaboor, *Thomas Hope.*

78 See Abigail Harrison Moore, 'Voyage: Dominique-Vivant Denon and the Transference of Images of Egypt', *Art History* 25: 4 (2002).

79 *London Courier and Evening Gazette* (6 May 1806).

80 Whitley, *Art in England,* I: 108.

81 'Elegant marble slabs. . .' from *London Courier and Evening Gazette* (6 May 1806). Thomas Tatham was one of the partners in the successful cabinetry and upholstery firm, Marsh & Tatham. Many thanks to Robert Copley of Christie's Furniture and Decorative Arts department for sharing his knowledge of these tables. See 'The Cleveland House Porphyry Tables' in *Christie's Exceptional Sale* (10 July, 2014).

82 *London Courier and Evening Gazette*, (6 May 1806); Tatham, *Etchings*. On Tatham's furniture design, see Proudfoot and Watkin, 'The Furniture of C.H. Tatham', *Country Life* (8 June 1972), 1481–86 and Pos, 'Tatham and Italy.'

83 Pos, 'Tatham and Italy', 67.

84 Tatham, *Etchings*, 7.

85 *London Courier and Evening Gazette* (6 May 1806).

86 My gratitude to Sue Stern, who generously shared her knowledge about these carpets and an unpublished section of her dissertation. See Susan Stern, 'Craftsman, Innovator and Entrepreneur: Thomas Whitty and the English Carpet' (MA diss., Birkbeck College and Wallace Collection, London, 2005).

87 *London Courier and Evening Gazette* (6 May 1806).

88 On the decoration of the gallery at the *Palais-Royal* see Rochelle Ziskin, *Sheltering Art: Collecting and Social Identity in Early Eighteenth-century Paris* (University Park: The Pennsylvania State University Press, 2012). For a new interpretation of this scheme in the context of early eighteenth-century court culture, see Aaron Wile, *Painting, Authority, and Experience at the Twilight of the Grand Siècle, 1688–1721* (PhD thesis, Harvard University, 2016).

89 Adriano Aymonino and Manolo Guerci, 'The Refurbishment of Northumberland House: Craftsmen and Interior Decoration in Mid-Eighteenth-century London Town Houses' in *The Georgian London Town House: Building, Collecting and Display* ed. Susanna Avery-Quash and Kate Retford (London: Bloomsbury, 2019), 71–98.

90 See, for example, Yonan, 'The Kunsthistoriches Museum/Belvedere, Vienna', 202.

91 Ian Jenkins, '"Athens rising near the pole": London, Athens, and the Idea of Freedom', in *London – World City 1800–1840* ed. Celina Fox (London: Yale University Press and the Museum of London, 1992), 143–66.

92 CM Westmacott, *British Galleries of Painting and Sculpture* (London: Sherwood, Jones & Co., 1824), 176.

93 I have also written about this idea in 'Beauty', *Interiors in the Age of Enlightenment*, 24–26.

94 Lawrence Klein, *Shaftesbury and the Culture of Politeness* (Cambridge: Cambridge University Press, 1994).

95 Cooper, *Characteristicks of Men, Manners, Opinions, Times* (London: John Darby, 1711), 338.

96 On the limit of Shaftesbury's influence in the first half of the eighteenth century see Matthew Craske, 'From Burlington Gate to Billingsgate' in *Articulating British Classicism* ed. Barbara Arciszewska and Elizabeth McKellar (Aldershot: Ashgate, 2004), 97–118.

97 'Chaste' in Britton, *Catalogue Raisonné*; 'Simple' in *The Times* (16 August 1806), 2; 'elegant' and 'tasteful' in 'The Marquis of Stafford's New Residence', *Press-cuttings*, 1282.

98 'The Marquis of Stafford's New Residence', *Press-cuttings*, 1282.

99 'Fashionable Furniture', *The Repository of Arts, Literature, Commerce, Manufactures, Fashions, and Politics* (April 1814), 236–37.

100 Tatham, *Etchings,* 4.

101 Pearce, 'Material as Style or Material as History?', 63.

102 Britton, *Catalogue Raisonné*, 1.

103 *Ibid.*, vii.

104 *Ibid.*, vii.

105 *Ibid.*, vi.

106 For an excellent, short introduction to the ideology of domesticity as it developed in the eighteenth century see Clara Tuite, 'Domesticity' in *An Oxford Companion to the Romantic Age* ed. Iain McCalman (Oxford: Oxford University Press, 1999), 125–33.

107 Amanda Vickery, *Behind Closed Doors: At Home in Georgian England* (London: Yale University Press, 2009), especially discussion of the meanings of the word home on 6–7. See also John Crowley, *The Invention of Comfort: Sensibilities and Design in Early Modern Britain and Early America* (Baltimore: Johns Hopkins University Press, 2001) and Witold Rybczynski, *Home: A Short History of an Idea* (New York: Viking, 1986).

108 Vickery, *Behind Closed Doors*. On how the ideology of domesticity permeated the acquisition and display of contemporary painting, see Kate Retford, *The Art of Domestic Life* (London: Yale University Press, 2006) and Retford, *The Conversation Piece* (London: Yale University Press, 2017).

109 Jane Austen, *Pride and Prejudice* (London: Penguin Classics, 1996), 202.

110 K Dian Kriz, *The Ideology of the English Landscape Painter* (London: Yale University Press, 1997), 40.

111 On the crowd at the Royal Academy, see Andrew Hemingway, 'Art Exhibitions as Leisure-Class Rituals in Early Nineteenth-Century London' in *Towards a Modern Art World* ed. Brian Allen (London: Yale University Press, 1995) and David Solkin, ed. *Art on the Line* (London: Yale University Press, 2002).

112 Britton, *Catalogue Raisonné*, vi.

113 Quoted in Whitley, *Art in England*, 1:109; *Daily Advertiser, Oracle and True Briton* (6 May 1806). This phrase was also adopted by the *London Chronicle and Evening Gazette* (6 May 1806).

114 Pearce, 'Material as Style or Material as History?', 63.

115 Richter, 'Cleveland House as Art Museum?'

2 'The high attraction of the spectacle': Displaying Sociability

1 Opening day was Wednesday 21 May 1806. James Greig, ed. *The Farington Diary by Joseph Farington, R.A.* 8 v. (London: Hutchinson, 1922–1928), III: 236.

2 John Britton, 'Notice respecting Tickets of Admission to the Cleveland-House Gallery', *Catalogue Raisonné of the Pictures Belonging to the Most Honourable the Marquis of Stafford, in the Gallery of Cleveland House* (London: Longman, Hurst, Rees and Orme, 1808), n.p.

3 'Monthly Retrospect of the Fine Arts', *Monthly Magazine* 21 (July 1806), 543–54.

4 Robin Evans, *Translations from Drawing to Building* (London: Architectural Association, 1997), 56.

5 Important touchstones in the literature on space and sociability include Michel de Certeau, *The Practice of Everyday Life*, trans Steven Rendall (Berkeley: University of California Press, 1984) and Jürgen Habermas, *The Structural Transformation of the Public Sphere*, trans Thomas Burger (Cambridge: Polity Press, 1989).

6 Henri Lefebvre, *The Production of Space*, trans Donald Nicholson-Smith (Oxford: Blackwell, 1991).

7 Hannah Greig, *The Beau Monde: Fashionable Society in Georgian London* (Oxford: Oxford University Press, 2013), 4.

8 'Spectacle' in the *Oxford English Dictionary* is defined as 'a specially prepared or arranged display of a more or less public nature . . . forming an impressive or interesting show or entertainment'.

9 On 'spectacle' in a private house, see Anne Nellis Richter, 'Spectacle, Exoticism and Display in the Gentleman's House' *Eighteenth-Century Studies* 41 (Summer 2008), 543–563.

10 Alice Barnaby, *Light Touches: Cultural Practices of Illumination, 1800–1900* (Abingdon: Routledge, 2017), 73.

11 Benjamin Heller, 'Leisure and the Use of Domestic Space in Georgian London', *The Historical Journal* 53:3 (2010), 643.

12 Heller 'Leisure,' 628–29.

13 Priscilla Wakefield, *Perambulations in London, and its Environs* (London: Darton, Harvey and Darton, 1814), 266–69. Wakefield writes that her description comes from a newspaper report that was written by 'a gentleman who visits my uncle'.

14 Wakefield, *Perambulations*, 266–69.

15 Peter Humfrey, *The Stafford Gallery: The Greatest Art Collection of Regency London* (Norwich: Unicorn Press, 2019), 148–67.

16 Alex Potts, *Flesh and the Ideal: Winckelmann and the Origins of Art History* New Haven: Yale University Press, 1994).

17 Michael Yonan, 'The Kunsthistoriches Museum/Belvedere, Vienna: Dynasticism and the Function of Art' in *The First Modern Museums of Art*, ed. Carole Paul (Los Angeles: J Paul Getty Museum, 2012), 197.

18 Andrew McClellan, *Inventing the Louvre: Art, Politics, and the Origins of the Modern Museum in Eighteenth-Century Paris* (Berkeley: University of California Press, 1999), 138–48.

19 On the system of entry to Cleveland House, see Anne Nellis Richter, 'Opening the Townhouse: Access in the Urban Environment in the Early Nineteenth Century,' in *Collecting and Access*, eds Andrea Gáldy, Susan Bracken, and Adriana Turpin (Newcastle: Cambridge Scholars Publishing, forthcoming). The tickets were supplied on a yearly basis by a printer. At least in later years, it seems likely that the printer was J Meeson, who also provided a picture list for distribution in the gallery in 1814. A bill from 'Meesons' for 'Bill of Admission Tickets to Gallery' was paid on 30 June 1820, Staffordshire Record Office D593/R/1/13/1.

20 Britton, *Catalogue Raisonné*, n.p.

21 Original emphasis, Kathryn Cave, ed *The Diary of Joseph Farington* (London: Yale University Press, 1982), VII: 2788.

22 Louis Simond, *Journal of a Tour and Residence in Great Britain* (Edinburgh: Archibald Constable, 1817), 235.

23 Constance Classen, 'Museum Manners: The Sensory Life of the Early Museum', *Journal of Social History* 40:4 (2007), 898.

24 'The Marquis of Stafford's New Residence,' [May 1806], *Press-cuttings, from English newspapers* . . . National Art Library, Victoria & Albert Museum, London (Shelfmark P.P.17.G), 1282.

25 *London Chronicle and Evening Gazette* (6 May 1806); *London Courier and Evening Gazette* (6 May 1806).

26 Wakefield, *Perambulations*, 267–69.

27 David Solkin, '"This Great Mart of Genius": The Royal Academy Exhibitions at Somerset House' in *Art on the Line* (New Haven CT: Yale University Press, 2002), 1–8.

28 Britton, *Catalogue Raisonné*, 1.

29 On the organization of pictures in houses see Frances Russell, 'The Hanging and Display of Pictures, 1700–1850,' in *Studies in the History of Art 25: The Fashioning and Functioning of the British Country House* (Washington DC: National Gallery of Art, 1989), 133–53 and John Cornforth, 'Symmetry and Shapes: Patterns of Picture Hanging II', *Country Life* 169 (11 June 1981), 1698–99. On the display of pictures alongside other decorative objects see Peter Thornton, *Authentic Decor: The Domestic Interior, 1620–1920* (New York: Viking, 1984), Gervase Jackson-Stops, *The Treasure Houses of Britain* (Washington DC: National Gallery of Art, 1985) and Charles Saumarez-Smith, *Eighteenth-century Decoration: Design and the Domestic Interior in England* (London: Weidenfeld & Nicolson, 1993).

30 See, for example, William Sanderson, *Graphice, or, The use of the Pen and Pensill, in Designing, Drawing, and Painting* (London: Robert Crofts, 1658), 24–27.

31 Philippa Simpson, 'Titian in Post-Orleans London' in *The Reception of Titian in Britain: From Reynolds to Ruskin* ed. Peter Humfrey (Brepols, 2013), 99–108.

32 William Thomas Whitley, *Art in England, 1800–1820* (New York: The Macmillan Company, 1928), I: 108; *The Times* (16 August 1806), 2.

33 Richard Rush, *Memoranda of a Residence at the Court of London* (Philadelphia: Key & Biddle, 1833), 155.

34 *London Courier and Evening Gazette* (6 May 1806); Whitley, *Art in England,* I: 108.

35 *London Courier and Evening Gazette* (6 May 1806).

36 Christopher Maxwell, 'People in Glass Houses: The Polished and the Polite in Georgian Britain' in *In Sparkling Company: Reflections on Glass in the 18th-Century British World* (Corning, NY: Corning Museum of Glass, 2020), 39–68.

37 See Maxine Berg, *Luxury and Pleasure in Eighteenth-century Britain* (Oxford: Oxford University Press, 2007), 114–15 and Lisa White, 'The Impact of Historic Lighting', in *Interior Finishes and Fittings for Historic Building Conservation* ed. Michael Forsyth and Lisa White (Oxford: Blackwell, 2012). On lighting and sociability in France see Mimi Hellman, 'Enchanted Night: Decoration, Sociability and Visuality after Dark' in *Paris: Life & Luxury in the Eighteenth Century*, ed Charissa Bremer-David (Los Angeles: J Paul Getty Museum, 2011), 91–113.

38 Barnaby, *Light Touches*, 122.

39 Rush, *Memoranda*, 155.

40 Cave, *Farington Diary*, VII: 2720.

41 Robin Evans, 'Figures, Doors and Passages', in *Translations from Drawing to Building* (London: Architectural Association, 1997), 56.

42 Feltham, *The Picture of London for 1815.*

43 Heller, 'Leisure', 628.

44 Britton, *Catalogue Raisonné,* n.p.

45 The *Morning Chronicle* (21 April 1806).

46 'Stafford House', *The Morning Post* (8 May 1806).

47 'Stafford House: Marchioness of Stafford's Grand Assembly', *London Courier and Evening Gazette* (6 May 1806).

48 *Ibid.*

49 The *Morning Chronicle* (21 April 1806).

50 *London Chronicle and Evening Gazette* (6 May 1806).

51 Greig, *Beau Monde*, 22.

52 'The Marchioness of Stafford's Assembly', *The Morning Post* (25 July 1807).

53 Jenny Uglow, *In These Times: Living in Britain Through Napoleon's Wars* (New York: Farrar, Straus and Giroux, 2014), 380.

54 Melanie Doderer-Winkler, *Magnificent Entertainments: Temporary Architecture for Georgian Festivals* (London: Yale University Press, 2013).

55 'Mr Lilleys Payments,' Staffordshire Record Office D593/R/1/13/1. On Smethurst, see bill in Banks Collection, British Library (Banks, 76.21) dated 1815.

56 *London Courier and Evening Gazette*, (6 May 1806); Wakefield, *Perambulations*, 267–69.

57 'Bill for Flowers at Covent Garden', 5 July 1806, 'Mr Lilleys Payments', Staffordshire Record Office D593/R/1/13/1.

58 'Stafford House: Marchioness of Stafford's Grand Assembly', *London Courier and Evening Gazette* (6 May 1806).

59 Ann Bermingham, 'Gainsborough's Cottage door in Sir John Leicester's "tent room"' in *Sensation & Sensibility* (New Haven CT: Yale University Press, 2005).

60 On the Bishop of London and the Marchioness of Stafford's concerts see Simon McVeigh, *Concert Life in London from Mozart to Haydn* (Cambridge: Cambridge University Press, 1993), 67.

61 *The Morning Post* (8 April 1807).

62 'Fashionable World', *The Morning Post* (29 April 1807).

63 Ibid.

64 Rush, *Memoranda*, 315.

65 Ibid., 316.

66 See for example Mary Douglas and Baron Isherwood, *The World of Goods: Towards an Anthropology of Consumption* (New York: Routledge, 1996) and Arjun Appadurai, *The Social Life of Things: Commodities in Cultural Perspective* (Cambridge: Cambridge University Press, 1986).

67 Douglas and Isherwood, *World of Goods*, 44.

68 Nicholas Tromans has written about the prescriptiveness of manners and social convention with regard to looking at pictures in the Victorian period in *The Private Lives of Pictures: Art at Home in Britain, 1800–1940* (London: Reaktion Books, 2022).

69 'Monthly Retrospect of the Fine Arts', *Monthly Magazine* 21 (July 1806), 543–54.

70 Wakefield, *Perambulations*, 414.

71 Britton, 'Notice Respecting Tickets of Admission', *Catalogue Raisonné.*

72 Greig, *Farington Diary*, III: 274, 251, IV: 115, V: 65.

73 On the timing of the social calendar in late Georgian London, see 'The Social Character of the Estate: The London Season in 1841', in *Survey of London: Volume 39, the Grosvenor Estate in Mayfair, Part 1 (General History)*, ed. FHW Sheppard (London, 1977), 89–93.

74 Opening day was May 21, 1806. Greig, *Farington Diary*, III: 236.

75 [Feltham, John.] *Picture of London for 1808* (London: Richard Phillips, 1808), 48ff.

76 Southey's book, written in the manner of Montesquieu's *Persian Letters* (1721), purported to come from the pen of a Spanish nobleman taking the opportunity of a trip through Britain to record the foibles of English society. Robert Southey, *Letters from England by Don Manuel Alvarez Espriella.* (London: Cresset Press, 1961), 81.

77 Greig, *Beau Monde*.

78 'The Marquis of Stafford's New Residence' [May 1806], *Press-cuttings*, 1282.

79 Christina Colvin, ed. *Maria Edgeworth: Letters from England 1813–1844* (Oxford: Clarendon Press, 1971), 388.

80 *The Morning Post* (8 April 1807).

81 'Fashionable World', *The Morning Post* (29 April 1807).

82 'Stafford House: Marchioness of Stafford's Grand Assembly', *London Courier and Evening Gazette* (6 May 1806); *Morning Chronicle* (21 April 1806).

83 Staffordshire Record Office D6579/21/1-133 /30.

84 Entry dated 29 May 1811 in Lady Theresa Lewis, ed *Extracts of the Journals and Correspondence of Miss Berry* (London: Longmans, Green and Co, 1865), II: 478.

85 Rush, *Memoranda*, 155.

86 Stella Tillyard, 'Celebrity in 18th-Century London', *History Today* 55:6 (2005), 20–27. On the correlation between aristocracy and 'celebrity' see Greig, *Beau Monde*, 20–23.

87 Letter dated 23 June 1806 in Augustus JC Hare, *The Life and Letters of Frances, Baroness Bunsen* (London: Daldy, Isbister and Co, 1879), 1:75.

88 *The Morning Post* (8 April 1807).

89 Edith Jackson, *Annals of Ealing* (London: Phillimore & Co, 1898), 174.

90 On Grosvenor House see Susannah Brooke, 'The Display and Reception of Private Picture Collections in London Town Houses, 1780–1830' in *The Georgian London Town House: Building, Collecting and Display* ed. Susanna Avery-Quash and Kate Retford (London: Bloomsbury, 2019), 149–67 and Dongho Chun, 'Noble Leisure: Lords [sic] Grosvenor's Art Patronage and Collecting in the Long Eighteenth Century,' in 미술사와 시각문화 2018년 | 제21호 (2018), 148–67.

91 'Old Grosvenor House', in *Survey of London: Volume 40, the Grosvenor Estate in Mayfair, Part 2 (The Buildings)*, ed FHW Sheppard (London, 1980), 239–50; John Cornforth, 'Old Grosvenor House', *Country Life* 154 (15 November 1973), 1538–41.

92 *The Examiner* (3 June 1832), 358.

93 Simond, *Journal of a Tour*, 229–31.

94 Mrs Hugh Wyndham, ed *Correspondence of Sarah Spencer, Lady Lyttelton, 1787–1870* (London: John Murray, 1912), 14.

95 *Ibid.*, 16.

96 Andrew Hemingway, 'Art Exhibitions as Leisure-Class Rituals in Early Nineteenth-Century London' in *Towards a Modern Art World* ed Brian Allen (New Haven CT: Yale University Press, 1992).

97 Britton, *Original Picture of London, Enlarged and Improved* (London: Longman, Rees, Orme, Brown and Green, 1826), 320.

98 Britton, *Original Picture of London*, 321.
99 Ibid.
100 Simond, *Journal of a Tour*, 229–331.
101 Hare, *The Life and Letters of Frances, Baroness Bunsen*, I: 75.
102 Greig, *Farington Diary*, III: 189.
103 Dror Wahrman, *The Making of the Modern Self* (New Haven CT: Yale University Press, 2004), 207.
104 Wakefield, *Perambulations*, 267–69.
105 Evans, 'Figures, Doors,' 56.
106 Lefebvre, *Production of Space*, 86–87.
107 Evans, 'Figures, Doors,' 88.
108 Ibid., 75.

3 'The superb furniture within': Materiality and the Domestic Interior

1 See for example Peter Humfrey, *The Stafford Gallery* (Norwich: Unicorn Press, 2019), 152, 158, 162.

2 Robin Evans, 'The Developed Surface: An Enquiry into the Brief Life of an Eighteenth-century Drawing Technique' in *Translations from Drawing to Building* (London: Architectural Association, 1997), 195–232.

3 Laura Jacobus has called the drawing technique used here the 'laid-out interior drawing'. Jacobus, 'On "Whether a Man Could See Before Him and Behind Him Both at Once": The Role of Drawing in the Design of Interior Space in England c. 1600–1800', *Architectural History* 31 (1988), 148–65. Robin Evans calls it the 'developed surface interior' in 'The Developed Surface', 195–232.

4 For the identification of the bust and sculptor, *London Courier and Evening Gazette* (6 May 1806). The bust is likely the one sold at Phillips auction house on 4 December 1979, lot 135, signed and dated 1805. A plaster cast is at Dunrobin Castle. See the Regency Portraits Catalogue at the National Portrait Gallery. Available at: www.npg.org.uk/collections/search/personExtended/mp04378/george-granville-leveson-gower-1st-duke-of-sutherland?tab=iconography.

5 Priscilla Wakefield, *Perambulations in London, and its Environs* (London: Darton, Harvey and Darton, 1814), 267–69.

6 Scott, *The Rococo Interior: Decoration and Social Spaces in Early Eighteenth-Century Paris* (London: Yale University Press, 1995), 245.

7 Benedict Leca, 'An Art Book and Its Viewers: The "Recueil Crozat" and the Uses of Reproductive Engraving', *Eighteenth-Century Studies* 38.4 (Summer 2005), 623–49.

8 Translation by the author from original French: 'Premiére piéce de l'appartement au rès de chaussée, Sur le Jardin. A droite en entrant, Un grand Dessein fait à la plume sur du Vélin, par Henri Goltzius, célébre Graveur . . .'. *Catalogue des Tableaux du Cabinet de M. Crozat* (Paris: Chez de Bure l'Aîné, 1755), 3.

9 The *Ædes Walpolianæ* is analysed in detail in *A Capital Collection: Houghton Hall and the Hermitage*, ed. Larissa Dukelskaya and Andrew Moore (London: Yale University Press, 2002).

10 *Ædes Walpolianæ* (London, 1747), 44.

11 Rochelle Ziskin, *Sheltering Art: Collecting and Social Identity in Early Eighteenth-century Paris* (University Park: Pennsylvania State University Press, 2012), 192–204.

12 Julius Griffiths, *Prospectus: Gallery of the Louvre at Paris* (1802).

13 Anne Nellis Richter, 'Taking the Museum Home: Maria Cosway's *Gallery of the Louvre* and the Domestic Interior' in Anca Lasc ed, *Visualizing the Nineteenth-Century Home* (New York: Routledge, 2016). At least one gentleman who encountered Cosway in the Louvre copying paintings for this project, an Hon Mr E–, was reported to have expressed his intention to do just this. See Henry Redhead Yorke, *France in Eighteen Hundred and Two*, JAC Sykes ed. (London: William Heinemann, 1912), 157.

14 Jacobus, 'On "Whether a Man Could See Before Him"', 148–49.

15 *Ibid.*, 158.

16 Peter Thornton, *Authentic Décor: The Domestic Interior 1620–1920* (London: Weidenfeld and Nicolson, 1984), 147–49. Thornton links this fashion to a variety of other developments in architecture relating to the fashion for the picturesque. The ideology of the *dérangé* scheme is also addressed in Evans, 'The Developed Surface'.

17 Jean-Jacques Rousseau's work, which promoted the notion of humans living in closer contact with the natural world, was embraced by the British upper classes; see Mark Girouard, *Life in the English Country House* (New Haven: Yale University Press, 1978), 213–44 and Thornton, *Authentic Décor*, 17. For an overview of these developments and how they related to other eighteenth-century decorative movements see Anne Nellis Richter, 'Beauty', in *Interiors in the Age of Enlightenment* ed. Stacey Sloboda (London: Bloomsbury, 2024).

18 Evans, 'The Developed Surface', 195–232.

19 On the particularly 'English' obsession with the single-family dwelling as the optimal form of housing in the nineteenth century, see Sharon Marcus, *Apartment Stories: City and Home in Nineteenth-century Paris and London* (Berkeley: University of California Press, 1999), 83–134.

20 See Witold Rybczynski, *Home: A Short History of an Idea* (New York: Viking, 1986), John Crowley, *The Invention of Comfort: Sensibilities and Design in Early Modern Britain and Early America* (Baltimore: Johns Hopkins University Press, 2001) and Amanda Vickery, *Behind Closed Doors: At Home in Georgian England* (London: Yale University Press, 2009).

21 *The Lady's Monthly Museum* 4 (Jan–June 1808), 49. On upper-class women and the embrace of the rhetoric of domesticity, see Amanda Vickery, *The*

Gentleman's Daughter: Women's Lives in Georgian England (New Haven CT: Yale University Press, 1998).

22 Letter from Elizabeth to Lady Wimbledon, 29 Nov 1793, National Library of Scotland, Dep 313 [744].

23 Letter dated Albemarle St, 14 Nov [1795]. National Library of Scotland, Dep 313 [744].

24 See Dror Wahrman for an analysis of how notions about private morality became central to public discourse in the late-eighteenth and early-nineteenth centuries. Wahrman, *Imagining the Middle Class: The Political Representation of Class in Britain, c. 1780–1840* (Cambridge: Cambridge University Press, 1995).

25 William Young Ottley, *Engravings of the Most Noble the Marquis of Stafford's Collection of Pictures in London, Arranged According to Schools, and in Chronological Order, with Remarks on Each Picture* (London: Longman, Hurst, Rees, Orme and Brown, 1818).

26 On the *Repository of Arts*, see John Ford, *Ackermann, 1783–1983: The Business of Art* (London: Ackermann, 1983) and Ann Bermingham, *Learning to Draw* (New Haven CT: Yale University Press, 2000), 140.

27 'The Marquis of Stafford's New Residence' [May 1806], *Press-cuttings, from English newspapers . . .* National Art Library, Victoria & Albert Museum, London (Shelfmark P.P.17.G), 1282.

28 Anne Nellis Richter, 'Cleveland House as Art Museum? The Short Life of the "Louvre of London"' in Margaret Iacono Wertz and Esmée Quodbach, eds *The Evolving House Museum: Art Collectors and their Residences* (Leiden: Brill, forthcoming) and Richter, 'Glitter and Fashion in the "Louvre of London"', in *The Georgian London Town House: Building, Collecting and Display* ed. Susanna Avery-Quash and Kate Retford (London: Bloomsbury, 2019), 233–46.

29 *London Courier and Evening Gazette* (6 May 1806).

30 Louis Simond, *Journal of a Tour and Residence in Great Britain* 2 vols. (Edinburgh: Archibald Constable, 1817), 2:193.

31 Longstaffe-Gowan, *The London Town Garden 1740–1840* (London: Yale University Press, 2001), 63. See also Mireille Galinou ed *The Glorious History of London's Parks and Gardens* (London: Anaya Publishers for the Museum of London, 1990).

32 Britton, *Catalogue Raisonné*, 40.

33 Britton lists this picture as cat 43, 'Landscape, with Figures'. Britton, *Catalogue Raisonné*, 51–53.

34 '*Crim. con*'., short for criminal conversation, refers to the contemporary legal framework under which a husband could sue for divorce on the grounds of adultery. Britton, *Catalogue Raisonné*, 52.

35 'Fashionable Furniture', *The Repository of Arts, Literature, Commerce, Manufactures, Fashions, and Politics* (May 1816), 307–08.

36 Ann Pullan, 'Conversations on the Arts': Writing a Space for the Female Viewer in the *Repository of Arts*, 1809–1815', *Oxford Art Journal* 15:2 (1992), 15–26,

Erin Mackie, *Market à la Mode: Fashion, Commodity, and Gender in The Tatler and The Spectator* (Baltimore: Johns Hopkins University Press, 1997), Elizabeth Kowalski-Wallace, *Consuming Subjects: Women, Shopping and Business in the Eighteenth Century* (New York: Columbia University Press, 1996).

37 See Clive Wainwright and Martin Levy, 'George Bullock (1818)' in British and Irish Furniture Makers Online (BIFMO). Available at: https://bifmo.furniturehistorysociety.org/.

38 Britton, *Catalogue Raisonné*, vi.

4 'We have lately been much attacked': Exhibiting Morality

1 Classic works on enclosure include EP Thompson. *The Making of the English Working Class* (London: Penguin, 1991) and JM Neeson, *Commoners: Common Right, Enclosure and Social Change in England, 1700–1820* (Cambridge: Cambridge University Press, 1993). Cultural historians have explicitly connected the social rupture of enclosure with the development of landscape painting in the eighteenth and early nineteenth centuries, see for example John Barrell, *The Dark Side of the Landscape: The Rural Poor in English Painting* (Cambridge: Cambridge University Press, 1980) and Ann Bermingham, *Landscape and Ideology: The English Rustic Tradition, 1740–1860* (Berkeley: University of California Press, 1986).

2 Marx described the clearances as the 'transformation [of land] into modern private property under circumstances of reckless terrorism'. Karl Marx, *Capital: A Critique of Political Economy* ed Frederick Engels (New York: Modern Library, 1906), 805; John Prebble, *The Highland Clearances* (London: Secker & Warburg, 1963).

3 Richards' enormous body of writing on this topic provides an even-handed scholarly treatment. In general, Richards argues that an unbiased interpretation of these events suggests that the actions of landlords were heavy-handed and even aggressive, but that charges of racial animosity toward the Highlanders are overstated. See Eric Richards, *The Leviathan of Wealth: The Sutherland Fortune in the Industrial Revolution* (London: Routledge and Kegan Paul, 1973), Eric Richards, *A History of the Highland Clearances: Agrarian Transformation and the Evictions 1746–1886* (London: Croom Helm, 1982) and *Patrick Sellar and the Highland Clearances: Homicide, Eviction and the Price of Progress* (Edinburgh: Polygon, 1999) and *The Highland Clearances: People, Landlords' and Rural Turmoil* (Edinburgh: Berlinn, 2000).

4 John Britton, *Catalogue Raisonné of the Pictures Belonging to the Most Honourable the Marquis of Stafford, in the Gallery of Cleveland House* (1808), i.

5 George Perry, *A Descriptive Catalogue of the Pictures in the Collection of the Marquis of Stafford in London* (London: J Walker, 1807), 31.

6 *Ibid.*, 1.

7 On Stafford's activities as a patron of British artists, see Peter Humfrey, *The Stafford Gallery* (Norwich: Unicorn Press, 2019), 110–20 and Holger Hoock, '"Struggling against a Vulgar Prejudice": Patriotism and the Collecting of British Art at the Turn of the Nineteenth Century', *Journal of British Studies* 49 (July 2010), 566–91.

8 Britton, *Catalogue Raisonné*, 110–11.

9 Humfrey, *Stafford Gallery*, 34–37.

10 G Reynolds, 'Turner and Dutch Marine Painting', in *Netherlands Yearbook for History of Art* 21 (1970), 383–90 and Martin Butlin and Evelyn Joll, *The Paintings of J.M.W. Turner* (London: Tate Gallery, 1984) I (Text): 12–13.

11 Hannah Greig, *The Beau Monde: Fashionable Society in Georgian London* (Oxford: Oxford University Press, 2013), 24–25.

12 Quoted in William Thomas Whitley, *Art in England, 1800–1820* (New York: The Macmillan Company, 1928), 1: 109

13 Linda Colley, *Britons: Forging the Nation 1707–1837* (New Haven CT: Yale University Press, 1992) and Gerald Newman, *The Rise of English Nationalism: A Cultural History 1740–1830* (London: Palgrave MacMillan, 1997).

14 During her minority the estates were managed by a board of Tutors, but by her eighteenth birthday she had begun actively participating in their management.

15 Prebble, *Highland Clearances*, 59.

16 David Cannadine, 'The Making of the British Upper Classes' in *Aspects of Aristocracy: Grandeur and Decline in Modern Britain* (New Haven CT: Yale University Press, 1994), 10–11.

17 Richards, *Patrick Sellar*, 38.

18 Richards, *History of the Highland Clearances*, 291.

19 Letter from Marchioness of Stafford to Marquess of Stafford dated 15 July 1805, in RJ Adam, *Papers on Sutherland Estate Management* (Edinburgh: Scottish History Society, 1972), II: 39.

20 KDM Snell, *Annals of the Labouring Poor* (Cambridge: Cambridge University Press, 1985). See Anne Janowitz's summary of these issues in 'Land' in *Oxford Companion to the Romantic Age* ed Iain McCalman (Oxford: Oxford University Press, 1999), 155.

21 Quoted in Prebble, *Highland Clearances*, 87.

22 Hugh Trevor-Roper, 'The Highland Tradition of Scotland' in Eric Hobsbawm ed *The Invention of Tradition* (Cambridge: University of Cambridge Press, 1983), 19.

23 Samuel Johnson and James Boswell, *A Journey to the Western Islands of Scotland and The Journal of a Tour to the Hebrides* (London: Penguin Classics, 1984), 51.

24 Prebble, *Highland Clearances*, 70.

25 Quoted in Richards, *Leviathan of Wealth*, 179.

26 David Solkin, '"Conquest, Usurpation, Wealth, Luxury, Famine": Mortimer's Banditti and the Anxieties of Empire' in *Art and the British Empire*, ed Tim

Barringer, Geoff Quilley and Douglas Fordham (Manchester: Manchester University Press, 2007).

27 Quoted in Richards, *A History of the Highland Clearances*, 74.

28 BG, 'On the Condition of the Highland Peasantry Before and Since the Rebellion of 1745', *New Monthly Magazine and Universal Register* XI (1 July 1819), 504–09.

29 Quoted in Richards, *A History of the Highland Clearances*, 294.

30 Letter dated 22 March 1813 in *Letters to Charles Kirkpatrick Sharpe* (Edinburgh: W. Blackwood and Sons, 1888), 2: 76.

31 *Ibid.*, 2: 77.

32 Quoted in Richards, *A History of the Highland Clearances*, 33–34.

33 Richards, *Patrick Sellar*, 45.

34 Quoted in Prebble, *Highland Clearances*, 112–13.

35 On reputation and the aristocracy at the end of the eighteenth century, see Paul Langford, *Public Life and the Propertied Englishman 1689–1798* (Oxford: Oxford University Press, 1991), 540–48 and Cindy McCreery, *The Satirical Gaze: Prints of Women in Late Eighteenth-century England* (Oxford: Clarendon Press, 2004).

36 *The Diaries of Sylvester Douglas (Lord Glenbervie)*, ed Francis Bickley (London: Constable & Co., 1928), 2: 15, 27–28.

37 Anne Nellis Richter, 'Changing Subjects: The Gallery at Cleveland House and the Highland Clearances', *British Art Studies*, Issue 2. Available at: https://doi.org/10.17658/issn.2058-5462/issue-02/anellisrichter.

38 Helen Smith, 'Acknowledgements and Dedications' in *Book Parts* ed Dennis Duncan and Adam Smyth (Oxford, Oxford University Press, 2019), 105.

39 'Mr Lilley's payments', 1805–1826, Staffordshire Record Office D593/R/1/13/1.

40 Smith, 'Acknowledgements', 104.

41 W Cantrill, *Etchings from Original Pictures in the Cleveland-House Gallery, Drawn, Etched and Dedicated to the Marchioness of Stafford by her Ladyship's Porter* (London: Published by subscription, 1812). The only known copies are in the libraries of the Society of Antiquaries and the British Museum. Many thanks to Charles Sebag-Montefiore, FSA, for arranging access to the Society's Library.

42 D.A Brunton, 'Todd, Henry John', *Oxford Dictionary of National Biography* (Oxford: Oxford University Press, 2004).

43 On genre painting in this period and its implications for issues of class, see David Solkin, *Painting Out of the Ordinary: Modernity and the Art of Everyday Life in Early Nineteenth-century Britain* (London: Yale University Press, 2008).

44 Quoted in Prebble, *Highland Clearances*, 87–88.

45 Richards, *The Highland Clearances* (Edinburgh: Berlinn, 2013), 185.

46 *Ibid.*, 182–89.

47 James Greig, ed. *The Farington Diary* (New York: George H. Doran, 1923–28), VII: 174.

48 Michael Levey, *Sir Thomas Lawrence* (London: Paul Mellon Centre, 2005) and Cassandra Albinson, ed *Thomas Lawrence: Regency Power & Brilliance* (London: Paul Mellon Centre, 2011). On the use of portraiture as image control see Michael Rosenthal, 'Public Reputation and Image Control in Late-Eighteenth century Britain', *Visual Culture in Britain* 7 (Winter 2006), 69–91.

49 Kate Retford, *The Art of Domestic Life: Family Portraiture in Eighteenth-century England* (London: Yale University Press, 2006), 187–214.

50 On Wilkie and his career see Nicholas Tromans, *David Wilkie: The People's Painter* (Edinburgh: Edinburgh University Press, 2007), W Chiego ed, *Sir David Wilkie of Scotland* exh. cat, (New Haven, CT and Raleigh, NC 1987) and Solkin, *Painting Out of the Ordinary.*

51 Allan Cunningham, *The Life of Sir David Wilkie* (London: John Murray, 1843), 1: 379. For more details on the commission, see Hamish Miles, 'The Breakfast' in the forthcoming *catalogue raisonné* of Wilkie's paintings. I thank Miles' editor, Alex Kidson, for sharing Miles' draft entry for *The Breakfast.*

52 Solkin, *Painting Out of the Ordinary*, 112–15.

53 Humfrey, *Stafford Gallery*, 114–15.

54 Cunningham, *Life of Sir David Wilkie*, 1: 440.

55 Wilkie to the Earl of Leven, Nov. 28, 1816, SRO GD/26/13/301.

56 National Library of Scotland MS 10995 (ff. 1–20, 23–29, 33–34). Thanks to Melinda McCurdy for sharing this reference.

57 Cunningham, *Life of Sir David Wilkie*, 1: 458–59.

58 Tromans, *David Wilkie*, 96.

59 See for example Arthur S Marks, 'Wilkie, Hogarth and Hazlitt: The Reading of a Will, its Origins and Legacy', *Studies in Romanticism* 48:4 (2009): 583+.

60 RH, 'Royal Academy Exhibition', *The Examiner* (8 June 1817), 363.

61 *Ibid.*

62 James Elmes, *Annals of the Fine Arts* 3 (London: Sherwood, Neely and Jones, 1819), 113.

63 *Ibid.*, 328.

64 *Oxford English Dictionary*, 'clearance': 'clearing of land by the removal of wood, old houses, inhabitants, etc.' See Richards, *A History of the Highland Clearances*, 5.

65 Embedded within this sense of the meaning of eviction is also an obsolete usage referring to the conquest of foreign lands. *Oxford English Dictionary*, s.v. 'eviction, n., sense 6'. Available at: https://doi.org/10.1093/OED/7961062227, accessed 9 November 2023.

66 *Oxford English Dictionary*, s.v. 'removal, n., sense 3.c'. Available at: https://doi.org/10.1093/OED/9475889706, accessed 9 November 2023.

67 Loch, *An Account of the Improvements on the Estates of the Marquess of Stafford, in the Counties of Stafford and Salop, and on the Estate of Sutherland* (London, 1820), 52.

68 *Ibid.*, 53.

69 Robert Southey, *Journal of a Tour in Scotland in 1819* ed CH Herford (London: John Murray, 1929), 137.

70 Quoted in Prebble, *Highland Clearances*, 70.

71 Quoted in Richards, *The Highland Clearances*, 180.

72 Loch, *An Account of the Improvements*, 63–64.

73 Quoted in Prebble, *Highland Clearances*, 124.

74 Southey, *Journal of a Tour*, 137

75 Thomas Bakewell, *Remarks on a Publication by James Loch, Esq.* (London: Longman, 1820), 38.

76 BG, 'On the Condition of the Highland Peasantry Before and Since the Rebellion of 1745', *New Monthly Magazine and Universal Register* XI (1 July 1819), 506.

77 'Sutherland Tenants', *The Morning Chronicle* (11 December 1819).

78 James Hunter, *Set Adrift Upon the World: The Sutherland Clearances* (Edinburgh: Birlinn, 2016).

79 Prebble, *Highland Clearances*, 22.

80 *Ibid.*, 60.

81 Hunter has written numerous books on Scottish history, the Clearances, and the Scottish diaspora, most recently *Set Adrift Upon the World* cited in n 78.

5 'To private collections alone': The Apotheosis of the Private Gallery

1 The earliest floor plan is dated 1808; the latest 1818.

2 William Young Ottley, *Engravings of the Most Noble the Marquis of Stafford's Collection of Pictures in London, Arranged According to Schools and in Chronological Order, with Remarks on Each Picture* (London: Longman, Hurst, Rees, Orme and Brown, 1818).

3 Carole Paul, ed *The First Modern Museums of Art* (Los Angeles: J Paul Getty Museum, 2012), Tony Bennett, *The Birth of the Museum: History, Theory, Politics* (London: Routledge, 1995) and Carol Duncan, *Civilizing Rituals: Inside Public Art Museums* (London: Routledge, 1995).

4 Giles Waterfield, *The People's Galleries: Art Museums and Exhibitions in Britain 1800–1914* (London: Yale University Press, 2015), Brandon Taylor, *Art for the Nation: Exhibitions and the London Public 1747–2001* (New Brunswick, NJ: Rutgers University Press, 1999), Christopher Whitehead, *The Public Art Museum in Nineteenth-Century Britain* (Aldershot: Ashgate, 2005) and Kate Hill, *Culture and Class in English Public Museums, 1850–1914* (Aldershot: Ashgate, 2005).

5 Morris Eaves, *The Counter-Arts Conspiracy: Art and Industry in the Age of Blake* (Ithaca, NY: Cornell University Press, 1993), 3–8.

6 'The Fine Arts', *The Literary Gazette* (5 April 1819), 219. Cutting in scrapbook assembled by Sir John Leicester, Tabley Hall.

7 Charlotte Klonk, 'The National Gallery in London and Its Public', in *Consumers and Luxury* ed Maxine Berg and Helen Clifford (Manchester: Manchester University Press, 1999), 228–50.

8 James Greig, ed *The Farington Diary* (New York: George H Doran, 1923–1928), IV: 107. Farington notes that Longman & Rees are hoping to compete with a similar publication already underway by a rival publisher.

9 Ottley and Tresham, *The British Gallery of Pictures, In Two Series* (Printed for Longman, Hurst, Rees and Orme, J White, Cadell and Davies and PW Tomkins, 1808), 1.

10 Peter Walch, 'Henry Tresham'. *Grove Art Online*. Oxford University Press. Accessed 23 May 2023. Available at: https://doi-org.libproxy.smith.edu/10.1093/gao/9781884446054.article.T086107.

11 Ottley, *Engravings*, prospectus.

12 See discussion of the challenge posed by the Louvre in Anne Nellis Richter, '"A Museum within His Own Apartments": Maria Cosway's *Gallery of the Louvre* and the Domestic Interior', in *Visualizing the Nineteenth-Century Home: Modern Art and the Decorative Impulse*, ed. Anca Lasc (Ashford: Ashgate, 2016), 93–95.

13 Martin Archer Shee, *Rhymes on Art* (London: John Murray, 1805), 66.

14 Peter Fullerton, 'Patronage and Pedagogy: The British Institution in the Early Nineteenth Century', *Art History* 5:1 (1982), 59–72.

15 Shee, *Rhymes on Art*, 66.

16 See Larissa Dukelskaya, 'The Houghton Sale and the Fate of a Great Collection' in *A Capital Collection: Houghton Hall and the Hermitage*, ed. Larissa Dukelskaya and Andrew Moore (London: Yale University Press, 2002).

17 Rosie Dias, *Exhibiting Englishness: John Boydell's Shakespeare Gallery and the Formation of a National Aesthetic* (London: Yale, 2013).

18 For more on this episode, see Morton D Paley, 'The Truchsessian Gallery Revisited', *Studies in Romanticism* 16 (Spring 1977), 165–77.

19 *Plan of Subscription Submitted to the Nobility and Gentry of Great Britain: And to continue Open during the Months February, March and April, 1804; for the Purchase of the Truchsessian Picture Gallery, Now Exhibiting in the New-Road, London; and for Converting It into a Grand and Permanent National Establishment* (London, 1804), 6.

20 Kenneth Garlick, Angus D Macintyre and Evelyn Newby, ed. *The Diary of Joseph Farington* (New Haven CT: Yale University Press, 1978–1998), XIV: 4930; XII: 3947, 4165; and XI, 4083. Quoted in Steven Parissien, *George IV: The Grand Entertainment*. (London: John Murray, 2001), 158.

21 Parissien, *George IV*, 159.

22 John Feltham, *Picture of London for 1802* (London: Richard Phillips, 1802), 226–234.

23 *Ibid.*, 302.

24 Susanna Avery-Quash, 'John Julius Angerstein and the Development of his Art Collection at No. 100, Pall Mall, London', in Avery-Quash and Retford, *The Georgian London Town House: Building, Collecting and Display* (London: Bloomsbury, 2019), 247–66.

25 Feltham, *Picture of London for 1809,* 305.

26 Britton, *Original Picture of London, Enlarged and Improved* (London: Longman, Rees, Orme, Brown and Green, 1826).

27 Feltham, *Picture of London for 1802,* 231.

28 Paul Langford, *Public Life and the Propertied Englishman 1689–1798* (Oxford: 1991), 30–31.

29 Ottley, *Engravings*, prospectus.

30 John Scott, *A Visit to Paris in 1814: Being a Review of the Moral, Political, Intellectual and Social Condition of the French Capital* (London: Longman, Hurst, Rees, Orme and Brown, 1816), 242, 266–67.

31 Ottley, *Engravings.*

32 Though this image was once thought to depict the gallery of Rowlandson's friend Matthew Michell, this identification is now less certain and it is unclear whether Rowlandson is depicting a real or fictional space. JH Plumb, *The Pursuit of Happiness* (New Haven CT: Yale Center for British Art, 1977), 49.

33 Sir Egerton Brydges, *Collins's Peerage of England* (1812), I: x, quoted in Linda Colley, *Britons: Forging the Nation 1707–1837* (New Haven CT: Yale University Press, 1992), 177.

34 Dongho Chun, 'Public Display, Private Glory: Sir John Fleming Leicester's Gallery of British Art in Early Nineteenth-century England', *Journal of the History of Collections* 13:2 (2001), 175–89 and Dongho Chun, 'Patriotism on Display: Sir John Fleming Leicester's Patronage of British Art', *The British Art Journal* 4 (Summer 2003), 23–28. On the upcoming class of art patrons see Dianne Sachko Macleod, *Art and the Victorian Middle Class: Money and the Making of Cultural Identity* (Cambridge: Cambridge University Press, 1996), 96.

35 Holger Hoock, '"Struggling against a Vulgar Prejudice": Patriotism and the Collecting of British Art at the Turn of the Nineteenth Century', *Journal of British Studies* 49 (July 2010), 566–91.

36 Elizabeth Helsinger, 'Land and National Representation in Britain', in *Prospects for the Nation: Recent Essays in British Landscape, 1750–1880* (London and New Haven CT: Yale University Press, 1997), 13–35; Andrew Hemingway, *Landscape Imagery and Urban Culture in Early Nineteenth-century Britain* (Cambridge: Cambridge University Press, 1992) and K Dian Kriz, *The Idea of the English Landscape Painter* (London: Yale University Press, 1997).

37 Chun, 'Patriotism on Display'.

38 Ann Bermingham, 'Gainsborough's *Cottage Door* in Sir John Leicester's "Tent Room"' in *Sensation & Sensibility: Viewing Gainsborough's Cottage Door* ed. Bermingham (New Haven CT and San Marino: Yale Center for British Art and The Huntington Library, Art Collections, & Botanical Garden, 2005), 136–61 .

39 For more on the relationship between the private interior and public taste, see Anne Nellis Richter, 'Improving Public Taste in the Private Interior: Gentlemen's Galleries in Post-Napoleonic London' in *Architectural Space in Eighteenth-Century Europe: Constructing Identities and Interiors*, ed Denise Amy Baxter and Meredith Martin (Burlington, VT: Ashgate, 2010).

40 Chun, 'Public display, private glory', 177.

41 The catalogue, published in 1819, which appears to have been based on Britton's, explicitly states that the regulations put in place are 'as at Cleveland House'. *A Catalogue of Pictures, by British Artists, in the Collection of Sir John Leicester, Bart.* (London 1819), cited in Chun 'Public display, private glory', 182.

42 Chun 'Public display, private glory', 182.

43 *The Morning Post* (20 May 1819).

44 *A Collection of Water Colour Drawings in the Possession of Walter Fawkes, Esq.* (London: Benjamin Bensley, 1819) and *A Collection of Water Colour Drawings, in the possession of Mr. Fawkes, 45, Grosvenor Place* (London: D Lewis, 1819). The catalogues differ on the precise details of the number of rooms allotted to the 'gallery' and the hanging of the pictures.

45 *A Collection of Water Colour Drawings in the Possession of Walter Fawkes, Esq.*

46 Richter, 'Improving Public Taste', 183–84; George Smith, *A Collection of Designs for Household Furniture and Interior Decoration* (London: J Taylor, 1808), 12. The object illustrated in Turner's view is clearly not the same as the type of ottoman described by Smith, since its design permitted views toward all of the room's four walls.

47 Christopher Rowell, Ian Warrell and David Blayney Brown, *Turner at Petworth* (London: Tate, 2004).

48 William Carey, *A Descriptive Catalogue of a Collection of Paintings by British Artists: In The Possession of Sir John Fleming Leicester, Bart.* (London: J Nichols and Son, 1819).

49 I discuss the engraving made for the catalogue in detail in Richter, 'Improving Public Taste', 174–75.

50 'Mr. Walter Fawkes's Gallery', *Repository of Arts* (May 1819), 297–301.

51 William Carey, *Some Memoirs of the Patronage and Progress of the Fine Arts* (London: Saunders and Ottley, 1826), 114.

52 William Carey 'Defence of the British Institution', *New Monthly Magazine and Universal Register* XII (1 Nov, 1819), 469.

53 WC [William Carey] 'Fine Arts', *New Monthly Magazine and Universal Register* XI (1 March 1819), 170.

54 'Sir J Fleming Leicester's Gallery', *The Literary Gazette* (22 May 1819).

55 'Mr. Fawkes's Pictures', *London Chronicle* (10 April, 1819), 347.

56 'Exhibition at the Leicester Gallery', *Repository of Arts* (April 1819), 230.

57 On the use of language and rhetoric in class construction in this period see Colley, *Britons: Forging the Nation* and Dror Wahrman, *Imagining the Middle*

Class: The Political Representation of Class in Britain c. 1780–1840 (Cambridge: Cambridge University Press, 1995).

58 *Press-cuttings, from English newspapers* . . . National Art Library, Victoria & Albert Museum, London (Shelfmark P.P.17.G), 1118.

59 Louis Simond, *Journal of a Tour and Residence in Great Britain* 2 v (Edinburgh: Archibald Constable, 1817), 1:229–331. For more on the practice of tipping in the country house and townhouse gallery, see Richter 'Opening the Townhouse: Access in the Urban Environment in the Early Nineteenth Century' in *Collecting and Access*, ed Andrea Gáldy, Susan Bracken and Adriana Turpin (Newcastle-upon-Tyne: Cambridge Scholars Publishing, forthcoming).

60 [Anon.], *Real Life in London; or, The Further Rambles and Adventures of Bob Tallyho, Esq. and his Cousin the Hon. Tom Dashall, &c. through the Metropolis* (London: Jones & Co. 1821–1822), 348–49.

61 'To Correspondents', *The Examiner* (March 1819), 207.

62 Jurgen Habermas, *The Structural Transformation of the Public Sphere*, trans Thomas Burger (Cambridge: Polity Press, 1989) and Terry Eagleton, *The Function of Criticism: From the Spectator to Post-Structuralism* (London: Verso, 1984).

63 *The Literary Gazette* (1819), 220.

64 *Ibid.*, 219.

65 'Mr. Walter Fawkes's Gallery', *Repository of Arts* (May 1819), 297–301.

66 [W], 'Sir John Leicester's Gallery', *The Literary Journal* (10 April 1819).

67 'Mr. Fawkes's Pictures', *London Chronicle* (10 April, 1819), 347–48.

68 William Paulet Carey, *Observations on the Probable Extinction of British Historical Painting* (London: Howlett & Brimmer, 1825), 34.

69 David Solkin, ed. *Art on the Line: The Royal Academy Exhibitions at Somerset House 1780–1836* (London: Yale University Press, 2001).

70 *Repository of Arts* (1 April 1819), 230–31.

71 On *The Microcosm of London*, see Bermingham, 'Urbanity and the Spectacle of Art' in *Romantic Metropolis: The Urban Scene of British Culture, 1780–1840*, ed James Chandler and Kevin Gilmartin (Cambridge: Cambridge University Press, 2005).

72 John Murdoch, 'Architecture and Experience: The Visitor and the Spaces of Somerset House, 1780–1796' in Solkin, *Art on the Line.*

73 On the publics at the Royal Academy exhibitions, see Matheson and Kriz in Solkin, *Art on the Line* and Andrew Hemingway, 'Art Exhibitions as Leisure-Class Rituals in Early Nineteenth-century London', *Towards a Modern Art World* ed. Brian Allen (London: Yale University Press, 1995).

74 Hemingway, 'Art Exhibitions as Leisure-Class Rituals'.

75 'Fine Arts. Whether they are Promoted by Academies and Public Institution', in PP Howe, ed. *The Complete Works of William Hazlitt* 21 vols (London: JM Dent, 1933), 18: 37–51.

76 John Barrell, *The Political Theory of Painting from Reynolds to Hazlitt: 'The Body of the Public'* (London: Yale University Press, 1986), 324. See also Peter

Funnell, 'William Hazlitt, Prince Hoare and the Institutionalisation of the British Art World', in Allen, *Towards a Modern Art World.*

77 'Fine Arts. Whether they are Promoted by Academies and Public Institutions', in Howe, *Complete Works of William Hazlitt*, 18: 45.

78 *Ibid.*, 46.

79 *Ibid.*, 38.

80 Hazlitt, *Sketches of the Principal Picture Galleries in England* in Howe, *Complete Works of William Hazlitt*, 10: 7.

81 These ideas are more fully elaborated and connected to other eighteenth- and early nineteenth-century aesthetic discourses in Jonah Siegel, *Desire and Excess: The Nineteenth-Century Culture of Art* (Princeton: Princeton University Press, 2000).

82 Howe, *Complete Works of William Hazlitt*, 10: 7.

83 *Ibid.*, 18: 44–45.

84 CM Westmacott, *British Galleries of Painting and Sculpture* (London: Sherwood, Jones & Co., 1824), vi–vii.

85 Maryanne C Ward, 'Preparing for the National Gallery: The Art Criticism of William Hazlitt and P.G. Patmore', *Victorian Periodicals Review* 23 (Fall 1990), 104–10 and Quentin Bailey, 'Hazlitt and the "Old Pictures": Westmacott, Patmore and the Role of Art Criticism', *The Wordsworth Circle* 41:2 (Spring 2010), 114–99.

86 PG Patmore, *British Galleries of Art* (London: G & WB Whittaker, 1824), 146.

87 Jocelyn Anderson, *Touring and Publicizing England's Country Houses in the Long Eighteenth Century* (London: Bloomsbury, 2018), 60.

88 See for example Brandon Taylor, *Art for the Nation: Exhibitions and the London Public 1747–2001* (New Brunswick, NJ: Rutgers University Press, 1999), 51–66.

89 Patmore, *British Galleries of Art*, 158.

90 *Ibid.*, 164.

91 *Ibid.*, 151.

92 Peter Mandler, *The Fall and Rise of the Stately Home* (New Haven CT: Yale University Press, 1997), 21–69.

93 Patmore, *British Galleries of Art*, 144.

94 *Ibid.*, 146.

95 *Ibid.*

96 CM Westmacott, *British Galleries of Painting and Sculpture* (London: Sherwood, Jones & Co., 1824), vi–vii.

97 *Ibid.*

98 Susanna Avery-Quash, 'John Julius Angerstein and the Development of his Art Collection at No. 100, Pall Mall, London', in Avery-Quash and Retford, *The Georgian London Town House: Building, Collecting and Display* (London: Bloomsbury, 2019), 247–66.

99 On the changes in strategies for display in public institutions after the 1830s see Charlotte Klonk, 'Mounting Vision: Charles Eastlake and the National Gallery of London', *The Art Bulletin* 82 (2000), 331–47 and Giles Waterfield, *Palaces of Art: Art Galleries in Britain, 1790–1990* (London: Dulwich Picture Gallery, 1991).

100 Quoted in Conlin, The *Nation's Mantelpiece: A History of the National Gallery* (London: Pallas Athene, 2006), 52.

101 *Ibid.*, 52.

Conclusion: The 'Home' of Art

1 Heidi Strobel, *The Art of Mary Linwood: Embroidery, Installation, and Entrepreneurship in Britain, 1787–1845* (London: Bloomsbury, 2023).

2 Mandler, *The Fall and Rise of the Stately Home* (New Haven CT: Yale University Press, 1997), 106.

3 Hazlitt, *Sketches of the Principal Picture Galleries in England* in PP Howe, ed *The Complete Works of William Hazlitt* 21 v (London: J.M. Dent, 1933), 10: 56.

4 Thanks to Tim Knox and Todd Longstaffe-Gowan for pointing me to the origin of this quote. Quoted in Christopher Hibbert, *Wellington: A Personal History* (Boston MA: Da Capo Press, 1999), 342.

5 Letter from Lord Francis Egerton, Dunrobin Castle, Sutherland to John Mountjoy Smith, 20 September 1841 in Charles Sebag-Montefiore with Julia Armstrong-Totten, *A Dynasty of Dealers: John Smith and Successors 1801-1924: A Study of the Art Market in Nineteenth-century London* (London: The Roxburghe Club, 2013), 85.

6 Colleen Denney, *At the Temple of Art: The Grosvenor Gallery 1877–1890* (Madison, NJ: Fairleigh Dickenson University Press, 2000).

7 Martha Ward, 'Impressionist Installations and Private Exhibitions', in *The Art Bulletin* 73:4 (December 1991), 599–622 and Morna O'Neill, *Hugh Lane: The Art Market and the Art Museum, 1893–1915* (London: Yale University Press, 2018).

8 For more on the metaphor of 'home' in Waagen, see Émilie Oléron Evans, 'Housing the Art of the Nation: The Home as Museum in Gustav F Waagen's *Treasures of Art in Great Britain*' in *Nineteenth-century Art Worldwide* 17: 1 (Spring 2018). Available at: https://doi.org/10.29411/ncaw.2018.17.1.2.

9 Gustav Waagen, *Works of Art and Artists in England* (London: John Murray, 1838), I: 14.

10 *Ibid.*, I: 42–43.

11 Mrs. (Anna) Jameson, *Companion to the Most Celebrated Private Galleries of Art in London* (London: Saunders & Otley, 1844), xxxiv–xxxv.

12 Mrs (Anna) Jameson, *Handbook to the Public Galleries of Art in and Near London* (London: John Murray, 1842), xxxiii–xxxiv.

13 *Ibid.*

14 Carol Duncan, *Civilizing Rituals: Inside Public Art Museums* (London: Routledge, 1995).

15 The series of essays, originally printed in *Artforum*, were collected in Brian O'Doherty, *Inside the White Cube: The Ideology of the Gallery Space* (Santa Monica: Lapis Press, 1986), 14.

16 O'Doherty, *Inside the White Cube*, 14. For two examples of scholarship that excavate the early twentieth century approach to museum display, see Charlotte Klonk, *Spaces of Experience: Art Gallery Interiors from 1800 to 2000* (New Haven CT: Yale University Press, 2009) and Kristina Wilson, *The Modern Eye: Stieglitz, MoMA, and the Art of the Exhibition, 1925–1934* (New Haven CT: Yale University Press, 2009).

17 O'Doherty, *Inside the White Cube*, 15.

18 Jonathan Conlin, *The Nation's Mantelpiece: A History of the National Gallery* (London: Pallas Athene, 2006), 422.

19 Georgina Adam, *The Rise and Rise of the Private Art Museum* (London: Lund Humphries, 2021).

20 Baigent, Elizabeth, and Ben Cowell, ed *Octavia Hill, Social Activism and the Remaking of British Society* (London: University of London Press, 2016).

INDEX

Italic numbers indicate illustrations. Places are in London unless indicated otherwise.

www.ingramcontent.com/pod-product-compliance
Lightning Source LLC
LaVergne TN
LVHW010555110826
845149LV00003B/670

9781350372788